English House Clocks: 1600–1850

BOOKS BY ANTHONY BIRD

Early Victorian Furniture
English Furniture for the Private Collector
The Damnable Duke of Cumberland
The Motor Car 1765–1914
The Rolls-Royce Motor Car
Roads and Vehicles
Lanchester Motor Cars
Steam Cars 1770–1970
(with Lord Montagu of Beaulieu)

English House Clocks: 1600–1850

An Historical Survey and Guide for Collectors and Dealers

Anthony Bird

Line drawings by George White of Thornbury

David & Charles
Newton Abbot

ISBN 0 7153 5767 0

Set in 12 *on* 13*pt Caslon*
and printed in Great Britain
by Redwood Burn Limited, Trowbridge & Esher
for David & Charles (Publishers) Limited
Brunel House Newton Abbot Devon

Published in the United States of America
by David & Charles Inc
North Pomfret Vermont 05053 *USA*

Published in Canada
by Douglas David & Charles Limited
1875 *Welch Street North Vancouver BC*

Contents

List of Illustrations

PLATES

LINE DRAWINGS IN THE TEXT

Preface

When I bought my first antique clock, the decayed remains of an eighteenth-century thirty-hour movement and dial, for which I paid half-a-crown in 1930, there were relatively few serious and knowledgeable clock collectors and only one shop in London, that of the late Percy Webster, which specialised in horology. Old clocks were the ugly ducklings of the antique trade, although the prettier sorts of French clocks in porcelain or gilt-bronze cases were sought by interior decorators, known unkindly as 'ormolulu boys'. Outside the 'magic circle' of Tompion, Knibb, Quare, Graham and a few more, antique English clocks fetched relatively little, and the majority of those able to buy in the 'magic circle' still bought for the name and, to a lesser extent, the outward appearance, and paid little heed to the mechanism. The first Tompion clock I saw in a private house, furnished with admirable eighteenth-century furniture and a rich display of Chelsea and Worcester china, was a lantern clock which had been ruined, as so many were, by the removal of its original weight-driven movement and the substitution of a Victorian spring mechanism. When I pointed this out to the owner, she replied with some hauteur (for I was only fifteen years old) that *real* antique collectors did not concern themselves with 'the works'; they were unimportant, she said, and it was only 'the name on the face' which mattered.

There was then little published material in English on the historico-mechanical aspects of antiquarian horology. Books on antique furniture understandably dealt rather cursorily with clocks and concentrated on the casework; Cescinsky and Webster's *English Domestic Clocks*, published in 1913, went into the subject more deeply but, again, the emphasis was rather more on casework than mechanism. The standard reference work, which is still of great value, was Britten's *Old Clocks and Watches and their Makers* which ran through six limited editions, with no major revision of the text, between 1899 and 1933. This definitive but in some respects outdated work (which was completely re-written by Ilbert and Clutton in 1956) was complemented by G. H. Baillie's *Watchmakers and Clockmakers of the World* which listed 35,000 names. There were also some technical treatises and handbooks for repairers which were usually rather disdainful in their references to antique movements. The Victorian attitude that the best thing to do with an old clock was to put a new movement in it, or, as a second best, to modernise the old one beyond recognition, died very hard.

Outside the small band of clock and watch collectors, the subject was not taken seriously. It was acceptable enough that enthusiasts should collect objects as diverse as Japanese netsuke and American matchbox labels and that serious books and periodicals should cater for them, but the horological enthusiast was chillingly dismissed by one high-toned periodical, in an article on antique collecting, with the words: '. . . and there are even some people who are interested in the insides of old clocks and watches.'

Today, the clock- and watch-collecting scene is very different. Even allowing for the depreciation of the currency, the rise in value has been startling and does not affect only the famous makers and their most notable works, but has spread to the humblest sorts of clocks, including many which were once virtually unsaleable. This has naturally brought about a marked increase in the numbers of dealers who specialise in horology, and has also fostered an equally natural and deplorable increase in the numbers of fakers, their whose works, thanks to corresponding growth of knowledge, are much more difficult to detect than once they were.

The application of modern scholarship to antiquarian horology stems largely from the thirties. The work done then has been continued and expanded since the war, and new information is constantly being published and old beliefs challenged. The changed attitude is also reflected in museums. Before the war, although many museums had notable horological collections (including some notable fakes), no museum curator was a specialist in the subject, clocks would be under the care of the department of mediaeval ironwork or something of the kind, whilst watches would usually be included under jewellery. The exhibits, clocks particularly, were often badly neglected and dirty. It was unthinkable for any museum-shown clock to be cleaned and occasionally set a-going, with the exception of the Wells Cathedral clock and one or two other turret clock movements in the Science Museum in London.

The extent of the change is reflected by the activities of the Antiquarian Horological Society which, at its inception nearly twenty years ago, was cynically described as a 'small body of antique dealers banded together to sell clocks to Courtney Ilbert', but which now numbers 2,200 members and has a very high reputation for the lectures, demonstrations and investigations it promotes. This society, which is one of several with similar aims throughout the world, sponsors a quarterly journal which is a model of its kind. Other publications on all aspects of horology, ranging from paperbacks to lavish 'coffee-table' books, sometimes seem almost as numerous as the clocks and watches they describe.

This being so it might seem presumptuous to offer yet another clock book to the public, and some explanation is needed. Many of the books published in the past ten or fifteen years have been written by specialists for specialists and have been too technical for the class of reader I hope to serve. Details about a rare type of experimental escapement, for example, with analyses of its theoretical advantages and practical drawbacks, may be of interest to me but can only confuse the tyro collector or dealer. I have often been told by antique dealers that they rarely buy clocks because 'they are so tricky unless you understand them'. This sort of statement is often qualified by an observation to the effect that the speaker wishes there were a book on clocks which would deal with matters other than casework and externals, without being too difficult for the layman to understand.

It is true that there are many excellent books, often splendidly illustrated, which are not crammed with technical details, but novices often find these unsatisfactory because they go too far in avoiding explanations of mechanical niceties. This leads to the annoyance of the reader when he finds, perhaps, an excellent picture with a descriptive caption which reads: 'Fine month long-case equation clock by Snooks, *c* 1740, with dead beat escapement and gridiron pendulum', but fails to find in the text any simple description of what is meant by an equation clock or a dead-beat escapement, and he is left in doubt as to whether the gridiron is of culinary or horological significance.

This book is intended to fill the gap between the extremes mentioned, and I can only hope that it does not merely fall between two stools. Whilst not neglecting casework and the various decorative and design features which mark changing fashions, the principal intention is to describe the technological aspects of English domestic clockmaking in language not too abstruse for the layman and not, I trust, too superficial and elementary for those who want to go beyond mere external features. It is also intended to point out some of the pitfalls, and the ways in which fakes and 'marriages' are foisted on the public as often through ignorance as by design.

Having made my living, or a large part of my living, for some years by buying and selling clocks on a fairly lowly scale (I have never been in the Tompion class except for brief ownership of one of his watches), I have had the non-specialist dealer and his non-specialist customers particularly in mind. Although the work and influence of the principal masters will be dealt with, the emphasis is upon the general rather than the particular. At the Fromanteel, Tompion, Knibb end of the spectrum there are admirable books dealing with particular makers or specific aspects of the craft.

Because what I have to write arises from personal experience and observation, personal opinions are occasionally allowed to intrude, particularly in relation to certain trade practices. Therefore I have not adopted the formal third-person usage normally employed in books of a more-or-less technical nature. I have also continued to express measurement in feet and inches. If any of my opinions seem tendentious, I must apologise.

ANTHONY BIRD

Potbridge, Odiham,
Hampshire

Chapter One

The Background to English Horology

If the man-in-the-street were asked which nation led the world in horology, he would unhesitatingly answer 'Switzerland'. With this would go the corollary, unspoken perhaps, that this was always so, and that the various inventions which transformed clockmaking from blacksmithery to precision instrument-making were also of Swiss, or at least of Continental, origin. Yet for more than a hundred vital years England was the horological centre of the world.

The renaissance reached Great Britain later and with less dramatic effect than Italy, Germany, France and the Netherlands. Although late in starting in the business of making chamber clocks, English manufacturing developed fast. There were certain fortuitous causes of this quick development, which were unrelated to the late start and the advantage gained by absorbing the experience of others. From somewhere, from nowhere, from everywhere a succession of great waves of scientific curiosity and inventiveness swept through Great Britain. There were many factors involved and the religious factions which dominated British politics for so long played a part. The men who had mental integrity and courage enough to be non-conformists were very often men of an inquiring turn of mind who developed new ideas and set up new industries.

Non-conformity flourished more freely at a distance from the capital. Quite apart from accidents of geography affecting transport and access to materials, this is one reason why the new industries of the eighteenth century developed in the north and midlands, as so many of the great industrialists came from the Quaker, Presbyterian or Methodist communities. This also explains why, although

London was the horological centre, many of the most famous clockmakers and inventors, although not necessarily dissenters themselves, were countrymen, such as Graham from Cumberland, Mudge and the Ellicots from the West Country and John Harrison, the Yorkshire carpenter, who finally solved that great conundrum 'the finding of the longitude of places'. It is also worth noting that the relatively large number of noted English clockmakers with French names reflect descent from Huguenot refugees.

Apart from these influences and the rapid growth of scientific knowledge, led by men such as Newton, Hooke and Boyle, seventeenth-century English rivalry with the Dutch must also be taken into account. This rivalry led English craftsmen first to imitate and then to surpass the Dutch. Despite frequent squabbles and occasional wars, there was a natural affinity between the two countries, and the quarrels did not materially affect the interchange of ideas. Most clock enthusiasts look upon the period between the Restoration of Charles II in 1660 and the abdication of his brother twenty-eight years later as the golden age of English clockmaking. At the start of this period Ahasuerus Fromanteel introduced Holland's great new contribution to horology, the pendulum-controlled clock. By the end of the century England had firmly taken the lead, and Dutch makers were freely borrowing such English inventions as the anchor escapement, the balance spring, the 'royal' or long pendulum and the rack striking mechanism.

Royal and governmental encouragement must also be taken into account. Charles II, James II and William III each had more than a layman's knowledge of clockmaking. Charles II in particular was a keen collector who was able to dismantle and clean his own clocks and watches; he took a lively interest in the latest inventions and patronised their authors, to whom he could talk technicalities without loss of face. The Royal Society, in whose formation and early activities he played an important part, devoted a lot of time to horological problems and ideas. Above all, the Royal Observatory, which Charles founded and supported (as far as his chronic shortage of cash allowed), was set up expressly 'for the finding of the longitude of places' and although this involved astronomical observations it soon resolved itself into a matter of timekeeping.

Though less knowledgeable than his brother, James II was

Page 17 PLATE I Made in England, but not yet English. Three-train musical clock by Nicholas Vallin, dated 1598. The wheel balance controller is in the space between the tops of the main pillars and the plate supporting the hammers of the thirteen-bell carillon

Page 18 PLATE 2 Transitional anonymous English lantern clock, with iron Gothic-buttress frame pillars, balance wheel control, no frets, *c*1620. The engraved brass dial plate and hand are twentieth-century replacements

PLATE 3 Fully-developed brass lantern clock by Peter Closon, London, *c*1640, with the bell structure removed to show the massive bell hammer; also visible are the powerful hammer spring attached to the bottom plate, the bulbous wheel arbors and the 'heraldic' frets

competent enough to adjudicate upon the rival merits of Barlow's and Quare's repeating watches, in order to settle a dispute about patents, and William III bought some of the finest clocks ever made. Royal interest under Anne and the first two Georges did not extend beyond the normal bounds of patronage, but King George III, that maligned man whom history has labelled stupid, equalled Charles II in his understanding of technical niceties. Unfortunatcly our knowledge of historical characters is still overlaid with Victorian moralising, and we therefore know more about Charles II's promiscuity than we do of his intelligence and encouragement of scientists. King George III kept no mistresses, but the facts that he gave the world's first practicable lever watch to his strait-laced, peppery wife and intervened in the dispute about chronometers between the government and John Harrison were of no interest to the Victorian school of biography which merely recorded, with characteristic disdain, that 'he had some liking for mechanics and, it is said, directed the construction of some interesting clocks'.

George IV's horological interest was rather less happy than that of his father, as his passion for punctuality was used as an excuse by his clockmaker, Benjamin Lewis Vulliamy, ruthlessly to 'modernise' many of the fine early clocks in the royal collection. The balance was redressed in some degree by one of George's brothers, the Duke of Sussex, who formed one of the finest horological collections of the time. Unlike most contemporary clock fanciers, the duke was not merely interested in decorative, ornate or elaborate clocks with musical work or automata. He had a keen eye for items of historical significance, or of mechanical peculiarity, and he also found a place for some early marine chronometers at a time when most collectors would not have given them house-room. Unfortunately, this royal collection was dispersed on the duke's death in 1843, and interest in clocks as clocks, apart from their decorative value, waned during the rest of the century.

Governmental encouragement to clockmakers in the eighteenth century was indirect, and took the form of an Act of Parliament in 1714 (12 Anne, *c*15), which offered a first prize of £20,000, a vast sum then, to the man who could devise a method of 'finding the longitude' within a specified degree of accuracy and in a manner which could easily be used by mariners. Lesser sums were offered for methods offering lesser degrees of accuracy. The loss of Sir Cloudesley Shovell's flagship, HMS *Association*, off the Scillies, which arose from accumulated errors in dead-reckoning which were unavoidable, led to the government's decision to offer such handsome prizes.

They were not the first to do so, for the French and Spanish governments had already offered rather smaller sums, but the Act of 1714 followed naturally on Charles II's encouragement of the Royal Observatory. It had been understood for many years that the easiest way to find the longitude at sea, would be to take suitable observations, which posed no difficulty, to determine noon (or any other hour, but noon was most suitable) by 'local apparent time' on board the ship, and then to consult an accurate timepiece which showed the 'local apparent time' of some known longitudinal location. Simple calculations, based on the difference between the two times, would then determine the precise distance by which the ship was east or west of the land-based longitudinal point.

The only flaw in this beautifully simple method, which had been outlined as early as 1530, was that at the time of the Act (and, of course, before it) no portable timekeeper was anything like accurate enough for the purpose. An ordinary pocket watch of 1714 construction would keep time within about two to three minutes a day, provided it had been fairly recently cleaned and oiled, kept at a steady temperature and not subjected to violent motion. Under less favourable conditions, inevitable at sea, the error would be greater, and as one minute of time equals nearly fifteen miles distance at the Equator, it is not surprising that the first Astronomers Royal and others busied themselves with an alternative method by lunar observations and measurement. They succeeded, but the lunar method was far too complicated and slow to be of much practical use at sea and so, spurred on by the prize, clockmakers worked away at the alternative solution. It took three-quarters of a century and the marine chronometer in its final form may appear to have little in common with the domestic clock, but it is impossible to do justice to the one without taking a look at the other. A not inconsiderable share of Britannia's ability to rule the waves and chart unknown waters in the late eighteenth century must be attributed to the invention of the marine chronometer.

It was in the domain of precision that clockmaking took a new direction in the second half of the seventeenth century. A clock made before that era was thought to be acceptably accurate if it kept time within ten or fifteen minutes a day. Indeed, a typical domestic clock, English or continental, of 1640 for example, would have kept no better time than one of 1440, as with a mere handful of exceptions, the escapement and its controlling balance had remained unaltered in principle during the four hundred years that mechanical clocks had been known. A mere forty years later one of the new-fangled English long-case clocks, with anchor escapement and long pendulum, could keep time with an error of no more than a minute a week.

Chapter Two

Pre-clockwork Time Measurement

By the time mechanical chamber clocks began to be made in Great Britain, the system of measuring the time by dividing the day into twenty-four equal portions, divided again for greater convenience into two sets of twelve, had been generally but not universally established for some centuries. As human beings usually start to learn their numbers by counting on their fingers, it might seem that ten rather than twelve would have been chosen as the bi-diurnal unit. That it was not may be a mere fluke; if so, it was a happy one for the makers of clocks dependent on arrangements of toothed wheels.

A day, measured by the rising or setting of the sun as seen from a given point—the solar day—may be conveniently expressed as the period between two successive returns of the sun to the meridian; if the clouds permit, this may be easily noted. Because the earth rotates about the sun in an elliptical path, and because the angle of tilt of its axis varies as it does so, the solar days are not of equal length, as they appear to be. By comparison with a perfect time-keeper going at a steady pace, solar time and clock time coincide only on 15 April, 14 June, 1 September and 25 December. The greatest variations are on 11 February, when the sun lags behind the clock by fourteen minutes and twenty-eight seconds, and 3 November when it is sixteen minutes and eight seconds ahead. Therefore the man who sets his stopped watch by a common sun-dial, without taking this 'equation of time' into account, may miss his bus by a quarter of an hour.

Mean time, or average time, by which we now order our affairs, is based upon equal subdivisions of the average length of all the days of naturally unequal length throughout the year. A more regular, natural division of the earth's annual excursion about the sun is used by astronomers and is known as sidereal time. This is measured by the rotation of the earth upon its axis in relation to the fixed stars. Owing to its progression round the sun, the earth revolves once more upon its axis in a year than is apparently the case, and the sidereal day is consequently shorter than the mean solar day by three minutes and fifty-six seconds. As the rotation of the earth goes at a uniform rate in relation to the fixed stars, stellar observations once provided a more convenient means of regulating accurate observatory clocks (by which other local timekeepers could be set) than solar observations as no 'equation' had to be calculated; it was only necessary to remember that the particular star being watched would cross the meridian on any day three minutes and fifty-six seconds sooner than on the preceding day.

To the first observers of natural phenomena, the various irregularities of the earth's motion (or the sun's motion as it doubtless appeared to them) cannot have been apparent, and it would have seemed that there were 365 intervals of alternating light and darkness between one spring equinox (or some other easily observed happening) and the next. At some uncounted number of years after this fact had been established, the need to chop each of these 365 days into smaller portions became apparent.

According to most authorities, our present system derives from that evolved during the earliest recorded period of Sumerian civilisation, but as the frontiers of archaeological and historical knowledge are constantly being widened this should not be accepted as final. Indeed, in the light of recent discoveries concerning Chinese horology it could well be that our modern time system dawned, with the sun, in the east. Whether ante-dated or not, the Sumerians appear to have evolved two systems, one beginning at midnight and dividing the day into six large portions, each sub-divided into sixty smaller ones, and the other measuring the start of the day from sunset and splitting it into twelve divisions each of which was subdivided thirty times.

In the absence of reliable clocks, a system which starts at midnight (or any other fixed point) and divides the day into equal portions, poses the problem of how to determine midnight. It is obviously easier to observe the sunset (or sunrise) and allocate portions until the next one. This carries the disadvantage that the 'hours' of night and day will only be naturally equal in number twice a year. Therefore if they are arbitrarily made equal in number throughout the year they have to vary in length with the seasons. This problem bedevilled the makers of mechanical clocks, when they first became known, as the design and construction of a machine to go at a steady pace was difficult enough, but to make one which could *regularly* go at *varying* rates proved almost impossible. Our present system of dividing the day into two sets of twelve equal hours, starting at midnight, originated in South Germany which may fairly claim to be the place where mechanical clocks first began to be made as regular articles of commerce.

Nevertheless, not all localities followed suit. In many parts of Italy, for example, a twenty-four unequal hour system, starting at sunset, persisted into the nineteenth century despite its inconvenience; whilst the Japanese continued with their even less manageable arrangements until 1868. This is no place fully to describe the Japanese system, which was based upon four sequences of six hours which, on their most highly developed clocks, were measured by a mechanism with two escapements, each beating at a different speed and each brought into action automatically to measure the long hours of night and the short hours of day, or vice versa according to season. The rates of going of the individual escapements had to be altered every few days. These Japanese clocks were not articles of ordinary domestic furniture, and the fact that none of those I have seen shows any perceptible traces of wear, suggests that their subtleties were too much even for the oriental mind. They were probably wound up only on high days and holidays (literally, as they were mostly used in temples) and valued more as status symbols than as timekeepers.

Whatever variations in methods of counting may have existed in different countries and different times, all known time systems that have been accepted have been based on a number divisible by three. That is, on six, twelve or twenty-four main divisions of the day. Whether this arose originally because of some religious or magical significance is not known, but it is probable that the remote, primitive arithmeticians who were responsible realised that a system based on a dividend of three is more flexibly sub-divided or multiplied than one based on five or ten.

The choice of a twelve- rather than a ten-hour system was fortunate for the makers of mechanical clocks, which depend upon the ratios of revolution of toothed wheels, of different sizes and tooth-numbers, in relationship with one another. When dealing with twelve, and the divisors and multipliers thereof, these gear ratios, as engineers call them, become quite complicated; but to achieve similar results on a decimal basis involves the use of much more complicated gearing. The only attempt, so far, made to introduce a decimal time and calendar system was foisted upon the long-suffering French by the Directory in 1794. Decimal timekeepers required gear trains of such complexity that they were priced out of the reach of ordinary people, which was just as well as ordinary people found the decimal time system so complex that they could not tell the time on the clocks they could not afford to buy. The French decimal clock and calendar were soon tactfully abandoned, but the idea crops up again from time to time. A recent letter to the *Sunday Times* of London advocated decimal time as a fitting accompaniment for decimal currency, and the writer was presumably unaware of the French attempt and the difficulties involved.

Another method of dividing the day was evolved in Nuremburg and was used throughout the almost autonomous district of which it was the principal city. The day was split into twenty-four hours divided into unequal night and day periods (except at the equinoxes); instead of having the individual hours of unequal duration, as in Japan, they were of equal duration but varied in number, by day and by night, as dictated by the changing seasons. As Nuremburg became an important clockmaking centre mechanical timepieces, particularly some important public clocks, made there conformed to this rather inconvenient arrangement. The numbers of the 'official' hours of day and night were proclaimed monthly, and such of the public clocks as had dials (a relatively new innovation) had moveable figures or shutters, painted pale and dark blue to suggest light and darkness, which could be adjusted to correspond with the proclaimed changes. This system lingered on into the seventeenth century, when Nuremburg gave up her 'moveable hours' in favour of the 'equal hours' of neighbouring districts.

It is fairly generally accepted that mechanical clocks, as we know them, were evolved for monastic use to supplement and then to supplant the sundials, sand-glasses and clepsydrae, or water clocks, by which the times of offices were regulated. The evidence so far available suggests that the clock was a thirteenth-century invention and that its first form was that of a simple, dial-less, alarum which rang a small warning bell at suitable intervals to attracted the attention of the 'tower warden' who rang a larger bell summoning the brethren to prayer.

The monastic brethren were not, at first, interested in ringing the equal or unequal hours of the secular day from their towers, but were only concerned to proclaim the irregularly spaced canonical hours which were bounded by sunset and sunrise. The canonical hours started with Matins at the third quarter of the night, followed by Prime at sunrise. Tertia fell half-way between sunrise and mid-day, which was originally called Sexta; Nona was at mid-afternoon, Vespers an hour before sunset, and Compline marked the close of monastic day. Tertia and Sexta were ultimately combined as one chapter, and Nona (or noon) was moved to midday. A code of varying numbers of strokes on the bell indicated these canonical hours.

As timekeeping became of greater consequence to the secular world, the monasteries began the practice of sounding the secular hours (according to local usage) from their belfries, but the influence of the canonical hours or chapters is still with us. What the layman would call the hour ring or numeral ring on a clock dial is still called the 'chapter ring' by horologists.

By the time the monasteries, or some of them, were proclaiming the secular hours to the outside world, as well as sounding the canonical hours for their own guidance, the use of the clock dial was becoming established. This was first developed as a revolving dial-plate or chapter ring with a fixed pointer to show the hour. No doubt this addition was originally only to make it easier to set the times at which the alarum should ring, but its general convenience would at once have become obvious. Next, some unnamed genius devised the 'count wheel' or 'locking plate' mechanism which enabled a clock to strike the hours (canonical or secular) automatically.

It is fairly certain that the first striking clocks were large machines, powerful enough to sound on large bells for the benefit of all those within a reasonable distance of the monastery or church. In other words, they were what we now call turret clocks, although they were not necessarily fitted in turrets. They had no dials although, very often, they worked quite large automaton figures of men, known as Jacquemarts or Jacks, who struck visible bells in simulation of the 'tower wardens' whose functions had been usurped by the new machinery.

At about the same time that these striking public clocks came into use, the striking mechanism, suitably scaled down, was applied to the small 'tower wardens' clocks' in place of (or in addition to) the alarum mechanism. So, what we now call the domestic or chamber clock was born and the moveable chapter ring rotating about a fixed pointer gave way to a moveable hand revolving round a fixed dial. This may originally have been changed for structural convenience, but it is a better arrangement as one tells the time by noting the position of the hands of the clock and it is not necessary to 'read' the numerals. It is in this respect that the conventional clock is superior to the newly fashionable contrivance (invented and re-invented many times in the past two centuries) which shows the time by changing numerals.

It is almost certainly because of the growing use of public striking clocks that a double-twelve-hour system supplanted the straightforward twenty-four hour usage in most countries. It is easy enough to make a mistake when counting eleven or twelve on a slow-striking clock, and the higher teens and twenties are even more misleading. A 'coded' system such as Knibb's Roman notation strike of the late seventeenth century would have got over the difficulty perhaps.

The addition of dials and hands to public, or turret clocks, came later than to the domestic variety. Indeed the 'faceless' public clock survived surprisingly late alongside the newer types. Tradition says that Queen Elizabeth I gave the Cinque Port of Rye its famous church clock, with its automaton figures of two fat gilded cherubs who strike the quarter bells. The dial, with hour and minute hands which the 'quarter jacks' now sit beside, dates from the mid-eighteenth century, and there is no reliable evidence to suggest that it ever had a predecessor.

Long before man had evolved these mechanical timekeepers to measure his fixed or moveable or canonical hours, the inaccuracies of the 365 day annual calendar had become apparent. In the northern hemisphere, it is convenient to measure the start of the year from the spring equinox when the sun crosses the equator from south to north—taking 1 January as New Year's Day is a relatively modern innovation. Between one spring equinox and the next, the earth makes 366 revolutions of sidereal time which equals 365 days, 6 hours, 9 minutes and 11 seconds of mean solar time. On completion of its excursion round the sun, the earth returns to the same place in relation to the fixed stars. However, because of the phenomenon known as the precession of the equinoxes—whereby, because of the retrograde motion of equinoctial points along the sun's apparent orbit, in each successive sidereal year the equinoxes occur earlier—this return does not exactly coincide with the spring equinox. In order, therefore, that the 'artificial' calendar may match the actual seasons, the sidereal year is disregarded and the solar or equinoctial year is adjusted to the nearest readily divisible factor of 365 days, 5 hours, 48 minutes and 48 seconds. The Julian calendar, which was adopted throughout the Roman Empire, disregarded the fraction until 45BC and allowed only 365 days to each year. The difference was then reckoned as six hours and every fourth year was made a leap year.

The difference between the six hours allowed in this new reckoning and the true fraction produced an error of about seven days in nine hundred years, and in 1582 Pope Gregory XII struck out ten days' accumulated error and ordained that three leap years should be omitted every four hundred years. Therefore, as 1600 was a leap year, 1700, 1800 and 1900 were not, but the year 2000 will have 366 days.

The Reformation left the English strongly anti-Papist and the Gregorian calendar was not adopted in Great Britain until 1752, although for nearly a hundred years some official documents and many private papers had been dated in 'New Style'. The 1752 adjustment required eleven days to be struck from the calendar, and this accounts for the apparently irrational start of the fiscal year on 5 April instead of on Lady Day, 25 March. The change provoked bitter opposition, riots, broken windows, street fighting and demands of 'give us back our eleven days'. Russia was the last major country using the western calendar to make the adjustment: this was in 1917 when the error had become one of thirteen days, and this is why the October Revolution took place in November by Gregorian reckoning.

We are apt to think of a clock as a machine which measures and indicates the time of day; but as the day is only a fraction of a year, and other larger units, clockmakers have often been concerned with machines contrived to show dates; lunar, tidal, stellar and planetary movements; eclipses and other occasionally recurring phenomena. Indeed, long before domestic clocks became common, elaborate 'clockwork' planetaria had been made to show the movements of the observable heavenly bodies in remarkably accurate fashion.

There is very strong evidence to support the theory that the first self-regulating machine controlled by an 'escapement'—that is the first 'artificial' timekeeper capable of a reasonably accurate performance—was a very large water-powered machine made in China before the Christian era as the heart and regulator of an elaborate automatic planetarium. As well as fulfilling a useful function by showing seasonal and lunar changes (information of great value to an agricultural community) the planetary and stellar motions indicated by machines such as these had astrological significance. Astrology, rather than astronomy as we know it, was at the root of most early planetaria, armillary spheres and similar devices both in the East and the West.

These planetaria were clockwork in a sense, but not clocks in our sense, as it was no part of their business to show the time of day; but as mechanical timekeepers became more common many were made, both public and domestic, which showed planetary and other astronomical information as well as the time. Their complex trains of gear wheels prove their makers to have been men of great ingenuity and mathematical ability. Yet, considered coldly, their efforts were misplaced as they had not yet solved the central problem of making the timekeeper, which controlled all the elaborate functions, keep time. This was well summed up by Mr George Daniels, in an article in *Antiquarian Horology* on the astronomical watches of George Margetts: '. . . long-period readings of the astronomical information . . . will, however, be unreliable because . . . the watch will have forgotten what time of day it is.' If this was true of an eighteenth-century watch capable of keeping time within about two minutes or less a day, how much truer it is of a sixteenth-century clock which, at best, probably had a daily variation of rate of some fifteen minutes.

There is also an inherent absurdity in making a machine to show celestial phenomena which occur and recur so infrequently as to be beyond the span of years during which the machine can be expected to keep going without pause. One of the lunar indications shown by the Margetts watch recurs at intervals of 18·61 years, and there is no possibility that the timepiece could run for that length of time without attention. Nevertheless, there was something heroic about the very impracticality of such splendid instruments, and they served a purpose by sharpening the wits of their makers, who achieved great feats of calculation in their design and miracles of workmanship in their execution with resources we would consider pitifully inadequate.

Naturally enough, these elaborate astronomical timepieces have always been rare, but even the simplest of English long-case and 'bracket' clocks, from the second half of the seventeenth century onwards, nearly always had a day-of-the-month indicator, and many country-made clocks also show the phases of the moon. In times and places where almanacs were scarce and regular newspapers unknown, the automatic calendar and the lunar disc were valuable adjuncts to the clock. The 'calendar work', as it is called, is usually of the simple variety, similar to that found on many modern watches, which has to be adjusted manually for those months with less than thirty-one days. What is known as 'perpetual calendar work' is not unknown: this is horological language for calendar indications, usually showing day of week, name of month, date, lunar phases and 'equation of time' so devised that the mechanism automatically adjusts itself to take note of the short months and remembers to put in the extra day at leap year.

At the heart both of the most elaborate astronomical clock and the simplest thirty-hour, single-hand, country-made 'grandfather' is a collection of toothed wheels, driven by falling weights or uncoiling ribbons of steel; and at *their* heart is a device to chop up the time into small and easily counted portions of precisely equal duration. This is the escapement, and the search for a perfect escapement must sometimes have seemed, to our ancestors, almost as hopeless as the quest for the philosopher's stone.

It is reasonable to suppose that man first measured the time of day by watching the sun and noting changing shadow-patterns, using first some natural object, a tree or a boulder, as his 'gnomon' before progressing to the construction of his own gnomon and other fixed indicators, in a series of ever more elaborate and accurately divided 'sundials'. The term covers great structures such as Stonehenge, and little folding contraptions to hang round one's neck or carry in a pocket. Sand-glasses, calibrated lamps or candles and a wide variety of clepsydrae or water-clocks followed the sundial, and the invention and application of toothed-wheel gearing antedate the mechanical clock by several centuries.

It is also reasonable to assume that the use of 'gear wheels', as they are now called, originated in connection with devices to raise and distribute water. The familiar shadoof, or rocking beam, bucket and counterpoise, still used in Egypt and elsewhere, is the oldest such machine with a probable life-span of some six thousand years; but rotary machines, often animal-powered, are scarcely less ancient.

There is little point in speculating upon the various stages of evolution from simple roller to the fully developed wheel, and then to the transmission of motion from one wheel to another. It is a reasonable guess that accident or some temporary need drove some ingenious man to drive pegs or spikes into the periphery of one wheel or drum and to cut suitable grooves or serrations in its fellow in order that the one might rotate the other without slipping. How long it then took to find out that if a ten-pegged wheel drove a twenty-grooved roller, the latter would always revolve only once for every two revolutions of its fellow is anybody's guess.

It is certain that complex systems of toothed wheels were known before the Christian era, and it is almost certain that China was their birthplace. Legend credits the Yellow Emperor with the invention of a 'South-pointing Chariot' four thousand years before Christ.

The chariot was surmounted by a full-sized carved figure of a god or immortal with outstretched arm and index finger, which always pointed to the south no matter in what direction the chariot turned. The Yellow Emperor used this chariot to guide his troops through an artificial fog which had been created by the enemy's necromancers to entrap them.

The Yellow Emperor is more a figure of myth than of historical fact, and so no doubt were the artificial fog—the first military smoke screen—and the magical chariot. Yet the legend was so interwoven with fact, or a sort of wish fulfilment, that three thousand years after the mythical chariot had shown the way, real South-pointing Chariots *were* made. They were probably only used in ceremonial processions, but their existence before the Christian era is fully documented and various accounts of them exist. It used to be assumed from these references that the Chinese had discovered the use of the magnetic compass some hundreds of years before, in fact, they did. Nobody was able to suggest how any magnetic system could have been used to turn anything as heavy as a life-sized carved wooden figure, but in the 1930s Sinologists came upon accounts of the chariots which described arrangements of toothed wheels used in their construction.

These 'specifications' made no sense, either because of repeated copying and mis-transcription or because the vital information had been deliberately concealed. The mystery was finally solved by George Lanchester, pioneer motor engineer, who concluded, and demonstrated with models, that the desired result could be attained by suitable gearing connected to the chariot wheels and acting upon the pointing figure through the medium of some form of the differential gear, now used in the final drive mechanism of motor vehicles. If this is accepted, and it provides the most logical explanation, Chinese engineers of the first century AD or before, would have been quite capable of making mechanical clocks. That they do not appear to have done so must be attributed to one of those quirks which occur so often in the history of technology.

Just as it is probable that toothed wheels first came into use in connection with irrigation works, so it seems likely that the use of a falling weight to provide motive power came from the same source. One of the earliest ways to ease the labour of hauling water from a deep well must have been by the 'windlass', or combination of cranked handle, revolving drum and rope. The inevitable accidents as the handle was released too soon and flew round under the impetus of the laden bucket, probably catching the operator a sharp blow as it did so, must have prompted certain lines of thought.

One of the merits of toothed wheel-work must have become apparent quite early. This is the readiness with which it may be made to transmit motion round corners. Primitive right-angled gearing lies at the heart of water-lifting or grain-grinding engines of great antiquity, and the origin of the first practicable clock escapement almost certainly stems from the same source.

If the pegs, or teeth, of one wheel (and it must be assumed that all gear wheels of antiquity were wooden) were fixed not radially around the periphery but axially, parallel with the axle, then the wheel could drive, or be driven by, a similarly pegged disc placed at right angles to it. The refinement of this crude system into the 'contrate wheel and pinion' still used in clock mechanism, and finally into true mitre, or bevel, gearing need not concern us.

At some time in the early stages of experiment, it was found possible to make the axially-toothed wheel cause alternating part-rotatory movement in a suitably shaped axle or 'staff'. A construction of this sort could easily be arranged to vibrate a hammer quickly to-and-fro against a bell to sound an alarum. At first, no doubt, the spiked disc or primitive contrate wheel was turned by hand to sound the tocsin, but the addition of a suitable 'barrel', rope and weight was an obvious way to make the alarum self-acting, once the human attendant had 'unlatched' it. It would then have been a fairly obvious refinement to add a large gear wheel to the primary, weight-driven, spindle which drove a small wheel or pinion on a second spindle to which the alarum-operating wheel was attached. This would greatly increase the duration of ringing in relation to the descent of the weight.

In *Weight-Driven Chamber Clocks of the Middle Ages and Renaissance*, Ernest L. Edwardes examines the possibility that mechanical clockwork alarums of this sort were eventually combined with clepsydrae. This seems a reasonable assumption, as all the known types of water clock in western usage share a particular shortcoming with sand-glasses or calibrated lamps. This is that no matter how elaborate they were, they depended in one way or another on the filling or emptying of vessels, and they required close attention towards the end of their period of going so that the necessary emptying and replenishing could be done without loss of time. Many of the clepsydrae of antiquity were of great ingenuity, showing equal or unequal hours in various ways. Plato is said to have had one with a whistling alarum, worked by a syphonic device from the water vessel, so that the machine could signal its need for attention. Except on very large machines such syphonic whistles would not have been as audible as a bell, and the combination of water-operated timepiece and weight-driven mechanical alarum seems logical.

The translation of the weight-driven alarum with its fast-vibrating hammer into the mechanical timepiece with its slow-vibrating controller seems to have been made by about 1270. The escapement which made this possible was still being made, unchanged in essentials, six hundred years later.

Page 35 PLATE 4 Bird's-eye view of restored single-spoke balance wheel and escapement wheel of lantern clock by Peter Closon, *c*1640. The vacant holes between the stalk of the bell hammer and the balance wheel, together with dark circles showing metal of different density, indicate an earlier conversion from balance control to anchor escapement

PLATE 5 Unrestored lantern clock dated (authentically) 1669, with heraldic frets, vase-shaped finials and inscribed numerals from 1 to 31 on the inner edge of the chapter ring suggesting the clock originally had a calendar hand

Page 36 PLATE 6 The 'grandfather' of all grandfather clocks. The definitive form by Ahasuerus Fromanteel, *c*1660–70, with eight-day striking movement, concentric minute hand, calendar, verge escapement with short 'bob pendulum' and bolt-and-shutter maintaining power. Height 6ft 3in, dial 9in across. Ebony case

Chapter Three

Early Mechanical Clocks

TIME never stands still, but the essence of an escapement is that it alternately arrests and releases the train of wheel-work in a clock, allowing it to run only in a series of jerks; each jerk being, theoretically, of the same duration as those that precede and follow it.

Sand-glasses and clepsydrae move without pause, and might therefore seem more naturally suited to the business of timekeeping than escapement clocks. For short intervals of time, they can be accurate enough. The Royal Navy used five- and fifteen-minute glasses to measure ships' speeds until the nineteenth century; and it is not difficult to make a sand-glass perform consistently for periods up to an hour or two. The tendency of the sand to run more slowly as the upper vessel empties can be counteracted by suitably shaping the glasses and the errors are self-cancelling, but a twenty-four-hour glass, or an eight-day glass (if such a thing could be made), would be both unwieldy and inaccurate.

Similar considerations apply to clepsydrae. These ranged from simple graduated basins from which (or into which) water flowed at a supposedly uniform pace, to more elaborate devices in which floats rose and fell to turn indicators by means of cords and pulleys, or toothed racks and pinions. The clepsydra was capable of almost unlimited elaboration; and a splendid contrivance, which was given to Charlemagne by the king of Persia in AD 807, is said to have had a 'dial' consisting of twelve small doors, each of which flew open at the hour it was supposed to represent. As each door opened it allowed the emergence of a number of metal balls, corresponding to the number of the hour shown, which rolled down inclined planes to fall upon and sound a large brass drum. At the twelfth hour automaton horsemen closed the doors.

Even with multiple supply tanks with suitable overflow pipes to maintain a constant 'head' of water, it is very difficult to ensure a constant rate of flow, particularly with vessels and pipes small enough to make the clepsydra a reasonably manageable size. The Chinese machine mentioned in the preceding chapter, though dependent on water, had an escapement device which alternately halted and released a large water wheel which both drove and regulated the elaborate wheelwork which moved the representations of the heavenly bodies. After each halt, the wheel could not move again until the next 'bucket' to be filled had received a definite weight of water. This tripped, or overbalanced, a series of weighted, links and levers which locked the wheel, but the action of withdrawing the first lock immediately interposed another, against which the next step of the wheel came to rest.

It is only during the last ten years that intensive deductive work from Chinese texts has laid bare the principle of this water-driven timekeeper, working models of which may be seen in the Science Museum in London. It is not yet confirmed, but it is believed, that knowledge of this system reached the Middle East and Europe, although it does not seem to have left any traces or records, and the invention of the mechanical escapement clock has no known connection with the water escapement clock.

The problem of adapting a weight-driven train of toothed wheels to the job of timekeeping doubtless exercised men's minds long before the escapement clock was evolved, and many expedients must have been tried. It is probably a safe guess that experiments were made with some form of fly wheel and then with a vaned fan or air-brake (a 'fly' in horological language), to keep the wheels turning slowly and steadily enough to be used for time measuring. The 'fly' is still used in clockwork to regulate the speed of the striking mechanism, by preventing undue acceleration. For this purpose it is adequate, but very few trials would have shown its unsuitability for the more precise business of timekeeping.

The supposition that the first mechanical escapement grew out of the mechanical alarum, cannot be verified but is probably true, and the family resemblance of the two pieces of mechanism is very marked. As Figure 1 shows, the work is done by an 'escapement wheel' with saw-tooth-shaped projections parallel with the axis. An uneven number of teeth is essential and there is little doubt that the first examples had plain pegs or pins: crude wooden clocks with such escapement wheels were made in the Black Forest until the eighteenth century; but the type of wheel shown, and normally used, probably dates from the twelfth century. A vertical 'staff' or 'verge' is so placed in relation to the escapement wheel that flat beds or flags, known as 'pallets', formed upon it engage with the wheel's teeth. The pallets are placed at an angle of approximately 90° to one another, and the distance between their centres is that of the diameter of the wheel.

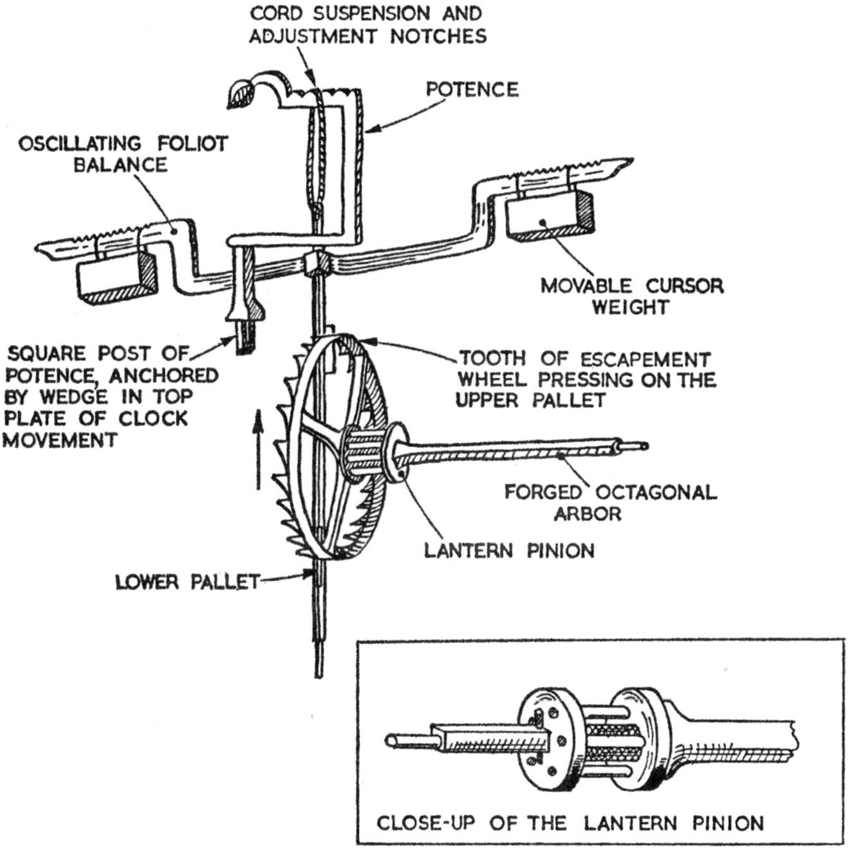

FIGURE 1 *The earliest form of escapement with foliot bar balance as arranged on fifteenth-century domestic clock*

At the upper end of the verge is a cross-piece, with moveable weights hanging from its arms, known as the 'foliot', and the complete assembly of verge, or pallet staff, and foliot is pivoted in a suitable bracket at its lower end whilst the upper end is held in place, and the weight supported, by cords from an upper bracket called the 'potence'.

The action of the escapement is easily seen. As drawn, the uppermost tooth of the escapement wheel is halted by the upper pallet; as the wheel tries to revolve it pushes this pallet aside, as though opening a door, and consequently sets the weighted cross-piece moving. When the tooth has escaped the pallet, the wheel is immediately halted again by, in effect, the lower door or pallet being slammed in the face of the next advancing tooth. The check is not 'dead', however, as the impetus given to the weighted foliot by the upper tooth causes it to continue travelling in the original direction for some distance. This means that the lower tooth is not only prevented from advancing but is actually forced backwards, and all the other wheels in the train, together with the driving weight are also put into reverse. In due time this 'recoil' is exhausted, the power of the driving weight, acting indirectly upon the escapement wheel, prevails over the inertia of the foliot and the lower tooth in turn pushes aside its door, gives contrary impetus to the balance and in turn slams the door in the face of the next upper advancing tooth. So the process continues, with the wheels of the 'going train' advancing in a series of measured steps—each step forward being followed by a lesser step back rather like the progress of a stage army in an old-fashioned melodrama.

The regulation of this series of steps, the necessary chopping of time into small, easily measured, pieces depends upon the inertia of the foliot fighting against the force trying to turn the escapement wheel. There is no naturally synchronous action inherent in such a combination of forces. Variations in the power reaching the escapement wheel directly affect the speed of the clock; and as there were many sources of variations, from imperfections in the shaping of the wheel teeth, changes in temperature, thickening of the lubricant and so on, the performance of a clock controlled by such an escapement is far from accurate.

The evidence so far available suggests that the 'verge escapement', as it is generally (though incorrectly) known, which made the mechanical clock a practicable proposition, was invented in the last third of the thirteenth century. 'Verge' in this context merely means a 'staff' or slender 'arbor', and is analogous with the wand of office carried by a verger. Therefore every 'arbor', 'staff' or 'axle' in a clock movement could properly be called a 'verge'. Until other types were invented, there was no need for any specific name for the old form of escapement. In the eighteenth and early nineteenth centuries, when it was necessary to distinguish between old and new escapements, the old type was described as the 'vertical escapement' (or 'vertical action'), particularly in watches, or the 'crown wheel escapement', and the word 'verge' came to mean the arbor or axle carrying the pallets of *any* type of escapement. Tautology crept in and it was often called the 'verge staff'. Only in the latter part of the nineteenth century did the term 'verge escapement' come into use in the present sense; dealers or repairers would speak of a 'verge watch' or 'verge clock' to signify one controlled by the oldest form of mechanical escapement. As in other fields, changed usage in horological nomenclature sets many traps for the unwary. In the eighteenth century for example, the term 'balance wheel' often signified what we now call the 'escapement wheel' of a watch, and it was so called because it gave motion to the 'balance'—the actual balance wheel (as we now know it) being called the 'swing wheel'. The escapement wheel of a clock was sometimes called the 'swing wheel' as it was responsible for imparting the swing to the pendulum. It would be too much to expect that this explanation does more than add further confusion to a confused subject.

Imperfect though this first escapement is, it is a great deal better than anything which had gone before it, and it probably had a longer 'production life' than any other mechanical device. As late as 1887, 300,000 watches were made in Switzerland with verge escapements; that is two hundred years after better escapements had been devised and six centuries after their first appearance.

Even if their timekeeping was erratic, the first mechanical clocks had the great advantage over clepsydrae and sand-glasses that they did not need such constant attention. Even those—the majority no doubt—which had to be wound every twelve hours had a safety margin of an hour or more in case the 'orologer' or custodian were late; but a sand-glass had to be turned at the instant its upper vessel emptied and this, in practice, meant punctual watchfulness every hour.

As already stated, the first mechanical clocks were probably monastic alarums, which then developed into striking clocks, probably without dials and powerful enough to be heard over a wide area. Domestic or chamber clocks, with or without striking work, followed soon after. The first type of striking mechanism is believed to date from about 1330, and is known as the 'locking-plate' or 'count-wheel' system. It survived into the twentieth century on some continental and American clocks, despite the introduction of a better mechanism in 1675. This was the 'rack' method, invented by the Rev Edward Barlow in England, and it will be convenient to consider the mechanical niceties of the two systems together in a later chapter.

The same sort of 'count wheel' mechanism which allowed a clock to strike the hours, secular or canonical, automatically in proper sequence, could also be adapted to sounding or 'chiming' the quarter hours. This necessitated adding another train of wheelwork to the assemblage, and one of the earliest surviving quarter-chiming clocks was that made for Wells Cathedral about 1390. The original movement, to which an anchor escapement and pendulum were added in the seventeenth century, is still to be seen going in the Science Museum. The oldest form of quarter chime was sounded on two bells of differing pitch and is known onomatopoeically as 'ting-tang', but more elaborate signals on greater numbers of bells soon followed. Quarter-chiming domestic clocks, although rare, were occasionally made before 1500.

It is perhaps necessary here to interpolate some horological language. The word 'clock', deriving from the low-German word for a bell, strictly speaking refers to a striking clock, meaning one which sounds the hours and, occasionally, gives some signal at the half hours, generally by a single blow on the bell or gong. Confusion arises because that which the horologist calls a striking clock is often referred to by the lay public as a chiming clock, although that term is properly reserved for one with full quarter-chiming mechanism in addition to the arrangements for striking the hours. The word 'timepiece' is generically applicable to any mechanical timekeeper, but it is specifically used by horologists to mean a clock with no chiming, striking or alarum work. More confusion arises here because a 'timepiece' in this sense was once often called a 'watch', irrespective of size or portability. The large long-case clock which Thomas Tompion gave to the Pump Room at Bath is referred to in a memorial tablet, placed near it, as 'this watch'. Similarly, what we now call the 'going train' of a striking or chiming clock was also once called the 'watch'. This usage applied particularly to turret clocks, and an item in parochial accounts: 'Pay'd XVIIJ^{d}. for mending of the watch' would refer to repairs to the going part of the church tower clock.

The verge and foliot combination is capable of adjustment by two means. The cursor weights on the cross-bar can be moved to or from the centre, thereby reducing or lengthening the time of each 'excursion'; or the whole assembly can be tilted, by moving the cord suspension along the notched potence, so as to increase or reduce the depth of engagement of the pallets with the wheel teeth. The more deeply they engage (up to the point at which they 'butt') the wider and slower the swing of the balance.

An alternative to the foliot, which was probably first used late in the fifteenth century, was a plain circular wheel balance with no moveable cursor weights. As made for domestic clocks, the pallet staff with its balance wheel was usually pivoted in a fixed bracket or 'cock' at its upper end and the arrangement of notched potence and cord suspension was gradually abolished. This meant that the pallets could no longer be moved in or out of engagement with the escapement wheel; and with the moveable cursor weights also gone, the only way of altering the clock's rate was by adding to or taking from the driving weight. The mass of the balance was supported on an 'end plate' below the bottom pivot and this, together with the pivoted upper support, meant that there was more friction for the clock to overcome than in the earlier system, and this added another source of inaccuracy.

The plain wheel balance therefore was inferior to the foliot and yet, although the latter survived on turret clocks until the seventeenth century, on crude Black Forest wooden clocks until the eighteenth, and on Japanese clocks until the nineteenth century, wheel balances appear to have outnumbered foliots on domestic clocks from about 1500 onwards. As far as is known, no English domestic clock was made with a foliot balance or with adjustable suspension for the wheel balance. The reason for this apparent illogicality is that the early clocksmiths must soon have discovered that the less opportunity the owner was given to meddle with his clock, the better. Adjustable balance weights and potences might be all very well on the church clock, which would probably be wound and adjusted by a competent man (very possibly at first by the maker himself), but domestic clocks, as present day repairers know full well, must be made proof against the worst that the cash customer can do to them; whether it is by boiling them or prodding their entrails with improbable implements.

So far, all the clocks we have considered were weight-driven and made entirely of iron by blacksmiths. Their constructional details are fascinating, showing a minimum of lathe-work and, usually, a total absence of screws, but lie beyond the scope of this book. As the domestic clock developed and grew smaller and more elaborate, the work began to savour more of the locksmith than the blacksmith and brass began occasionally to be used for some of the parts. Whilst all clocks were weight-driven and had to hang on the wall or stand on a suitably pierced bracket, they were not easily transported from house to house. Yet the man rich enough to own a clock in the fifteenth or sixteenth century, when domestic clocks were still expensive rarities, was also the man rich enough to move, with all his furnishings, from one property to another at fairly frequent intervals, in order to supervise different estates and to allow time for each house to 'sweeten'.

The invention of the spring-driven mechanism in the late fifteenth century got over the difficulty, and the clock could be not only moved from house to house without trouble, but from room to room: or, if it were made small enough, it could be hung round the owner's neck and become not only a 'watch' but a costly and highly-prized status symbol.

The business of making a coiled ribbon of elastic metal suitable to drive a train of wheels as it uncoiled was a difficult one. The first mainsprings may well have been of brass (as is the oldest known surviving example, dating from 1525), but the art of making them of steel, which probably originated in Italy, was mastered and developed in South Germany during the first years of the sixteenth century. The spring clock, and then the watch, were Germany's particular contributions and for some time Nuremburg was the horological centre of the world.

The oldest and simplest way of applying the power of a coiled ribbon spring is that still found in cheap alarm clocks. That is, the inner end of the spring is hooked to the 'arbor' of 'the great wheel', with the usual arrangement of ratchet and pawl connection to allow the arbor to be turned in one direction for winding, whilst the other end of the spring is formed into a loop and anchored to one of the pillars or supports of the frame.

If an exposed spring of this kind breaks (and one may suppose breakages to have been common whilst the techniques of spring-smithing were in their infancy) it may bend or break adjacent parts as it flies asunder. An early refinement was to enclose the spring in a 'barrel' or circular box attached to the great wheel as shown in Figure 2. The inner end of the spring is again anchored to the arbor, which is free to turn in its bearings in the barrel. A ratchet wheel and 'click' (as clockmakers always call what engineers refer to as a pawl) allows the arbor to be turned to wind the spring, but prevents it

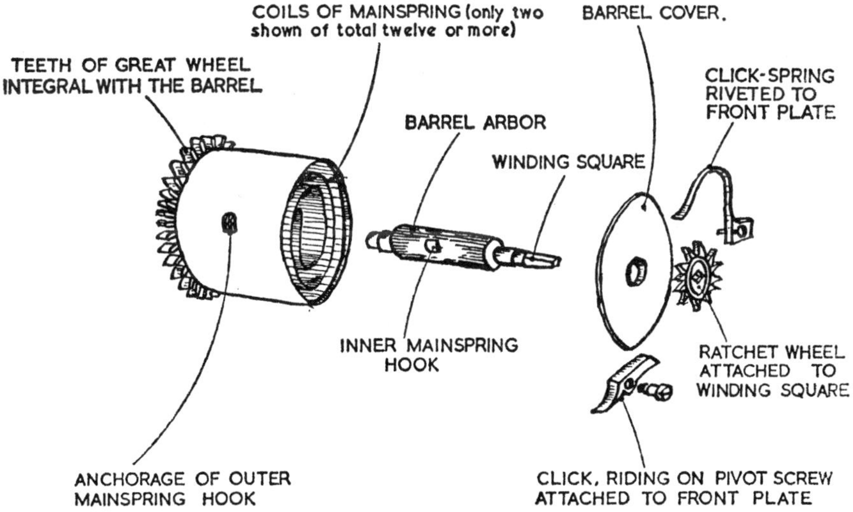

FIGURE 2 *'Going barrel' integral with great wheel; in practice there would be between ten and twenty or more turns of spring coiled in the barrel*

from turning the other way and the transmission of the power is from the outer end of the spring which is hooked to the inner circumference of the barrel. In addition to safeguarding the clock if the spring breaks, the 'going barrel' system has the merit that there is no interruption of the power supply during winding, as there is with the normal arrangement of weights and the cruder arrangement of spring connection.

Whether exposed or enclosed, spring power has the disadvantage that the force it exerts decreases as it runs down. With the verge escapement and unsprung balance controller being very susceptible, as we have seen, to any change in the power delivered to it, this variation in the driving force added another source of error and two methods were devised to deal with it. The first was by means of a device called a 'stackfreed' which was used in Germany and not, apparently, elsewhere. The second was by a 'fusee' which is of Italian origin and which is as perfect a solution to the problem as the stackfreed was imperfect.

As no stackfreed clock or watch is known to have been made in England, it is only necessary to say that the contrivance was supposed to work as a brake of diminishing power opposing the mainspring for about half the duration of the run after which, as it were, it gave a push to reinforce its waning effort. Although the fusee appeared in Germany early in the sixteenth century and is immeasurably superior to the stackfreed, it is one of the oddities of horological history that some German craftsmen were still making stackfreed clocks and watches (the latter particularly) in the seventeenth century.

The fusee is one of those perfectly logical and beautifully simple inventions that occasionally spring from the minds of a Leonardo da Vinci or a Frederick Lanchester. Da Vinci did indeed show a fusee in one of his many drawings of machines, but he did not relate its application to clockwork, and it is believed that a craftsman named Jacob Zech (or the Czech) of Prague made the first fusee clocks in about 1520. The evidence that Jacob Zech was the first to apply the fusee principle is, like so much in the history of inventions not conclusive. It rests upon a splendid table clock, made for King Sigismund I of Poland, which is now in the possession of the Society of Antiquaries of London, and which is dated 1525. Some

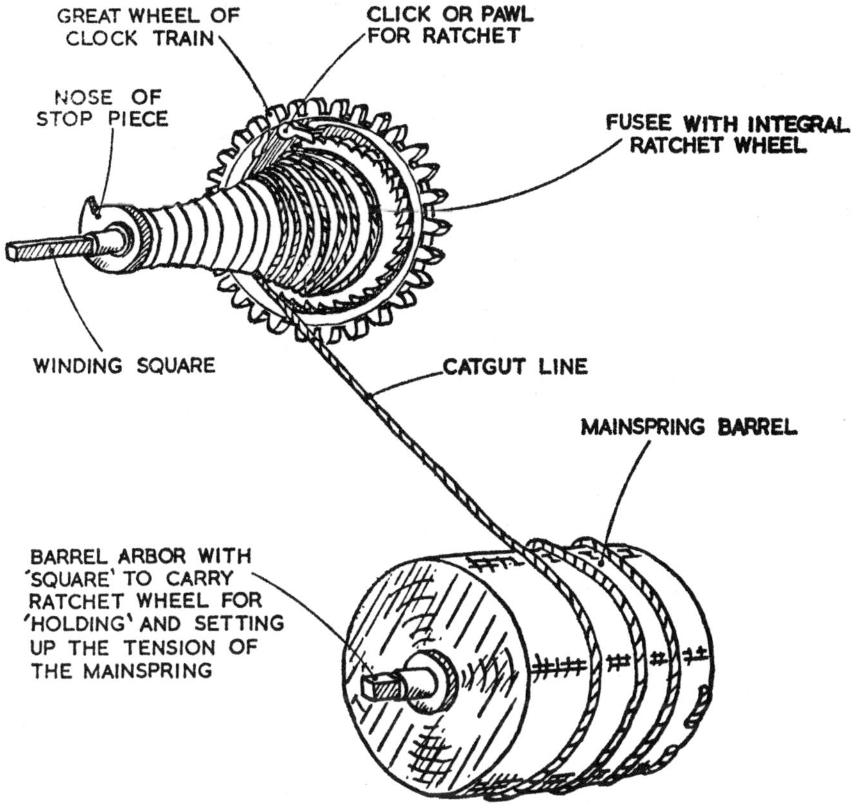

FIGURE 3 *Simplified diagram of spring barrel and fusee*

authorities are sceptical of the date. Even if it is authentic, this earliest known fusee clock is not necessarily the first and Jacob Zech may not have been the originator of the mechanism. So much has been discovered about horological history in the past ten or fifteen years that we can no longer accept some attributions of invention which were once stated as articles of faith.

As Figure 3 shows, the mainspring is enclosed in a barrel of which the arbor is normally prevented from turning. The first wheel, or great wheel, is no longer attached to the barrel, but is connected by ratchet and click to the fusee which is a conical grooved pulley. Mainspring barrel and fusee are connected by a catgut cord (or a fine chain), and as the fusee is turned by the winding key the gut line is pulled from the barrel, thereby turning it and coiling the spring inside it. When the spring is fully wound the catgut line has reached the last turn on the narrow end of the fusee; consequently the declining power exerted by the spring, as it uncoils and rotates the barrel, is compensated by the increasing leverage as the line travels from the narrow to the wide end of the fusee. If the strength of the spring is carefully matched to the angles of the fusee, the pull of the former is given uniform effect throughout the whole run.

A little lever, with a step formed in it, is pivoted to the frame of the clock, and as the catgut or chain approaches the last few turns of the fusee during winding, it pushes this lever before it, against the resistance of a light spring, so that the step on the lever moves into the path of a projection on the 'nose' of the fusee. This prevents the gut from running off the end and jamming between fusee and frame, and also prevents straining the mainspring. This contrivance is known as the 'stop-work', though seventeenth-century craftsmen referred to it with graphic simplicity as the 'garde-gutt'.

The initial tension on the mainspring, necessary to keep the gut line taut at the end of the run, can be varied by turning the barrel arbor (which is normally held stationary), and a ratchet and click or worm and wheel arrangement allow this to be done. Varying the initial (and therefore the overall) tension of the spring provided the only means of altering the rate of early spring clocks and watches; but when the verge escapement was transformed by the addition of the balance spring in the late seventeenth century, or when the pendulum was applied in suitable conditions, other means of regulation became possible and it was no longer necessary to regulate a timepiece by interfering with the power supply. The arrangement for varying the tension was retained as a means of 'setting up' the spring during assembly.

Unlike the 'going barrel' arrangement, the fusee system has the disadvantage that the power is cut off during winding, and this affects the timekeeping, but as the inherent timekeeping of a pre-pendulum, or pre-balance spring, piece is so bad this drawback was of little consequence. When more accurate methods made the short-coming apparent, an arrangement known as 'maintaining power' was fitted to good-quality timekeepers to obviate the difficulty.

Otherwise, the combination of mainspring, barrel, fusee and stop-work represents one of the most perfect in the history of mechanical engineering. It survived in production for the finest English work until very recently; and only now that the marine chronometer is being finally put out of business by radio time signals, is the fusee becoming obsolete after 450 years of useful life.

The framework and cases of early clocks assumed a wide variety of forms. The earliest types, known generically as 'Gothic clocks', which survived into the seventeeth century, had no cases in the accepted sense; but the framing carrying the wheelwork and supporting the bell, or bells, was pierced, arched, crocketed and finial-adorned in profuse, often beautiful, adaptations of Gothic architectural forms. The 'crossings', or spokes, of the exposed wheelwork, and particularly the balance, were also shaped or faceted to correspond. Simpler weight clocks of rectangular form began to be fitted with panels between the posted framework, and these panels, of iron or gilded brass or copper, were soon found valuable not only to keep dust and prying fingers out of the mechanism but as suitable areas for decoration.

Some of these hanging weight-driven clocks may have been protected by glazed wooden 'hoods' but wooden-cased clocks as such are not known to have existed before the seventeenth century, and their development is particularly associated with the rise of English clockmaking. Similarly, weight clocks were occasionally designed to be supported by wooden pedestals which enclosed, or partly enclosed, the weights, pulleys and cords. It is sometimes argued that these 'pillar' or 'pedestal' clocks are the true ancestors of the English long-case or 'grandfather' clock; but there is no clear line of descent and the long-case clock was more probably a spontaneous invention arising from the development of the pendulum mechanism in England between 1660 and 1670.

A peculiarity of early clocks (as distinct from timepieces in horologists' language) is that the two trains of wheelwork are seldom side by side, but nearly always back to back. The going train was, logically enough, placed immediately behind the dial, with the striking work parallel to it at the back of the framing. In more complex clocks, it was not unknown for one or more trains of wheelwork to be at right angles to the dial; a 'four train clock' might therefore have its going and striking trains back to back, parallel with the dial, in the usual way, with quarter-chiming and alarum work at either side of them and at right angles to the dial or front plate. Such an arrangement often involved complication, but was economical of space.

Spring-driven movements were easily adapted to all manner of cases and shapes, and had the additional advantage that they could be disposed horizontally. As the sixteenth century advanced, the clockmakers of Germany, Italy and France vied with one another in the design and construction of very elaborate and costly spring clocks.

A favourite conceit appealed to the popularity of automaton figures and satisfied religious influence at the same time. 'Crucifix' clocks had the horizontal movement concealed in the plinth; the time was shown by a band with the hours engraved upon it rotating in relation to a fixed pointer encircling or surmounting the top of the cross. Examples with striking work sometimes had automaton figures at the base of the cross which moved when the hours sounded. A more elaborate variety had a figure of the Virgin Mary, with the hours engraved upon a rotating crown on her head; the figure of Jesus indicated the time with an outstretched hand and, as the clock struck, the Virgin raised a sceptre in her right hand at each blow on the bell.

Much more elaborate automata, also usually of religious significance, were to be found on scaled-down and spring-powered versions of some of the great public automaton/astronomical public clocks of the period. Isaac Habrecht, who made the second great Strasburg clock, was responsible for a famous example, now in the British Museum, which has many intricate moving figures in addition to dials for hours, quarters, feast days, holy days and solar and lunar movements. It is doubtless apochryphal, however, that on one of Habrecht's masterpieces the twelve apostles, passing in procession as noon strikes, inclined their heads before a figure of the Almighty, but bowed from the waist before a representation of the Holy Roman Emperor.

Among the plainer sorts of spring clock of this period, the so-called 'table clock' remained in common use on the continent until well into the eighteenth century. A few examples of English manufacture are known, but it was not as popular in Great Britain. Table clocks were circular, square, hexagonal or sexagonal. The angular ones often had glass or rock crystal windows in their panels, so that the decorated movements could be seen. The cases were of metal—bronze, gilded brass or occasionally silver—and the metal dials were, like the movements, horizontal. The time could not, consequently, be read across a room and in view of this inconvenience it is a little difficult to account for the popularity of the style.

Whether large or small, plain or bizarre, these domestic spring- or weight-clocks of the sixteenth century might be occasionally equipped to show all manner of astronomical motions, but they were rather at a loss to know the time of day. The majority of them show only the hours; although there was a fashion for a separate dial marked to indicate the quarter hours. The hand traversing this quarter dial necessarily revolves once in an hour and could consequently be used for telling the minutes and, indeed, the minute divisions were occasionally marked.

The use of concentric hour and minute hands in the modern fashion is exceedingly rare (non-existent, some experts say) before 1600, and uncommon before 1660. This used to lead antique dealers and collectors to conclude that earlier craftsmen were incapable of devising the necessary 'motion work' to drive concentric hour and minute hands. The corollary to this was the belief, still widely held, that clocks without minute hands must be of great antiquity. Neither is true. A craftsman able to calculate and make the gear trains to show astronomical and lunar movements, would obviously have been fit for the simpler task of making the mechanism to operate concentric hands; and single-hand clocks were still being made in the nineteenth century.

It is reasonable to assume that the majority of clockmakers, as resistant to change as the majority of their customers, were content to continue with the old and tried type of escapement and the traditional forms of construction. They doubtless saw no point in putting minute hands and markings on machines which suffered unpredictable variations of rate up to a quarter of an hour in twelve; similarly the majority of their customers were content with a clock which showed hours and quarter-divisions by means of a single hand, and they would have been confused by a concentric minute hand. So it was that sales resistance to the new arrangement by a large conservative body of users influenced the manufacture of single-hand clocks for more than 150 years after the concentric minute hand had been standardised by leading makers. Nevertheless, during the second half of the sixteenth century, when domestic clocks began to be made in England (at first, mostly by immigrant craftsmen) a few of the leading continental makers began to feel their way towards more precise methods of timekeeping.

One obvious way to improve performance was by improving the accuracy of dimensions and standards of finish of the wheels, pinions and other parts, so as to make the force reaching the escapement less inconstant. Early domestic clocks, following the turret clock pattern, had wheel teeth which were rectangular in shape, or nearly so; but in the better sixteenth-century clocks the teeth, though still cut and filed to shape by hand, assumed curvilinear forms which, though far from correct as a modern gear-cutting expert would judge them, ran with less friction and back-lash.

Similar improvements were made in the 'leaves' of the pinions or small gear wheels. It is probable that the first clocks had 'lantern' pinions, formed by fixing two discs of appropriate diameters to the spindle or arbor, drilling holes near their peripheries, fixing pins or rungs across from hole to hole and riveting them fast. Such a lantern pinion can, indeed, give excellent results in the larger sizes, particularly if it is so constructed that the pins or 'trundles' can rotate; but in the smaller sizes needed for domestic clocks they were difficult to make accurately. Consequently solid pinions, forged in one piece with the arbor and finished by filing, come into use. As with the larger wheels, the tooth forms became less crude as experience was gained. Solid-drawn pinions, not introduced until the seventeenth century, were shaped by drawing soft bar or 'pinion wire' through hardened dies, then turning away the surplus pinion leaves to form the arbor and hardening the complete arbor/pinion assembly. Figures 1 and 22 illustrate two types of pinion.

Also in the sixteenth century, it began to be realised that iron wheels meshing with iron pinions and turning in iron bearings run with more friction than a combination of iron and brass. Although all-iron construction remained common for the larger weight-driven clocks, the smaller pieces, particularly spring-driven clocks and

Page 53 PLATE 7 Side view of the Edward East movement showing the wheel work of the striking train, the crown wheel of the escapement, directly under the bell, and the calendar ring and one of its rollers on the back of the dial plate

PLATE 8 The movement of a clock by Edward East similar to that in Plate 6, showing shaped plates, great wheels and ratchets, a Continental type horizontal bell hammer. The lever and pull-cord, top left, are to operate the maintaining power. Between pendulum and bell hammer is the 'locking plate' for the strike. *c*1670

Page 54 PLATE 9 Spring-driven eight-day striking clock by William Clement, putative inventor of the anchor escapement, 1675. The walnut case is here shown standing on its acorn 'feet', but is really designed to be hung on the wall

PLATE 10 Movement of the William Clement spring clock, with bell removed, showing the shaped decorative 'apron' to the pendulum cock; the movement is otherwise undecorated

watches, began to be made with brass wheels meshing with steel pinions and with the steel arbors turning in brass frame-bars or plates. Or, if iron frames were retained, the 'pivot holes' were bushed or lined with brass.

No matter how much the wheelwork might be improved really consistent accuracy could not be attained with the verge escapement and foliot or unsprung wheel balance. At the time when English domestic clockmaking began to develop distinctive native characteristics, a few leading continental makers began experimenting with new forms of controller. Nicholas Radeloff of Schleswig and Jöst Burgi of Vienna, for example, both attained a commendable degree of accuracy, said to be within two or three minutes in twenty-four hours, with an ingenious variant of the old verge and balance, known as the 'cross-beat' escapement. These developments followed soon after Gallileo's observation of the naturally synchronous action of a simple pendulum, and the application of pendulum control to clock escapements is particularly associated with the rise of English horology.

Chapter Four

The First English Chamber Clocks

CHAMBER clocks were made in England in the reign of King Henry VIII, possibly earlier; but English clockmaking as we know it did not really start until the reign of James I. The clockmakers had no guild of their own until 1631, previously the principal London craftsmen had been members of the Blacksmiths' Company.

Henry VIII's principal resident clockmaker, 'deviser of the King's horologies and astronomer', was a Bavarian, Nicholas Cratzer (or Kratzer), who is said to have lived thirty years in England without learning the language and who is shown in the Book of Payments kept by the Treasurer of the Household to have been paid at the rate of £20 a year in 1538. It is not known which of the clocks mentioned in the Wardrobe Inventories of the time were made by Cratzer and which were importations, but it is apparent that Hans Holbein collaborated with him over case design and decoration. In addition to the construction and care of mechanical clocks, Cratzer was also responsible for designing sundials and, in conjunction with Holbein, he made at least one most elaborate combination of mechanical clock, fore and after noon sundials and clepsydra with automata.

Coincidentally, following Henry's precedent with Cratzer, Queen Elizabeth I had three clockmakers with the first name of Nicholas. These were the Urseaus, father and son, who were French and the Flemish Nicholas Vallin. One of Vallin's clocks, dated 1598, is the oldest known surviving musical clock, with a carillon of thirteen bells on which rather muddled jangles—one can scarcely call them tunes—are played at each quarter hour. It is unfair perhaps to impugn Vallin's musical ability as the pin barrel, from which the bell hammers are worked, has been repaired and re-pinned so many times in its life that even that admirable craftsman, the late Philip Coole of the British Museum was unable to make much sense of it. It is greatly to his credit that he resisted the temptation to re-pin the barrel yet again to play *Greensleeves*; though it is on record that once, when the clock was being over-hauled, it was temporarily altered (it being very easy to re-arrange the hammer-pins) and was heard to play Colonel Bogey.

This important sixteenth century crypto-English clock has all three trains, for going, hour strike and music, at right angles to the dial and it is one of the rare examples of the period with concentric hour and 'minute' hands. The word minute is in inverted commas because when the clock was discovered in the 1920s it had a chapter ring with each minute marked which, with the two hands, was palpably of fairly late seventeenth-century origin. When the clock was acquired by the late Courtney Ilbert he caused the removal of these later additions and substituted hands of more authentic sixteenth-century style and a chapter ring with no minute markings, but with the four quarters marked on the inner edge of the ring. The motion work shows no sign of alteration and was designed to work the two concentric hands; therefore the clock in all probability now appears to the visitor to the British Museum much as it appeared to its original owner. (See Plate 1.)

Queen Elizabeth also appointed Bartholomew Newsam clock-maker in 1572. Newsam is believed to have been a Yorkshireman who moved to London in about 1560, and he must be one of the first makers of chamber and portable clocks of wholly native origin. A very small spring clock in the British Museum, signed *Bartilmewe Newsam*, is of distinctively English flavour as far as the decorative engraving of the gilded brass case is concerned, and although the movement is arranged horizontally, in two storeys, like many continental table clocks, the dial is set vertically. The dial plate is below the surface of the case so that the latter may be lifted bodily away from the base leaving movement and dial exposed. Small doors in the side panels allow the fusees to be seen without removing the case, so the owner may judge whether the clock is nearly run down and in need of re-winding.

Bartholomew Newsam appears to have founded, or at least been an important member of, a dynasty of clockmakers, for on his death in 1593 he bequeathed to John Newsam, clockmaker of York, his second-best vice and some other tools, whilst the rest of his workshop equipment went to his son Edward. A second Bartholomew Newsam, son of Edward it is believed, was one of the pioneer makers of pendulum clocks in the second half of the seventeenth century.

Before the end of Queen Elizabeth's reign, native-born makers of chamber clocks and watches began to outnumber the immigrant craftsmen. Rainulph, or Randulph, Bull, who was appointed keeper of the great clock at Westminster Palace by James I in 1617, is known to have made portable spring clocks and watches nearly thirty years earlier, and the most famous native maker to have been in business before the end of the sixteenth century was a Scotsman, David Ramsay. Ramsay's early work, exemplified by a beautiful watch inscribed *David Ramsay, Scotus, me fecit,* in the British Museum, is in the French style and he appears to have been working in France when Queen Elizabeth died, whereupon James I sent for him. The esteem in which he was held is shown by his being made page of the bedchamber, as well as keeper of the king's clocks and watches. Nor were the material rewards despicable, as he was paid, from 1613 onwards, a pension or retaining fee of £200 a year, increased soon to £250, and also received substantial payments for clocks or watches supplied and work done. On his accession in 1625, Charles I continued Ramsay's appointment and rates of payment. Between 17 March 1627 and 13 July 1628, in addition to his annual retainer, Ramsay was paid £856 for clocks supplied and work done and £358 16s 8d 'in lieu of diet and bouche of Court'. All told therefore, his receipts for this sixteen-month period were worth more than £20,000 in terms of 1972 values.

These were the plums of the trade, but the business of clockmaking had become important and influential enough for its practitioners to demand protection under the guild system, even though that meant submitting to regulation. A proposal in 1627 to grant letters patent authorising French clockmakers to work in the City of London precipitated affairs, and negotiations were put in hand which culminated in the grant of a charter of incorporation to the Clockmakers' Company on 22 August 1631.

The charter to the 'Master, Wardens and Fellowship of the Arts or Mystery of Clockmaking of the City of London' named David Ramsay Master though, as an elderly man, he does not seem to have played a very active part in its affairs. Henry Archer, John Wellowe and Sampson Sheldon were his Wardens and the 'Assistants of the said Fellowship' were James Vautrollier, John Smith, Francis Fórman, John Harris, Richard Morgan, Samuel Lynaker, John Charlton, John Midnall, Simon Bartram and Edward East. Apart from Vautrollier, all these names were British and the birth of the Clockmakers' Company coincided with the emergence of the first distinctive or definitive type of English clock—the brass lantern clock which, in debased form, is still extensively reproduced today.

It used to be thought that the English lantern clock, of which Figure 4 is a fairly typical specimen of about 1665, was a wholly new conception developed towards the end of the first quarter of the seventeenth century. This was an over-simplification and the line of descent should be traced between the true lantern clock and the most common type of hanging-weight clock made in the latter part of the previous century. The construction of these 'posted' or 'framed' iron clocks was in turn derived from the 'Gothic clocks' of the fifteen century which were shorn of their elaborately shaped and pierced framing, crockets, spires, pinnacles and other decorative features to become plain rectangular shapes with side doors and back plate supplementing the dial plate to enclose the mechanism.

With its side, back and dial plates removed, such a clock is seen to be composed of two horizontal plates separated and supported by four corner posts. Until the seventeenth century was well advanced, these iron corner posts were rectangular and so forged and file-shaped as to suggest the buttresses of Gothic buildings. (See Plate 2) The bottom plate was pierced to allow the passage of the cords or thin braided ropes from which the driving weights hung, and the top plate was also pierced and slotted to allow room for the bell hammer to move and for the escapement arbor to pass through it; the balance wheel was above the top-plate and immediately below the lower edge of the bell, which formed an ornamental domed top to the structure and kept dust from falling into the escapement. Other holes and slots cut in the top and bottom plates served to

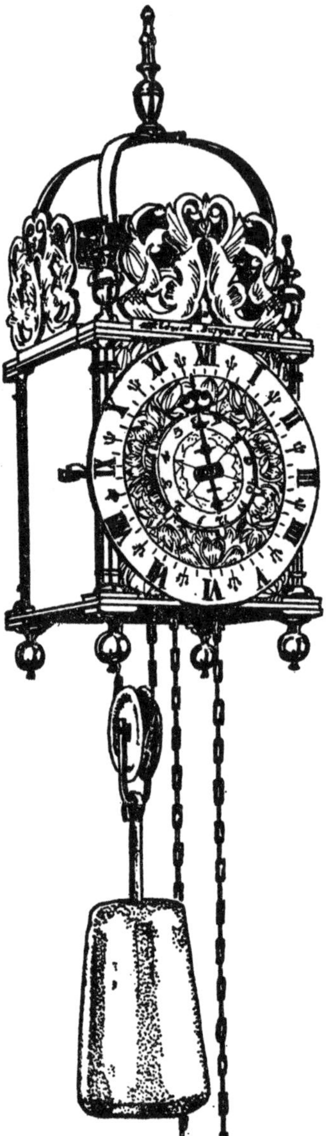

FIGURE 4 *Typical London-made lantern clock, by Edward Burges, with strike and alarum, c1665. Originally with wheel balance and rope drive converted in the nineteenth century to anchor escapement, short pendulum and chain*

accommodate three bars, or narrow plates about an inch wide, which carried the pivots of the wheelwork. The foremost bar was usually about half an inch behind the dial plate, the second bar in the middle and the third bar not far from the back edge of the movement. These bars were held in place by wedges.

The front and back bars of English hanging clocks, of the fully developed lantern type, had narrow 'arms' extending to either side, the whole roughly forming a Roman cross. The purpose of these extensions was to provide bearings on one side for the two pivoted levers concerned with unlocking and re-locking the striking train, flanked on the other side by the arbor carrying the hammer. On early examples, in which continental influence is still strong, these pieces were pivoted in the frame posts or in separate supports. Before the lantern type was fully developed the English makers also broke away from the continental way of working the bell hammer whereby, although the tail of the hammer moved in the same plane as the pins on the great wheel of the strike train, the hammer head itself was on a short stalk at right angles to the vertical hammer shaft and moved horizontally. This wayward arrangement persisted on some types of continental clock until the nineteenth century, to be cursed by repairers as inevitable lost motion in the linkage at every change in direction made it difficult to adjust the hammer correctly. The English arrangement was simpler and better, with the hammer tail, stalk and head all in one piece, moving in the same plane. Therefore the hammer head moved vertically and there was no lost motion. The hammer tail was pushed aside by the pins in the great wheel against the resistance of a stiff plate spring attached to the bottom plate, and the combination of large bell, heavy hammer and stout spring ensured that when an English lantern clock struck, all but the stone deaf within a tolerably wide radius were left in no doubt about it. In the days when the average household could afford but one clock, it was an advantage to have it audible throughout the house.

The space between the dial and the front bar was occupied by the small pinion on an extension of the great wheel arbor (or, in many instances, the arbor was saw-cut and filed into the shape of a crude four-leaf pinion at its extremity) to drive the hour wheel, to which the 'pipe' carrying the hour hand was frictionally fixed.

Behind the hour wheel, and integral with the pipe, was a twelve-pointed star wheel which raised and released a lifting piece to unlock the strike train at appropriate intervals. Between the front and middle bars were the wheels, usually three, of the going train; between centre and rearmost bar were the wheels of the striking train; whilst the 'locking plate' or 'count wheel' and its detent occupied the space between the rearmost bar and the back plate or door enclosing the movement.

This basic structure of the sixteenth-century iron chamber clock remained unaltered, and its transition into the lantern clock began with a greater use of brass. Brass side and dial plates were combined with iron corner posts, iron wheels and top and bottom plates and bars in transitional pieces. Like their all-iron forbears these usually had the numerals of the chapter ring engraved directly on the dial plate. Brass wheels became commoner at the turn of the century and, to have the necessary strength, they had to be thicker than their iron predecessors. The use of brass for the corner posts, top and bottom plates and movement bars followed logically, as it was not only mechanically sensible to have the arbors turning in brass bearing surfaces, but these brass bars and plates could also be cast and hammered or 'planished' to a finish with less work than went into forging and filing all the parts of an iron frame and its appurtenances.

Soon after brass began to replace iron for the plates, the side posts lost their rectangular Gothic buttress form and became slender turned brass pillars, finished at top with elegant vase-shaped finials and at bottom with globular ball 'feet'. Similarly the bell was no longer supported from below on a 'stalk', but was hung from four interlaced brass straps, surmounted by another finial, which sprung from the four corner finials. This increased the height of the clock and improved its appearance, but left a large gap between the top plate and the underside of the bell. This space was filled at front and sides by pierced and engraved brass galleries or 'frets'.

The final stage in the transfiguration was to engrave the hour numerals, and half and quarter divisions, on a separate chapter ring mounted on the front plate so as to leave the recessed central portion of the dial plate to be filled with decorative engraving and, very often, the maker's signature. This is not an invariable rule, and many lantern clocks, particularly before 1660, have the signature on the front fret. The separate chapter rings were occasionally of silver, some were 'close-plated', but the majority were brass 'silvered' by a chemical process which will be dealt with later. Many lantern clocks had an alarum as well as the striking train, and the alarum mechanism was fixed to the back plate of the 'case', whilst the time at which the alarum was to sound was set by turning an engraved and silvered disc in the centre of the dial plate, as on the clock shown in Figure 4, so that the appropriate number was in line with the 'tail' of the hour hand.

The engraving of the numerals, the decorative work and the maker's name and address was filled with black wax. It is known that some of the finest early lantern clocks had the external brass work gilded, but the majority were finished by burnishing to a high polish which was then preserved against oxidisation and tarnishing by a coat or two of lacquer. The use of lacquer as a varnish to protect polished metal from the atmosphere was well understood early in the seventeenth century, and it was soon discovered that the rich colour of gilt brass could be simulated by using suitably tinted lacquers. The process of 'gold lacquering' was not quite as durable as fire gilding, but it gave nearly as handsome an effect at far less cost.

The lantern clock, with its turned pillars and finials, pierced frets and combination of burnished gold-colour and matt silver, was as much a creature of the Renaissance as its all-iron predecessor had been a child of Gothic architecture. Architectural influence was not lost, however, and the side pillars of a good lantern clock are not cylindrical but have a slight swell or entasis in the tradition of classical architecture. Where the sixteenth-century plain hanging clocks tended to look squat and rather clumsy, the bell supports, finials and frets added stature to the lantern clock and gave it good proportions. This is particularly true of early examples where, though it is not immediately apparent, the distance from the top of the dial plate to the tip of the upper finial is fractionally greater than that from the same point down to the bottom of the 'feet'. The chapter rings of early clocks were narrow, which added to the good effect, but after about 1680 wider rings became fashionable and rather spoilt the appearance.

That the brass-and-silvered lantern clock is extremely attractive, is borne out by the continued popularity of reproductions. Furthermore, the use of cast brass and turned, rather than forged, posts enabled costs to be reduced. The domestic clock was still expensive but no longer confined to the very rich. It is difficult to equate early to middle seventeenth-century values with our own, but the lantern clock became cheap enough to find a place in relatively modest households. Long before Mr Pepys had amassed the prosperity which allowed him to buy his own coach and a watch—in that order—he was able to afford a lantern clock with which to regulate the affairs of his household.

Most of the lantern clocks that have survived were made after 1660–70 when the pendulum control came into use, and of the surviving pre-pendulum examples most were converted to pendulum control relatively early in their lives. The conversion was not difficult and transformed their timekeeping from an erratic gain or loss of about 10 to 15 minutes a day to an error of only a second or so. It would be rash to say that *no* English lantern clock survives with its original wheel balance controller, but in recent years many of those which were converted to pendulum in the late seventeenth century have been re-converted to the original type of mechanism. If it is done by a clever craftsman, with good historical knowledge, the traces of the conversion and re-conversion can be successfully obliterated. The methods and ethics of the operation will be discussed later.

On pre-pendulum lantern clocks each train of wheels had its own driving weight (later types had a single weight acting on an endless cord for reasons which will appear), and so that the clock would not tend to tilt sideways, or the weights foul one another, the two great wheels revolved in opposite directions; this arrangement brought the weights well clear of one another, at the sides of the clock. As there was one reversal of direction between it and the hour wheel, the going train great wheel turned anti-clockwise. The weights were hung on soft braided ropes which passed over spiked pulleys on the arbors of the great wheels; the pulleys were free to revolve in one direction for winding up and, in the other direction, they drove their great wheels by the simple 'click' arrangement shown in Figure 5. Small counterweights on the 'free' ends of the ropes held them down between the pulley shrouds and enabled the spikes to grip. It is possible that the going weight was made with a brass canister half-filled with molten lead, leaving space for lead shot to be added to or removed from the vacant space to regulate the speed of the clock. Alternatively, solid lead weights may have been used with arrangements for adding discs or washers on the going side.

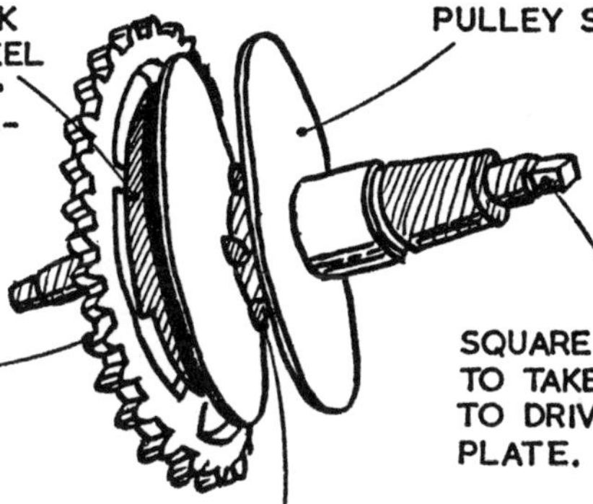

FIGURE 5 *Great wheel, pulley and click of the early form still used throughout the eighteenth century in thirty-hour long-case clocks, and others derived from the original lantern clock type of mechanism*

If an early lantern clock is hung at a convenient height, with its dial not much more than six feet from the floor, the drop will be enough to run it only about fifteen hours between windings. This means it must be wound morning and evening, but there is an ample margin of safety if the winding is delayed.

As stated earlier, there is no known example of an English clock with a cross-bar or foliot balance, and all the pre-pendulum lantern clocks had plain, heavy wheel balances as in Figure 6, large enough to extend about half an inch from the edges of the top plate. With the balance wheel occupying so much space, the 'cock', in which the upper pivot of the pallet arbour is supported, had to be mounted inside the circumference of the wheel. Space also had to be provided for the movement of the bell-hammer shaft, which traversed almost two-thirds of the width of the clock near the centre line.

Consequently the balance wheel had only one spoke, arranged so that it pointed directly forwards or backwards when the escapement was midway between beats and the arrangement allowed rather more than 180° of arc to the balance before the single spoke 'banked' on the bell-hammer. The upper balance cock was, and is, still often called the 'potence' although the word, which means a gallows, only properly refers to the type of support from which the old foliot balance had been supported by cords. It will be convenient to consider other constructional details in connection with post-pendulum lantern clocks.

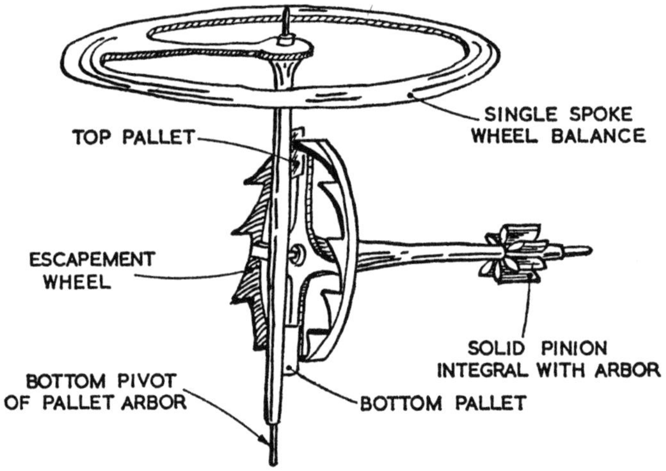

FIGURE 6 *Escapement wheel, pallet arbor and single-spoke wheel balance as used on pre-pendulum English clocks*

In its general design characteristics, the lantern clock became standardised surprisingly early. This is not to say that those of one maker would be identical with those of a rival, but the differences are only trifling and it seems clear that a certain number of 'bought out' components, supplied 'in the rough' and finished and assembled under the eye of the ostensible maker, were used very early in the business. This particularly applies to such things as frets, bell straps and other frame castings. Wheel-cutting probably became a separate craft before the adoption of Robert Hooke's wheel-cutting engine and I suspect that most of the engraving, including the beautiful, flowing 'signature' was jobbed out to specialists by mid-century.

Just as the clock and watch trade fathered modern precision engineering, so the sub-division of labour which began in the first half of the seventeenth century was the true progenitor of the factory system and of mass-production. This is not to say that the seventeenth-century clockmakers were mere retailers, as their nineteenth-century counterparts became. The ordinances of the Clockmakers' Company ensured that every practitioner was fully capable of making his wares, entirely by hand, from raw materials on his own premises. They also ensured that the 'masters' in the various components trades were also subject to similar regulation. What Campbell wrote in 1747, in *The London Tradesman*, of the watchmakers of that time was true of the master tradesman of the previous century; he concluded:

> The Watch-Maker puts his Name upon the Plate, though he has not made in his Shop the smallest Wheel belonging to it. It is supposed, however, that he can make all the Movements: and Apprentices are still learned to cut them [the wheels] by Hand. He must be a Judge of the Goodness of Work at first Sight and put his Name to nothing but what will stand the Severest Trial . . .

There were some exceptional lantern clocks for which bought-out components cannot have been suitable. Exceptionally small and exceptionally large clocks come into this category, as well as a few rare and highly-prized examples in silver cases.

A fair average size of lantern clock has top and bottom plates 6in square and measures 16in from the bottom of the feet to the top of the upper finial. The dial plate of such a clock will be about 6½in, or slightly more, from top to bottom and 6in across. Therefore a chapter ring of 6½in outside diameter will touch top and bottom of the dial plate and overlap at the sides by an amount sufficient to mask the centre portions of the side pillars. Smaller clocks are fairly often seen, such as the one in Figure 4 which is 12in high and has a 5in diameter chapter ring. True miniatures are rare. The smallest lantern clock I have seen was just under 5in high, beautifully proportioned and of the finest quality, worthy of its famous maker, John Ebsworth. When I recall that the price asked in 1932 was fifty shillings and that I did not buy it because of the parental fury which would have been provoked by spending so much of my savings on so worthless a piece of old rubbish, I may be forgiven if I shed a retrospective tear. Its present day value would exceed £800.

Lantern clocks much above 16in high, and with their other dimensions correspondingly enlarged, generally belong to a later period; but oversize pre-pendulum examples were made. Not infrequently the extra size was used to accommodate a third train, giving ting-tang quarter chimes. More elaborate quarter chimes, or hourly music on eight or more bells, are known but are very rare.

The general run of lantern clocks have an hour hand only, and on the early ones only the half hours are marked, by an engraved diamond, fleur-de-lys or other decorative device between the numerals on the chapter rings. After mid-century these ornamental half-hour marks were supplemented by quarter divisions, engraved within a narrow border, between fine concentric circles, on the inner edge of the chapter ring.

When horological history began to be studied seriously in the 1920s and 1930s, most authorities maintained that no pre-pendulum lantern clock existed with *original* motion work to drive a concentric minute hand. Undoubtedly some of the old balance-wheel clocks, which were converted to pendulum control, were modernised by the further refinement of additional motion work and a minute hand, with the necessary markings added to the outer edge of the chapter ring—or, if there was no room, a new ring would be fitted. The belief that none of these clocks had had a minute hand originally is now challenged. Ernest L. Edwardes maintains in *Weight-Driven Chamber Clocks:*

> There are early English lantern clocks having balance control (or having been designed for such) which possess apparently original minute hands. . . Some few of these—a very few indeed—must surely be genuine . . .

One of the 'very few', which passed through my hands about twenty years ago, not only had a minute hand which, together with its motion work, was unquestionably original, but calendar and lunar work as well. These most rare, probably unique, attributes were clearly designed all of a piece with the dial of the clock, which was not only elaborately engraved with zodiacal signs but had a curved 'apron' between the feet of the clock which accommodated a 'day of the week' indicator. As these unusual features were clearly part of the original design, it is fair to assume that the extra wheelwork to drive the extra 'motions', including the concentric minute hand, was also original.

For good measure this splendid clock also had a ting-tang quarter chiming train and had originally been controlled by a balance wheel. It had suffered the usual late seventeenth-century conversion to anchor escapement and long pendulum and, as I found it, it had also lost its front fret. As most of the recessed centre of the dial was occupied by the calendar engravings and lunation disc, the maker's signature had presumably been on the missing front fret in the early style. Unfortunately, as ever, the need to earn a crust obliged me to pass this clock on 'in the trade' after a short while, and it has now been admirably re-converted to balance control and has mysteriously grown a suitable front fret which bears the engraved signature of a most illustrious early maker. Lest the present owner of this rare clock should read these words, prudence sternly represses further comment.

Considering the shortcomings of the escapement, the English pre-pendulum clock was not a bad performer. Given reasonably frequent cleaning and re-oiling (which most of them did not get) and a reasonably stable temperature (which no seventeenth-century house can have had) I have proved one able to keep within ten minutes a day. Although the scientific or geometric determination of the correct shape for wheel teeth lay in the future, the English makers had achieved tolerably accurate forms empirically before mid-century, and this mitigated the defects of the controller. To a modern eye the wheels, and the bars in which they are pivoted, look needlessly thick and a little clumsy, but the excess metal contributed to longevity and the method of making the wheel blanks and other parts from hammered castings resulted in a hard, close-grained brass.

The only glaring piece of bad design, common to all lantern clocks and persisting as a sort of mechanical coelacanth for 150 years after they were no longer made by the top-flight London men, is found in the 'fly' or air-brake which regulates the speed of the striking train. The purpose and effect of an air-brake demand that it be as large and as light as possible, but those found in lantern clocks are always extraordinarily thick and heavy, and invariably much smaller than the available space. Consequently, when the strike train is suddenly halted by the stop-piece falling into the space in the hoop wheel the inertia of the heavy, fast-turning fly makes it try to go on spinning, straining against the locked wheels. In theory, this was dealt with by having the fly loose on its arbor and frictionally connected to it by a light springy tongue which was supposed to allow it to go on spinning freely after the arbor had stopped. In practice, this arrangement works badly or not at all, because if the spring is stiff enough to drive the fly it is too stiff to let it slip as it should. The result is a great deal of bouncing to and fro as the fly comes to rest, with consequent fretting and wear of the engaged teeth of its pinion and the wheel which drives it. Despite this bad design, many a 300-year-old lantern clock is still running without too much noise from its original fly pinion and wheel.

The empirical good sense which made the lantern clock a thing of sound and long-lasting design was reinforced by excellent workmanship, considering the relative newness of many of the processes. The strict rules of the Clockmakers' Company discouraged the production of inferior clocks as the officials had the power, often used, of inspecting premises and destroying badly-made pieces on the spot. These powers lapsed early in the eighteenth century, and before the end of the seventeenth some decline in standards can be noticed. This seldom affected the mechanical parts, which, indeed, tended to improve as knowledge grew, but one finds such things as frets and bell straps less well finished than once they had been. On early clocks all three frets were engraved, but after about 1660, when newer types began to oust the lantern clock, the side frets were usually left blank and the decoration of the front fret became nothing more than a little perfunctory hatching. Quite often, also, the side frets were not properly 'cleaned' with file and graver but had their undersides left rough, as they came from the foundry, with some of the pierced work 'blind', or nearly so, from casting 'rag'.

Early lantern clocks seem always to have been mounted by hanging them on the wall by a hook or staple passing through wrought-iron, semi-circular 'stirrups' riveted to the top plates; these were supplemented by pointed iron 'spurs' designed to dig slightly into

Page 71 PLATE 11 Fully developed bracket clock by John Knibb, Oxford, *c*1695 with verge escapement and pull-quarter repeat on three bells. The curved slot marked S-N above XII is for the strike/silent and the calendar is at the top of the dial centre, Knibb fashion, which precludes fitting the then-usual mock pendulum

Page 72 PLATE 12 Early, probably experimental, form of anchor escapement pallets from a small long-case clock made by Joseph Knibb *c*1670–75

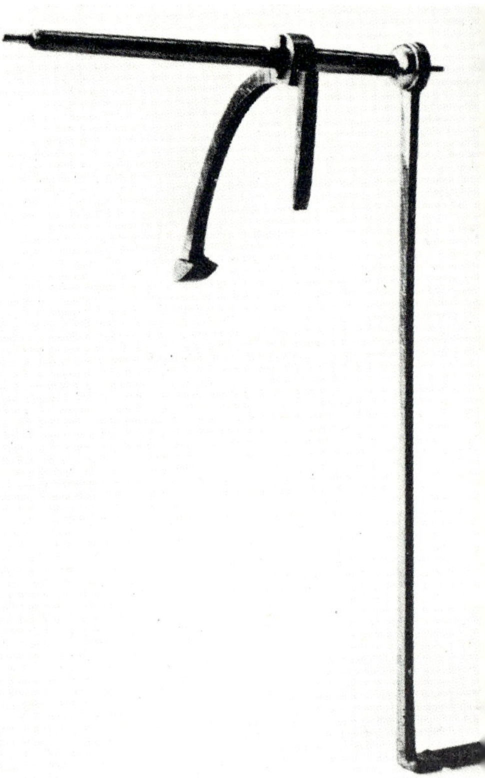

PLATE 13 Fully developed form of anchor escapement in a Joseph Knibb long-case clock *c*1680. Also visible are the characteristic deep beel, baluster pillars between movement plates and the spring suspension for the pendulum

the plaster or wainscot in order to keep the dial parallel with the wall and to prevent the clock slipping during winding. The spurs were at first attached to the back-plates, but were later screwed into the back 'feet'. The feet therefore were originally non-functional, but no doubt many clocks were placed on suitable wooden brackets early in their lives. This may sometimes have been done as an alternative to repairing a broken stirrup or spur, but as some late lantern clocks appear to have been made without these appendages it may be assumed that the use of brackets became more fashionable as time went on. After the 'hooded wall clock' (designed as such) and the long-case clock came into use, some lantern clocks on brackets were protected by little glazed hoods, and a few had trunks or pedestals added to enclose the driving weights, thus becoming cousins of the true long-case clocks.

The different patterns of fret and the changes in decorative engraving and proportions of chapter rings will be dealt with in connection with post-pendulum clocks. In the lantern clock, we see for the first time that blend of harmonious proportion and fitness of purpose, which was for so long the particular attribute of English clocks.

Lantern clocks seem to have been known in the seventeenth century by the simple designation of hanging clocks. Their likeness to the common form of eighteenth-century square-section, steeple-topped lanthorn adequately justifies their most usual name. The lesser-used terms, 'bedpost' and 'birdcage' are not too inept; but the trade name of 'Cromwellian' cannot be too much deplored. It is much favoured by auctioneers and was probably coined by one of that class of late-Victorian dealer who dreamed up 'grandfather' clock, 'cockfighting' chair, 'bachelor's' chest and other antique-trade misnomers.

Chapter Five

The Bob Pendulum

It is necessary to turn our attention away from Great Britain again to consider the invention of the pendulum clock. Galileo Galilei discovered the naturally isochronous action of a simple pendulum in the sixteenth century; Christiaan Huyghens van Zulichem successfully combined the pendulum with clock mechanism in 1656; Salomon Coster of The Hague produced commercially the first domestic pendulum clocks on Huyghens' principles, soon after, and imparted all he knew about their principles and the methods of construction to John Fromanteel in 1657. This Fromanteel, second generation member of a notable 'Anglo-Dutch' clockmaking family, having spent some months with Coster, introduced the new designs to England and the first English-made pendulum clocks were sold by John's father, Ahasuerus Fromanteel, and bore his name, in 1658. In the same year, Huyghens published a full account of his pendulum clocks, and in the following year Coster died. Huyghens died in 1696, by which time Isaac Newton's work on the laws of gravitation provided 'philosophers' with the scientific rationale for the action of pendulums.

The common description of the Fromanteels as Dutch or Anglo-Dutch requires some qualification. John (or Johannes) Fromanteel's father Ahasuerus I (there was a second clockmaking Ahasuerus, the son of John) was a part of the 'Dutch colony' in London by virtue of being a member of the Dutch Reformed Church. This, together with the fact that his son had been sent to work under Coster in Holland, naturally suggests that the family was of fairly recent Dutch origin. The signature 'Fromanteel, Amsterdam' on some late seventeenth-century clocks suggests that a branch of the family was still resident in Holland. This has led one author to assert positively that Ahasuerus I 'came from Amsterdam', and that at the time when 'Ahasuerus I and Ahasuerus II were at the peak of their fame there must have been a large family of Fromanteels working in Holland'.

It seems there is little 'must' about it, as Ahasuerus I was born in Norwich, as were many other Fromanteels, and the member of the family who worked in Amsterdam is now thought to have gone there from London. The 'Dutch colonies' in Norwich, and other parts of East Anglia, together with that of London, were not Dutch in the modern sense and most of the members were French or Flemish Protestants. Recent investigations by Dr R. Plomp (*Antiquarian Horology* vol 7, no 4) indicate that the Fromanteels were French-Flemish rather than Belgian or Low Countries Flemish, and he points to the existence of two French villages, one in Normandy and one farther south, named Fromental. It is certainly true that Ahasuerus I and his family were fully assimilated and accepted as English by their contemporaries; and in connection with the introduction of the pendulum, John Evelyn proudly refers to Ahasuerus as 'our own Fromantil'—that being one of the many variations in the spelling of the name.

However, to return to the discovery of the pendulum, Galileo's observation that a hanging lamp in the cathedral at Pisa, having presumably been set swinging when it was lit or trimmed, continued to swing at the same rate throughout the service, although the extent of its swing naturally lessened, was timed against his pulse-beat. More precise experiments followed, from which he determined that the length rather than the weight of a pendulum was the critical factor and that the excursions were performed in equal time irrespective of their amplitude. It was later discovered, by Huyghens, that the latter assumption was not true and that the wider the swing the slower by a very small amount. It was established, though, that if the total swing was itself small, around 10° or 15°, variations of 2° or 3° were of little consequence. It was also established that because of the diminishing force of gravity the greater the distance from the Equator, the length of pendulum to beat a given time varies slightly with the latitude. The ratios of length to duration of swing were also established, as it was clear that doubling the length did not halve the rate, for which a fourfold increase is necessary. For all practical purposes, in English latitudes, a pendulum to take one second to swing from one extremity to the other must be fractionally more than 39in long, from the point of suspension to the centre of gravity of the bob weight; and it must be approximately 13ft long to take two seconds.

These facts having been established, the simple pendulum was used before the end of the sixteenth century to time astronomical observations, and the increased precision of time measurement enabled new knowledge to be gained. The pendulum used for the purpose was usually a light chain with a heavy, spherical weight attached; and it was generally the duty of the astronomer's assistant to count the beats and to give the pendulum an occasional push to keep it swinging.

Patience and concentration were needed to avoid errors of counting and Galileo himself, in his later years, turned his attention to ways of combining the pendulum with clockwork. He sketched designs, but as he was nearly blind, he entrusted his son with the practical work in 1641; there were unexplained delays and, at his death in 1649, Vincenzio Galileo had only one unfinished pendulum clock to show for his pains. From his drawings a model of the mechanism has been made in the Science Museum, from which it may be seen that the elder Galileo had devised an ingenious escapement not dissimilar in principle from that of the 'duplex' watch escapement of a century later. The Galileo escapement and pendulum would be capable of quite good performance if they were applied to a clock.

Huyghens' first application of the pendulum was made by removing the cross bar foliot balance from the escapement arbor of an old clock and substituting for it a single arm extending over the back of the movement, so that its upturned extremity engaged with a horizontal fork attached to the rod of a separately suspended pendulum. He converted two old turret clocks in this way (at Scheveningen church and Utrecht cathedral) and got good results, as their 'slow' escapement allowed the use of long, heavy pendulums, which had plenty of room to swing through wide arcs. Their powerful movements could cope with the friction of the rather crude way in which the escapement gave impulse to the pendulum. Although this simple system was used for nearly two hundred years on two types of Dutch domestic clock, the Zaansklokken and Friesian Stoelsklokken, Huyghens realised it would not give him the accuracy he sought in an observatory clock.

The arrangement gives the pendulum a wide arc of swing and therefore, for practical reasons in domestic clocks, demands a fairly short one. Huyghens was anxious to use as long a pendulum as possible—a seconds pendulum preferably—but this seemed incompatible with the conventional verge escapement which requires a wide movement of its pallets, so, instead of trying to devise a new form of escapement as Galileo had done, Huyghens got over the difficulty by interposing a reduction gear between escapement and pendulum, as shown in his own drawing at Figure 7. Here the escapement wheel and vertical escapement staff are exactly as in the conventional balance or foliot clock of the time, but instead of a balance the top of the pallet arbor carries a pinion 'O' meshing with a contrate wheel 'P' (only a few teeth of which need be cut as the wheel does not rotate fully); the arbor 'Q' of this contrate wheel carries the forked 'crutch' 'R' which engages the pendulum hanging on a cord from the bracket 'S'. Huyghens apparently stipulated a two-to-one reduction between pinion 'O' and wheel 'P' which enabled a seconds pendulum to be used, as the reduction gear kept the oscillations down to about 15° of arc which was manageable enough even with a 39in pendulum.

Coster apparently made some clocks to this plan, but a grave drawback must soon have been apparent. Whatever merit the gear had in reducing the arc is nullified by friction in that gearing, and by lost motion as soon as any wear occurs between the few teeth of the pinion 'O' and the fewer teeth of wheel 'P', on which all the work is concentrated. The alternative of applying the verge escapement more directly meant a wide pendulum arc of about 40°–50° and for obvious reasons this meant having a short pendulum. The next step, made jointly by Huyghens and Coster, was to let a short, directly-connected pendulum swing widely but to find a way to correct the tendency of such a pendulum to be 'slow in the long arcs', as horological language puts it.

In his first drawings of the mechanism with reducing gear and a long pendulum, Huyghens had shown the suspension cords hanging between curved flat strips of brass called 'cheeks'. It was hoped that

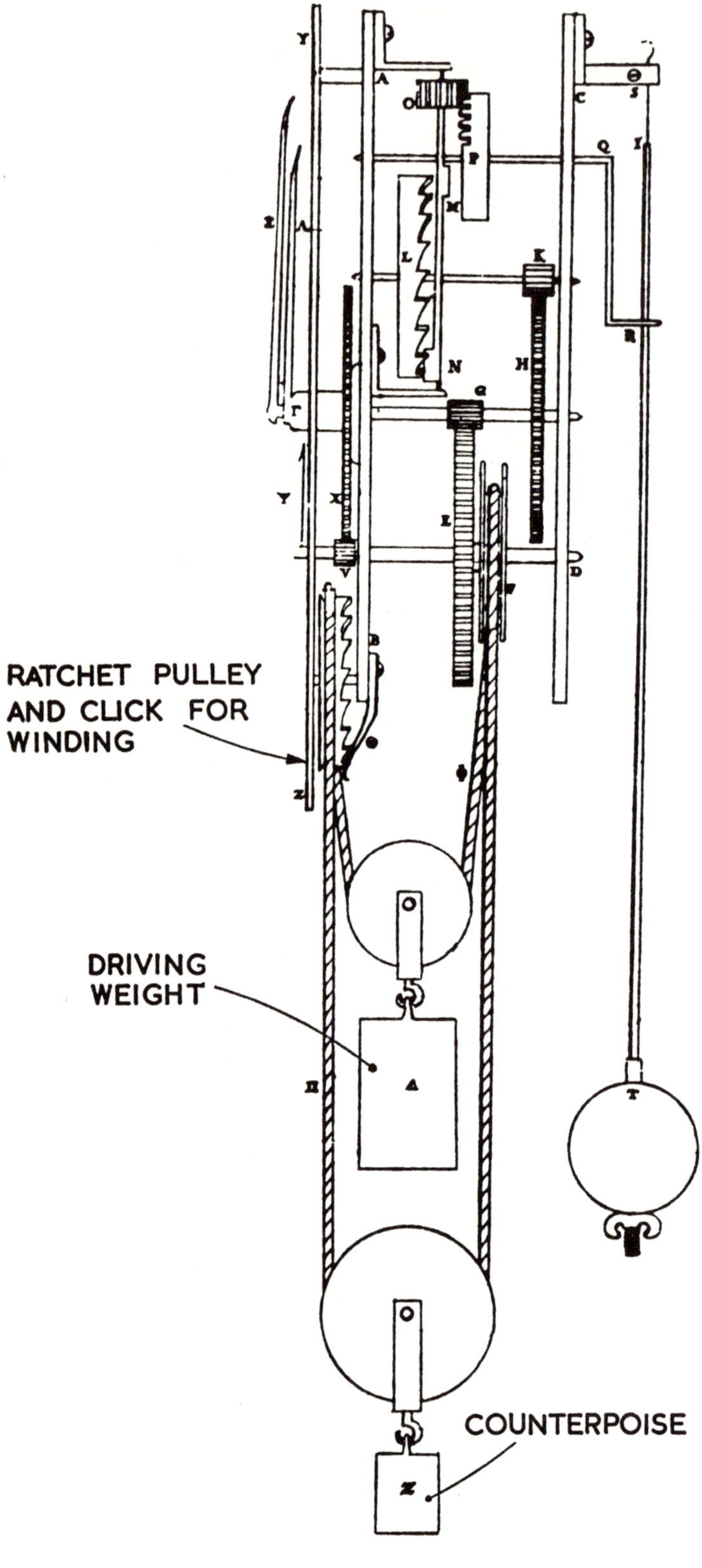

FIGURE 7 *Huyghens' own drawing of his pendulum clock u reducing gear between the palle arbor and the crutch, and with the endless cord winding system which provided 'maintaining power'*

these would correct errors arising from variations in arc. The cheeks were shaped as segments of circles and appear to have been applied to only a very few clocks. As Huyghens experimented, he was able to work out the formula which governs the pendulum clock. This is that the time occupied by the swing of a pendulum varies as the square root of its arc, and inversely as the force of gravity. He christened the first variation 'circular error', and went on to discover that a pendulum would be isochronous, irrespective of the extent of its swing, provided its bob weight traversed a cycloidal curve and not the arc of a circle. A cycloid is the path traced by a point on the circumference of a circle if that circle rolls along a flat plane. A pendulum following a cycloidal curve would thus get shorter the further it swung, and this is presumably what Huyghens had tried to achieve empirically with his part-circular cheeks which could not, in practice, have served any useful purpose.

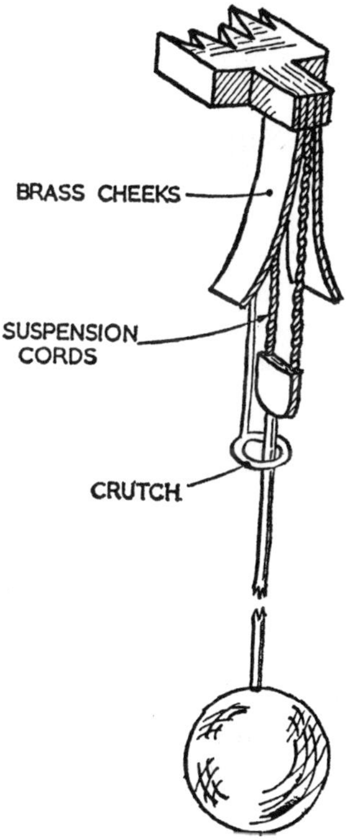

FIGURE 8 *Pendulum suspension between cycloidal cheeks*

By making cheeks of truly cycloidal form, Huyghens expected the problem to be solved.

Consequently the next generation of pendulum clocks had no reducing gear, and short 'bob' pendulums with cord suspension hung between accurately formed cycloidal cheeks as in Figure 8. To adapt the old-style escapement so that the crutch moved in the same plane as the pendulum, without the change of direction provided by the reducing gear, it was necessary to plant the arbor of the escapement wheel vertically, as shown in Figure 9, so that the pallet staff

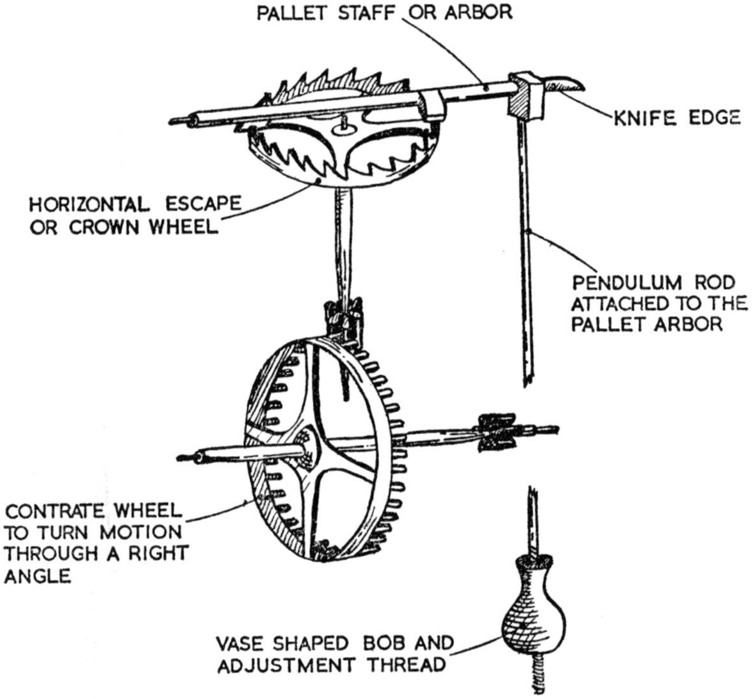

FIGURE 9 *The old type of escapement arranged horizontally for direct pendulum control*

lay horizontally across the wheel. This necessitated having a contrate wheel to drive the pinion on the escape wheel arbor, in order to turn the motion through a right angle.

It was with the pendulum clock in this stage of development that

John Fromanteel came to work under Coster in order to learn how to calculate pendulum lengths, and the various details of construction of the new timekeepers. In a broadsheet published at the end of October 1658, the Fromanteel firm advertised English pendulum clocks for sale. *The Commonwealth Mercury* carried this longer advertisement a month later:

> There is lately a way found out for making of clocks that go exact and keep equaller time than any now made without this Regulator (examined and proved before His Highness the Lord Protector by such Doctors whose knowledge and learning is without exception) and are not subject to alter by change of weather, as others are, and may be made to go a week, a moneth or a year with once winding up, as well as those that are wound up every day, and keep time as well, and is very excellent for all house clocks that go either with springs or weights; and also steeple clocks that are most subject to suffer by change of weather. Made by Ahasuerus Fromanteel, who made the first that were in England. You may have them at his house on the Bankside, in Mosses Alley, Southwark, and at the sign of the Mermaid in Lothbury, near Bartholomew Lane end, London.

Although Salomon Coster died in 1659, the types of pendulum clock he had evolved, particularly a spring-driven variety, were made by other leading Dutch makers with little mechanical change for some years. The thread suspension and cycloidal cheeks gradually became obsolete; and although the first Fromanteel pendulum clocks had cycloidal cheeks few other English makers followed suit and the Fromanteels themselves very soon gave them up.

The most usual alternative arrangement, with the short 'bob' pendulum was to attach the pendulum rod directly to the pallet arbor. The objectionable friction set up by the weight of the pendulum (however slight) on the back pivot of the pallet arbor was avoided by English makers by substituting a steel 'knife edge' rocking in a V-shaped notch as shown in Figures 9 and 10. With the pendulum attached in this way, the flexible suspension and cycloidal cheeks had no part to play and were abolished. At first glance the new 'English' arrangement has nothing to recommend it, except a reduction of complication and cost ,as it appears to provide the very situation Huyghens had been at such pains to avoid—a short, and necessarily light, pendulum swinging through some 50° of arc, with no provision for correcting circular error.

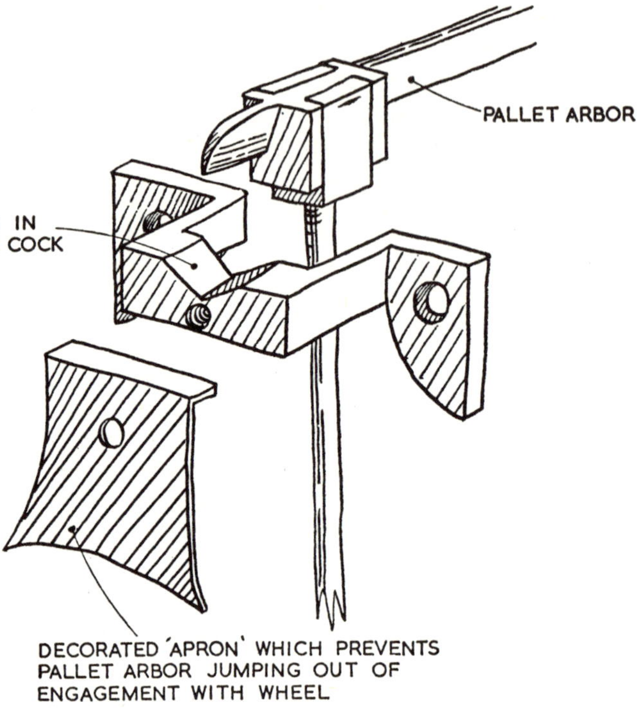

FIGURE 10 *Detail of knife edge suspension*

In practice though, as the Fromanteels and those who so quickly followed their example soon realised, the elegantly contrived cycloidal cheeks served no useful purpose, and under certain conditions they could introduce into the action of the pendulum an error worse than that they were intended to cure. They could induce an unpredictable change in the *effective* point of suspension of the pendulum which, with flexible cord or spring suspension, is the point at which the suspending medium flexes at each swing and not the point from which it is hung. Therefore the cycloidal cheeks, instead of counteracting the pendulum's tendency to be 'slow in the long arcs', by causing a minute and scientifically accurate shortening of its effective length, might induce unpredictable and excessive changes in effective length by causing the suspension to flex at varying points.

More simply expressed, the cycloidal cheeks could only function properly, in effect, if the pendulum maintained a consistently wide arc, in which event they were unnecessary because if the width of arc was constant the circular error was also constant and self-cancelling. Also the cord suspension was badly affected by changes in humidity and caused more error. It is true that the English makers soon substituted flat, thin, spring-steel suspension pieces for the cords, in those movements for which the knife-edge suspension was not used, which overcame that particular drawback of the original Dutch system; but on practical grounds, they were undoubtedly right to abolish the cycloidal cheeks and to concentrate on so refining all the constructional details as to keep the power reaching the escapement, and hence the swing of the pendulum, as nearly constant as possible.

The Fromanteels were no sluggards. John, or Johannes, Fromanteel's first period with Coster lasted from September 1657 to May or June 1658, during which time, on the evidence of surviving Fromanteel movements, he had mastered all the necessary new knowledge. It is still not uncommon for manufacturers to advertise new products some months before they actually have any ready for sale, but Ahasuerus' advertisement of November 1658 seems to have lived up to its promise. Although the year had only a few weeks to run, it does seem that those who had called at his house on the Bankside, or at the sign of the Mermaid, could have bought a pendulum clock 'over the counter', or with very little delay.

Perhaps the evidence is not wholly reliable, as it rests principally on a spring clock which was found in a decayed and altered condition, without a case and with only a fragment of dial (but still with its beautiful original hands), in the 1930s. On the evidence of the vacant holes, the movement has been sympathetically restored by the removal of the more modern escapement and the fitting of a verge, bob pendulum, cord suspension and cycloidal cheeks. The back plate of the movement bears a beautifully engraved signature and inscription which runs:

A. Fromanteel. London
Fecit 1658

Although dated movements are very rare, this example has had wide acceptance amongst experts. In his monograph, *The First*

Twelve Years of the English Pendulum Clock, published as an accompaniment to a splendid exhibition which included the clock in question, Mr Ronald Lee says: 'Amongst the known pendulum clocks of the Fromanteel family this table clock is the earliest recorded example and the only one to be dated, made during the year when Ahasuerus advertised his new clocks in . . . 1658.'

Some other observers, myself amongst them, are less happy about the date. It throws out of balance an inscription which would otherwise be symmetrical, or almost so, and the numerals are less well engraved than the rest of the flowing script. It is not unknown for legitimate restoration to step over the dividing line and become improper enhancement, as when a furniture dealer turns a Victorian sideboard into a Regency chiffonier by the removal of some carved flummery and the addition of some gilt-metal grilles and mounts; and the date on this particular clock should be treated with reserve. For our purposes it is of little importance as it is undeniably one of the first English pendulum clocks; and whether it was actually made in 1658 or 1659 is of less consequence than the fact that in the latter year, within twelve months of publishing his advertisement, the most characteristically English of all domestic timekeepers, the long-case clock, was brought into the world by the skilled midwifery of Ahasuerus Fromanteel.

In the seventh edition of *Britten's Old Clocks and Watches and Their Makers* the writer, C. Clutton, states that: 'The earliest long-case clocks are all English and it seems reasonably certain they are an English invention.' He also asserts: 'No wood long-case clock was made before 1659.' These assertions are challenged by reference to the continental 'pedestal' clocks of the sixteenth century, but in the sense that the true long-case clock was designed as a complete entity (though made by the joint efforts of clockmaker and cabinet-maker) Clutton's statements are not unjustified. The object was the same in either case, to support a heavy clock from the floor in preference to hanging it precariously on the wall; the pedestal or pillar clocks were more in the nature of hybrids from which the clock part could always be removed, one feels, and function as a hanging clock without looking naked—as would the movement and dial of a long-case clock similarly divorced from its case.

It was the advertised undertaking to make clocks to go 'a week, a moneth or a year with once winding-up' which lay behind the design of the long-case clock. The use of the pendulum so improved timekeeping that it was not only practicable to fit a concentric minute hand (and, at first to mark each minute) almost as a matter of course, but it was no longer essential to correct the clock by the sundial every day—or as often as the weather allowed. With the need for daily correction removed, it was an obvious added attraction also to remove the need for daily winding.

The first step in the process of increasing the duration of going, was to increase the overall ratio between the first and last wheels of each train. There were two ways of doing this, either by greatly increasing the tooth-numbers, and sizes, of the primary wheels or by adding one or more extra wheels and pinions. The latter was the more convenient way, and where, for example, the going train of a thirty-hour clock almost always has three wheels, that for an eight-day clock has four; and comparable additions have to be made for month, three-month or year timepieces. Each increase in the multiplication requires a corresponding increase of the driving power. Also, to increase the number of times the great wheel may revolve in relation to a given descent of the driving weight, the simple arrangement of a cord or soft rope passing over a spiked pulley no longer sufficed. Instead of the pulley a grooved 'barrel' or drum was connected to the great wheel arbor by ratchet-wheel and click, (see Figure 11) to permit winding up, and the weight hung from a line of fine catgut which was wound round this barrel, passed through a single pulley hooked to the weight and then passed back to an anchorage below the clock movement. This arrangement of line and idler pulley also economised the rate of descent but required a further increase in the weight; so, broadly speaking, the weights needed to drive an eight-day clock so rigged need to be more than twice as heavy as those for a thirty-hour piece of comparable workmanship. The increased mass made the complete clock too heavy to be conveniently fixed to the wall, and the 'trunk' of a long-case not only enclosed the driving weights and kept them from childish fingers but put the weight of the whole affair where it belonged, on the floor.

The new arrangement of barrel and thin gut line meant that winding a weight clock was no longer a matter of merely pulling up

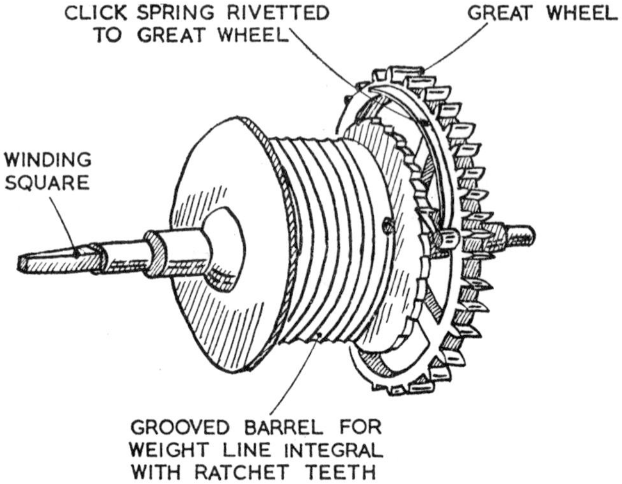

FIGURE 11 *Long-case clock barrel, great wheel and click; the ratchet teeth cut for anti-clockwise winding as used on month-duration clocks*

the weight, by hauling down the free end of the rope. A projecting 'square' and key was required, as for a spring-driven clock; but the early spring clocks, with balance control, could be turned about with no risk of stopping the movement so it was of no consequence that the strike or quarter trains had to be wound from the back or side of the case. It was at once apparent that a pendulum clock could not be treated in this way, and the old back-to-back juxtaposition of going and striking trains could no longer be used. In any event, the old arrangement of wheels, directly one above another, meant an inconveniently high movement if more than three main wheels were to be used in each train. These considerations forced a fundamental change of plan with the trains of wheelwork (usually two but sometimes three if a quarter-chiming train were included), side by side so that the winding squares could all be reached through holes in the dial plate. Another advantage was that the wheels did not have to be directly above one another, but could be staggered to save space. This was of great advantage later, when repeating work and other complications were added.

Instead of a 'frame' consisting of fairly small, widely spaced, horizontal top and bottom plates supported and tied together by four vertical corner 'posts', the new style movement became a thing of larger, rectangular, vertical back and front plates, spaced only two to three inches apart (the length of the winding barrels being the determining factor), held together by four, five or occasionally six, horizontal 'pillars'. All the main wheel work was pivoted between the plates, and the motion work for the hands, together with the striking detents, were mounted on the front plate which was also pierced to receive the short pillars, or feet, carrying the dial plate. For convenience of dismantling and re-assembly some of the first long-case clocks had two or three narrow plates in front instead of one wide one, but this is rare.

Also, a few of the new-style eight-day pendulum clocks were made as 'hooded wall clocks' on brackets; but they too are rare, and appear to have been cheaper alternatives to the new style long-case clocks and not their progenitors. Those that exist appear mostly to have been made between 1660 and 1675 or thereabouts, and they should not be confused with later varieties of 'hooded wall clocks' which had thirty-hour movements and derived from the later lantern clocks. These simpler hooded clocks, and alarum timepieces, were made in country districts until the nineteenth century and retained the old style 'posted' movements.

The new style long-case clock was established in time to greet King Charles II at his restoration, and the horological enthusiasm of that discerning monarch gave a fillip to the clock and watch trade. As may be seen in Plate 6, the first of the new clocks were almost small enough to qualify for the coy designation of 'grandmother' clocks; they were seldom above 6ft high and the dials were 8 to 9 in square. A very dark wood, ebony or ebonised fruit-wood or laburnum veneered upon oak, was almost universal. The sides of the trunk, as well as the flush-fitting door, were each divided into three panels—a small square one in the centre, with long rectangular ones above and below. In accordance with the rules of proportion of classical architecture, the upper panels were a trifle shorter than the lower ones, but generally only sufficiently so as to deceive the eye, viewing them from a distance, into seeing them as equal. Architectural influence also shaped the 'hood' which was topped by a triangular moulded pediment. The sides as well as the front of the hood were glazed so that the movement could be seen; this served the practical purpose of allowing the owner to judge whether the clock needed winding without opening the trunk door. The base or plinth was plain and joined to the trunk by an ogee moulding, whilst a bold convex moulding swelled out from the top of the trunk to meet and support the wider dimensions of the hood. Concave mouldings at these points came into fashion in the early years of the eighteenth century.

A peculiarity of early long-case construction is that the hoods have no hinged door in front, and to get at the dial to wind or set the clock it is necessary to raise the whole hood upwards. The back-board of the case fits into grooves in the sides of the hood and a spring-loaded metal catch holds the hood sufficiently high to give access to the winding holes and hands. The object of this rather awkward arrangement was to prevent unauthorised people from interfering with a highly-prized and very expensive piece of domestic equipment, as the affair was so contrived that the hood could not be raised unless the trunk door was opened, and the trunk door was fastened by an ordinary small tumbler lock of which, no doubt, the master of the house kept the key. As the clock could not be wound until the trunk door was opened, the arrangement had the further advantage that the owner could watch the weights as they were wound up and could stop winding before their pulleys crashed into the seat-board below the movement.

The device which made this possible was an ingenious iron catch, pivoted below the seat-board, and with a spoon-shaped projection lying in the doorway; the upper end of the spoon was turned into a forwards-facing tongue which fitted into a socket in the base of the hood, and the affair was so weighted that the tongue automatically fell clear of the socket as the trunk door opened. Though ingenious, the arrangement of lift-up hood and automatic catch became inconvenient as clocks grew taller, and in low-ceilinged rooms they could not function at all. It is therefore uncommon to find an *original* lift-up hood, as nearly all were converted, either to slide forwards or to have a hinged door in front, early in their lives.

Other clockmakers soon followed Fromanteel's example in making long-case clocks. Notable amongst them were William Clement, Joseph Knibb, Edward East and Hilkiah Bedford, but Fromanteel's may be taken as archetypal. It is not possible to say

Page 89 PLATE 14 Typical fine London long-case clock dial and hood. By Edward Card, *c*1690. The 'blind' winding holes indicate the presence of bolt-and-shutter maintaining power. The admirable proportions and legibility of the 10in dial need no emphasis

Page 90 PLATE 15. This 10in dial by Joseph Windmills, London, *c*1700, shows the next stage of development from Plate 14, the hour hand is less bold, there is no maintaining power and the cherub spandrels have been extended by foliage and entwined curlicues whether the clockmaker or the casemaker was primarily responsible for the overall design, but the balance of probability is that the clockmaker dictated the form and laid down the general proportions. Mr Ronald Lee's researches show with tolerable certainty that Joseph Clifton made the first-long cases for Fromanteel, and doubtless for others.

Some of the long-case clocks of the first dozen years perhaps lack the harmonious proportions which followed the introduction of the long pendulum, but they are as superbly made as the mechanical parts they enclose. They established, from the start, a principle that was seldom departed from by English clockmakers for the next two centuries: that the case and its decoration must never subordinate the clock. This is particularly true of the earliest examples, where the severe architectural lines of the case focus attention on the dial.

What superb dials they are, too. Figure 12 shows one of Ahasuerus Fromanteel's long-case clock dials of about 1660 which could not be improved upon for elegance and legibility. By contrast, most dials and hands in the modern idiom appear to have been designed by a specialist in fairground furnishings and executed with knife and fork. Some of the first English pendulum clocks, weight- or spring-driven, had engraved 'spandrels' or corner ornaments, and engraved decoration in the dial centre; but separate mounts soon became general, although the attractive pierced and gilded, or silver, central boss did not survive long. The whole dial plate was gilded, and the areas outside the chapter ring burnished; though the centre portion, including that beneath the pierced boss, was 'matted' before gilding by a delicate punching process, or by the use of special rollers similar to those used for preparing plates for the contemporary invention of mezzotint engraving. The edges outside the applied chapter ring were generally left plain except for the maker's signature, but later specimens with larger dials often have a little decorative engraving between the cast spandrels, and wholly-engraved borders are found on many first quality clocks of *c*1700. Some few clocks of the first period had solid silver chapter rings, but the majority were chemically 'silvered'; Fromanteel and some of his contemporaries favoured a form of 'close plating', with a very thin sheet of silver soldered to a thicker plate of brass. Although the chemical silvering needs occasional renewal, as described in Chapter 14, it can be given a soft, matt finish which is preferable to the brighter surface of the close-plated or solid silver.

The earlier the dial, generally speaking, the finer the grain of the matted surfaces. Those of the 'Fromanteel period' have a particularly fine satiny quality which not only served as a perfect foil to the chapter ring and the gilded spandrels but also cut down reflected light behind the hands. Dutch and French makers of the period often achieved a similar effect by covering the dial plate, behind the

FIGURE 12 *Showing the proportions of Ahasuerus Fromanteel's elegant and legible long-case clock dial and hands, c1665*

applied chapter ring, with dark red or black velvet, to provide a most attractive contrast to the metal ring. Elegant though they were, these velvet-covered dials suffered the defect of growing shabby fairly quickly; whereas the English combination of matt and burnished gold with matt silver chapters needs only occasional attention.

In addition to the quarter- and half-hour marks on the inner edge of the chapter ring, the minute divisions were scribed on the outer edge with each fifth minute numbered; the numbers being engraved inside the minute circle and not outside it, as later became fashionable. It will be seen that the winding holes are 'blind'. This is because they have moveable shutters behind them forming part of a device known as 'bolt and shutter maintaining power', which will be dealt with later. Tradition says, perhaps with little justification, that the beautifully cast, tooled and gilded winged cherubs' head spandrels of this period were designed by Sir Christopher Wren.

The drawing says all that needs to be said of the hands, which were of chiselled and burnished steel made blue-black by heat treatment. The proportions should be noted, with the tip of the hour hand encroaching on the inner edge of the chapter ring by a tiny amount, and the tip of the minute hand just short of the outer edge by a similar amount. This relationship of hand length to chapter markings was maintained by English dial-makers until the mid-nineteenth century and, again, cannot be improved upon for appearance and legibility. Many continental styles, and most modern clocks, are less attractive and much less readable because the hands are too much alike in pattern and length.

It will be seen that the Fromanteel dial has no seconds hand; this refinement did not materialise until the next mechanical innovation was established with the invention of the 'anchor' escapement. There is, however, a day-of-the-month indicator in the shaped 'window' between the winding holes. This day-of-the-month indicator was to be a feature of all first-grade English clocks spring- or weight-driven, for the next 150 years.

The mechanism to work the calendar consists simply of a twenty-four-hour-wheel in the motion work geared one-to-two with a pinion carried on the hour wheel. This twenty-four-hour-wheel has a pin or lug protruding from it, which engages the saw-teeth cut round the inner edge of the calendar ring on which the thirty-one date numerals are engraved. This ring is necessarily of large diameter, and rotates on rollers mounted on suitably placed feet, projecting from the back of the dial plate. If the clock is correctly assembled, the pin on the twenty-four-hour wheel begins to engage and move the calendar ring at about 10 o'clock (arranged for obvious reasons as 10 o'clock at night), and completes the movement soon after midnight. Thereafter the pin is clear of the ring, which may be moved by hand during daytime hours in order to set the correct date, or to make the necessary adjustment at the end of a month with less than thirty-one days.

Simple though it is, this calendar mechanism could get out of adjustment and stop the clock. Many generations of clock bodgers have dealt with the problem not by restoring the proper adjustment, but by removing the twenty-four-hour wheel and telling their customers that the mechanism was worn out. A special place in Hell is reserved for these vandals.

Although Ahasuerus Fromanteel's 1658 advertisement had promised clocks to go 'a moneth or a year at once winding up', it seems that most of the early long-case clocks were of the type known generically but a little inaccurately as 'eight day'. That is, they had to be wound once a week, but had a margin of excess duration of about twelve to sixteen hours. The general arrangement of an eight-day clock, weight- or spring-driven, has four main wheels in the going train, and five in the striking train if one includes the fly; with the great wheels and their barrels revolving twice in twenty-four hours. Unlike earlier productions, in which the motion work was driven from a small pinion of four or six leaves mounted on an extension of the great wheel arbor, the hands were driven from the second wheel of the going train (or the third or fourth wheels in later clocks of a month or more duration), which wheel consequently became known as the centre wheel and had an arbor long enough to protrude through the centre of the dial plate. This extended arbor had the minute wheel and 'pipe' for the hand frictionally mounted on it; and the centre wheel was always so geared in relation to the others that it turned once an hour; the minute wheel drove a simple twelve-to-one reduction gear to drive the concentric hour hand. Unlike previous motion work, geared down from the great wheel, this new arrangement avoided the annoying backlash characteristic of the older sort, which nevertheless persisted in many types of continental clock until the mid-nineteenth century.

The plates carrying the two (or three) trains of wheelwork were fairly narrow in early specimens and were cut away to an arched or truncated triangular form at their tops; the great wheels protruded beyond the edges of these narrow plates for almost half of their diameters as may be seen in Plates 7 and 8. The 'bob' pendulum was generally just over 10in long and swung from one side to the opposite in half a second. The pear-shaped brass bob had a wooden core forced into a hole drilled through it and this engaged with a screw thread cut on the last inch or so of the pendulum rod, and the bob could consequently be raised or lowered to regulate the rate of going.

Cord suspension and cycloidal cheeks were not much used in Great Britain, as we have seen, and the directly-attached pendulum soon became the general rule, with the arbor rocking on a knife-edge at the end carrying the pendulum. There is evidence though that Fromanteel, and perhaps some others, occasionally used an alternative arrangement with the rear pivot of the escapement arbor supported in the 'V' formed between two overlapping pivoted discs, known as 'friction rollers'. Anti-friction rollers would be more apt, and although such rollers were not used after the first year or so for the escapement arbor, they appear often in other parts of fine quality precision clocks in the eighteenth century; they form, in effect, an embryonic roller bearing.

One notably Dutch feature of long-case clocks of the 'Fromanteel period' is the continental type of bell hammer, bracketed to front or back plate, and with the hammer head on a short arm moving in the horizontal plane. Also popular was a method of sounding the half hours by a system known as 'Dutch striking'. This provides for striking the same number of blows at the half hour as at the preceding hour, but striking them on a smaller bell of higher pitch.

The disadvantage of 'Dutch striking' is that it requires the mechanism to strike 312 blows in twenty-four hours instead of 156, when the hours only are struck, and this calls for a 'high numbered train' and a lot of power. Although it did not materialise until a little later, the need to economise power on the striking side of clocks designed to go a month or more without winding led Joseph Knibb to devise a system known as 'Roman notation striking'. This used two bells of different pitch and two hammers, the latter being actuated by pins protruding from both sides of the appropriate wheel. The high-pitched note, 'ting', represented the 'I' of the Roman numerals and the lower note, 'tang' represented the 'V'. Therefore, for example, 'ting, ting' indicated 2 o'clock but 'ting, tang' indicated 4 o'clock (or IV). Ten or 'X' was indicated by two blows on the deeper bell so the signal for 12 o'clock was 'tang, tang, ting ting', requiring only four movements of the hammer instead of the usual twelve. There were corresponding economies for all the other hours except the first three, with a total of only sixty blows in twenty-four hours.

This most ingenious system was occasionally used by other makers, and still more occasionally is found on eighteenth-century clocks, but it is particularly associated with the Knibbs and with the latter half of the seventeenth century. Clocks with Roman notation strike were distinguished by having the Roman four engraved on the chapter ring as IV instead of IIII, which is otherwise almost universal if Roman numerals are used. This peculiarity of clock dialling is attributed to many reasons, but most probably it was done for the sake of symmetry with the IIII balanced by VIII on the other side of the dial plate. People generally read the time merely by noting the position of the hands; and if asked to write the Roman numerals of a clock dial, the majority would incorrectly write the four as IV, although it is tolerably certain that none of them will have seen a clock so marked.

The combination of verge escapement and directly attached 'bob' pendulum soon found its way into clocks other than those of the new long-case type. However, some country makers continued to make balance-wheel lantern clocks until the end of the century (probably because their sense of thrift would not allow them to waste stocks of castings and other parts), and it seems that some London-made lantern clocks were still being made in the old style until about 1670. These were probably in the minority though and the leading makers, London or provincial, began making lantern clocks with 'bob' pendulums by 1660. The change to the new escapement was accompanied by a change to a system using only one weight, instead of two, to drive both going and striking trains. This apparent impossibility was brought about by an arrangement of endless cord and pulley of the most engaging ingenuity, which had been devised by Huyghens, originally as a form of maintaining power, in which connection it will be discussed more fully later. This new system necessitated having both great wheels turning in the same direction, and this in turn entailed moving the bell hammer from the right-hand side of the clock (as seen from in front) to the left, with a corresponding shift from left to right of the lifting piece and the count wheel detent arbor. The use of the single weight system meant that only one great wheel pulley had to be able to turn back, by the usual ratchet device, for winding; consequently, the pulley of the going train great wheel was permanently fixed to its arbor and the winding was done on the striking train, so that the weight continued to exert a downwards pull on the going side, equal to half the normal power exerted, whilst the clock was being wound up.

Most bob pendulum lantern clocks had the pendulum swinging behind the back-plate, between clock-case and wall (the common arrangement of 'stirrup and spurs' allowed room for this). The continental fashion for some types of wall clocks, with the short pendulum swinging in front of the dial, was not adopted in England, but some lantern clocks were made with the pendulums swinging between the two trains of wheelwork. This required four bars to support the arbors, instead of the usual plan of having one central bar common to both going and striking trains. With a central pendulum, the bob was no longer of the usual pear shape but was formed like an anchor with upturned scrolled ends to the flukes; these swung through slots cut in the side doors and gave a pleasing effect as they bobbed into view, first on one side of the clock and then on the other.

A few lantern clocks with central pendulums have glazed semicircular 'wings' attached to the side doors, which totally enclose the pendulum whilst still allowing it to be seen. The 'wings' are surmounted by pierced brass frets corresponding to those between case and bell. I have never seen a 'winged' lantern clock on which the wings did not have that indefinable something which suggested they were reproductions, and I believe them to be 'reproductions' of something which never existed originally. They may well have been 'invented' during the early years of this century by a noted antiquarian horological dealer, who was much given to causing engraving of 'more than oriental splendour' to appear on surfaces which the original craftsman had been content to leave plain, and to arranging that once-simple country-made oak long-case clocks should burst forth in a rash of carving of the sort known to the printers of Victorian pattern-books as 'Jacobean'.

Although the long-case clock was an innovation with no direct continental parent or counterpart, the first English spring-driven pendulum clocks in wooden cases were almost exact replicas of a type laid down by Salomon Coster. Their development into the typically English 'bracket' clocks (the term is more than a little inappropriate but must suffice as it has become widely accepted) will be considered later, but one or two aspects of their mechanism are appropriate here.

Following their Dutch forbears, the first examples were made with flexible suspensions and cycloidal cheeks. This arrangement very soon gave way, as on the long-case clocks, to directly attached pendulum and knife-edge suspension—or, very occasionally, spring suspension without cheeks. Also following the Dutch example, the earliest specimens were made without fusees. In his pamphlet, Huyghens had argued that the superiority of the pendulum over the uncontrolled balance made the fusee unnecessary. He went on to say:

> Although it is admitted that by this method [without a fusee] the motion of a pendulum is not equally vigorous in the beginning and at the end [of the spring power], nevertheless the effect is not to reduce the time of the concluding oscillations as has been proved earlier.

Despite Huyghens' conclusion and the Dutch examples, English practitioners soon found that better results were to be had with the fusee than without it, and with rare exceptions all English spring clocks from 1660 onwards have fusees, and have them, moreover, for the striking (and quarter-chiming) trains as well as for the going part. Some kinds of continental portable clocks were made with fusees for the going trains, but with the striking mechanism driven by a 'going barrel'. This saved space and cost and was sensible because few customers were likely to complain if the rate of striking declined as the clock ran down; but this never appealed to British makers, who continued to fit fusees to their strike and quarter-chiming trains until the twentieth century.

Chapter Six

The Royal Pendulum

If it is sufficiently well made, in good, clean condition, properly adjusted and lubricated, a weight-driven verge escapement clock with a short bob pendulum will keep time within three minutes a week or a little less. Therefore the new generation of timekeepers, which the Fromanteels and their contemporaries produced in the first years of the Restoration, were to their predecessors what a 'Silver Ghost' Rolls-Royce must have seemed to those pioneers who had started motoring in the 1890s with one of Karl Benz's single-cylinder, belt-driven, horseless carriages. Nevertheless, the clock-makers were not satisfied; one of the drawbacks of the verge escapement clock is that it will keep going even when its parts are dirty, hampered with thickening oil and badly out of adjustment, and its performance then becomes very erratic. Even at its best the accuracy fell short of that attained by the simple pendulum used to time astronomical observations.

The reason for the disparity is that the laws governing the action of the pendulum, and the conditions under which its oscillations may be isochronous, apply only if it is free. The simple weight swinging on a light chain, and given an occasional push by an astronomer's assistant, was for all practical purposes a free pendulum; but the controller of the new style clock was never disconnected from the mechanism it governed and which gave it impetus. Consequently it still suffered (though to a lesser extent because of its obedience to the force of gravity) as the old balance had done from the effects of variations in the amount of power reaching it. This was much more serious in its effect than the expansion and contraction of the pendulum rod by change of temperature—a source of error only just beginning to be considered by the mid-seventeenth-century clockmakers.

It was obvious that one way to lessen the 'interference' of the escapement with the pendulum, or to increase the 'dominion' of the latter as seventeenth-century usage had it, was by increasing its weight and, if possible, its length. However, a heavy pendulum swinging through a wide arc was not a practicable proposition; nor was reducing gear such as Huyghens had devised, even though it had enabled a verge escapement to work a heavy 39in seconds pendulum. A new mechanism was needed, and the answer was provided by the invention of the anchor escapement in about 1670.

Like most great inventions, the anchor escapement is so simple that it is remarkable that nobody thought of it earlier. Although the proportions, angles and radii of the various parts involve some geometrical nicety in calculation, the action of the mechanism may be understood almost without explanation by reference to Figures

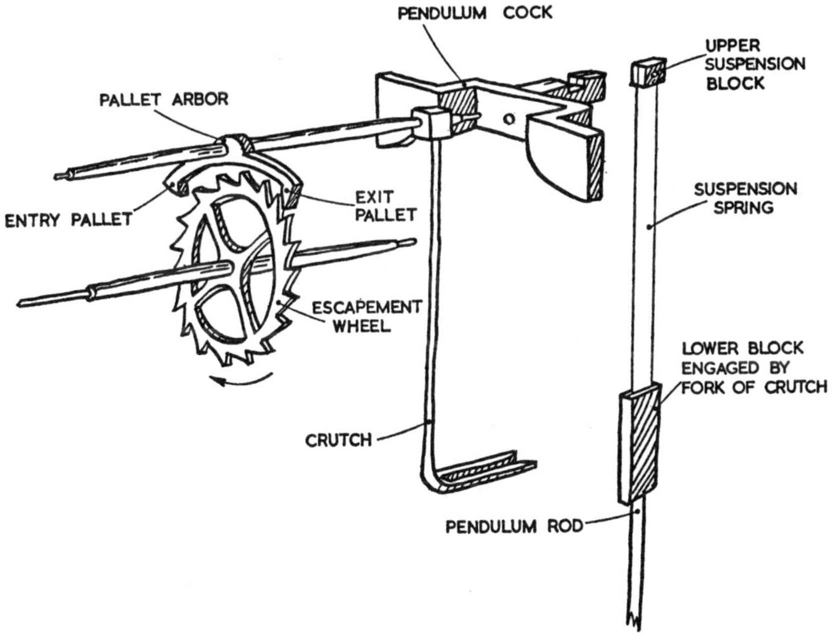

FIGURE 13 *Anchor escapement parts as arranged in English long-case and late-type bracket clocks*

13 and 14. The escapement wheel has undercut 'saw' teeth very similar to those of the verge escapement wheel, except that they travel with their curved rather than their straight faces foremost, but they are set radially instead of axially; this is of advantage because it avoids the rather inefficient contrate wheel needed with the verge escapement and pendulum in order to turn the motion through 90°.

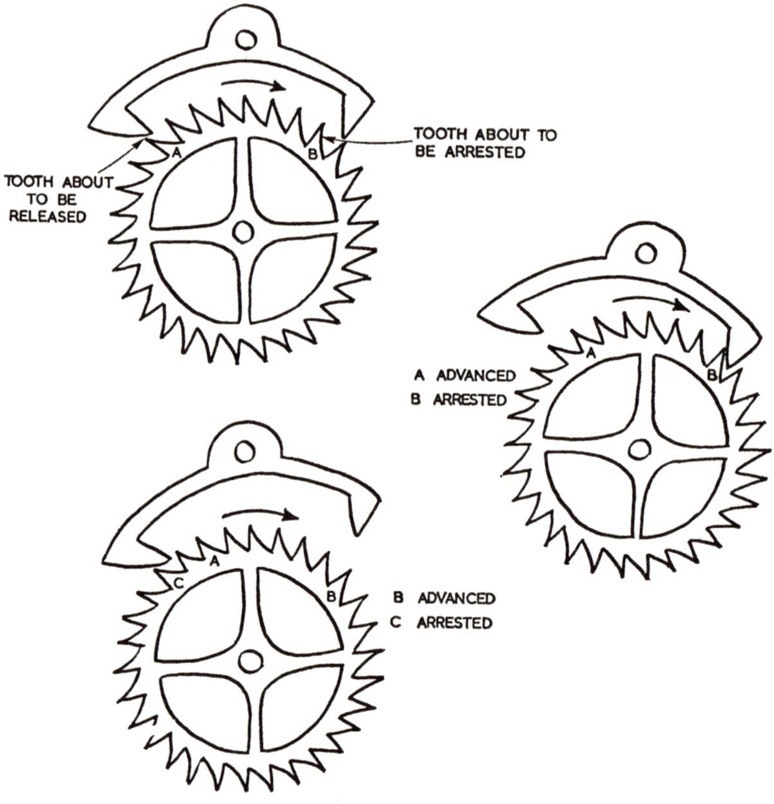

FIGURE 14 *Three consecutive movements of anchor escapement pallets and wheel*

As the drawings show, the 'bow' carrying the pallets has its shank protruding, unlike a real anchor, from the convex rather than the concave side of the curve, otherwise, the resemblance to the mariners' 'killick' is sufficiently close to justify the name of anchor.

As the anchor see-saws to and fro on its pivots, the pallet faces alternately check the advancing wheel teeth and receive impulse from them as they pass. The faces of both the 'entry' and the 'exit' pallets, as they are called, are curved and the relationship of these curves with the curvature of the wheel teeth is such that the two surfaces act upon one another rather in the fashion of tiddleywinks, and tend to force one another apart. This tiddleywink action involves sliding friction, and means that the pallet faces have to be oiled; however, it gives the necessary impetus to the pendulum with less waste of power than in the old verge escapement.

The connection between escapement arbor and pendulum rod was through Huyghens' 'crutch' piece, but in English anchor escapement clocks the pendulum itself hung from a piece of thin spring steel, not from cords, and cycloidal cheeks were never used. One tooth of the escapement wheel having passed the entry pallet, the wheel advanced by half a tooth space until the next advancing tooth was arrested by the exit pallet as the pendulum swung. The continued swing of the pendulum, in the direction previously given to it, gave a slight but perceptible recoil to the wheel, as with the verge escapement, until the intertia of the pendulum was exhausted and its motion reversed. The pendulum was, indeed, no more 'free' of the clock than formerly but the effect of the interference was very much less and the recoil considerably smaller. The principal merit of the anchor was that it functioned with a much smaller angular movement of the pallets than the verge mechanism, and consequently the arc of movement of the pendulum was reduced from some 40°–50° to something of the order of 6°–8°. This allowed the weight of the bob to be greatly increased, with a corresponding increase in the 'dominion' of the pendulum over the clock.

In practice, the use of the anchor escapement meant that a clock with the train of wheels suitably geared could be controlled by a seconds pendulum, 39in long, with a 'lenticular' bob weight of lead covered with brass, 2–3in in diameter and weighing about 1½ lb, having a total swing from one extremity to the other of no more than 7 to 8in. This swing could easily be accommodated within the narrow trunk of the early-style long-case clock and some of the first examples with the new mechanism had second-and-a-quarter pendulums, 61in long. This extra length increased the distance covered by the extremity of the rod to about 12in which, again, could easily be accommodated in the base of the clock.

Until recently, it was generally said that the anchor escapement was first made by William Clement and fitted to a turret clock which he made for King's College, Cambridge, in 1671. As Clement was a maker of the first rank but was not known to have shown any other evidence of inventiveness, it was thought probable that the actual invention came from Robert Hooke, and that Clement was the craftsman who gave his idea practical shape. That irascible genius, Dr Hooke, certainly contributed as much to horology, in the shape of the wheel-cutting engine and the balance spring, as he did to the motor-car in the shape of the universal joint, but there is no direct evidence that he invented the anchor escapement. Recent investigations show that there was a preliminary stage in the development of the anchor, and that the missing link is no longer missing but is to be found in a variant of the cross-beat escapement applied to the long pendulum.

The cross-beat had been occasionally used by some of the leading continental makers, as we have seen, towards the end of the sixteenth century. The central feature of it was a radial-toothed escape wheel, almost exactly the same as that used in the anchor mechanism but with the straight sides of the teeth travelling foremost. This wheel acted on two pallets, as usual, but each pallet was carried on a separate pallet arbor and carried its own cross-bar balance oscillating in the vertical plane. The two pallet arbors were geared together by small toothed wheels which ensured not only the relative movements of the pallets but the opposing oscillations of the balances. Although the cross-bar balances had no naturally isochronous tendency, their linked contrary movements tended to make their variations contra-cancelling. Given careful construction and very frequent cleaning and oiling, a cross-beat balance clock can keep time, it is said, within a minute a day; but the performance deteriorates very quickly even with modern oils. The extra frictional points in the additional pallet arbor and the connecting gears very largely nullified the advantages of the system, much as the reducing gear did in Huyghens design for a long pendulum clock.

Figure 15 shows the escapement parts of a cross-beat, long-pendulum clock made by Samuel Knibb of Oxford in about 1668.

There is also in existence a long-case clock by William Clement which has a conventional anchor escapement and a 1¼ seconds pendulum; however, scribed marks and vacant pivot holes show that the clock was designed for a verge and bob pendulum, but was made with a cross-beat of the type shown and altered to its present system very early in its life—the anchor, pallets, and associated parts all being of very early type. Whether Knibb ante-dated Clement in this combination of cross-beat and long pendulum is

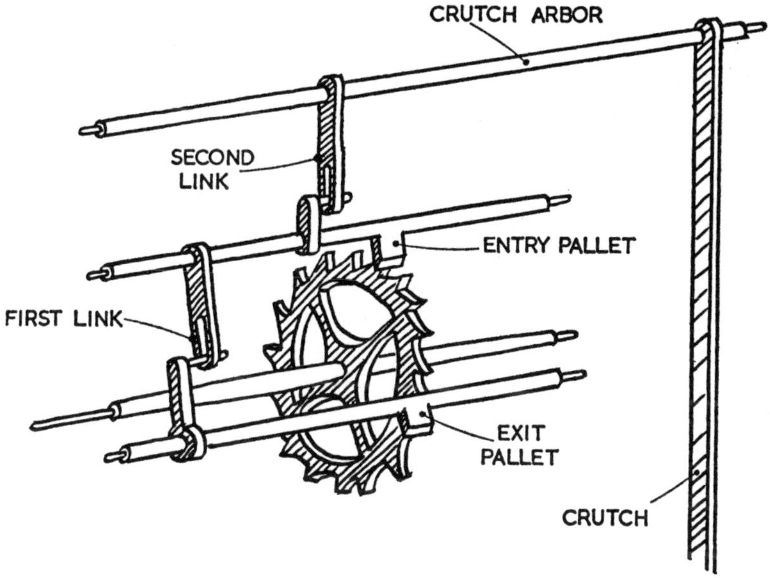

FIGURE 15 *Joseph Knibb's variant of the cross-beat escapement applied to a long seconds pendulum*

not known. The necessary connection between the two pallet arbors, to keep the motions of the pallets in phase, is done not by gear wheels, as in the earlier type of cross-beat, but by the arrangement of pin and slotted link shown; similar linkwork transmits the motion to the crutch arbor and thus to the pendulum. Given a craftsman as good as Knibb, links such as these work with less lost motion than toothed wheels but suffer more from sliding friction; indeed, the escapement has five points of sliding friction and six pivot holes which need oil, against the three sliding contacts and two pivots of the conventional anchor escapement. In fact, the surviving example referred to works well and shows little sign of wear, but this is more a tribute to Knibb's skill than to the merit of the design and it is not surprising that some bright mind, whether Knibb's, Clement's, Hooke's, soon saw the drawbacks and probably almost by chance hit upon the idea of substituting the action of a simple see-saw for the complexity of separate pallet arbors linked together.

The niceties of who did what, and when, need not concern us and it is clear that the combination of the anchor escapement, in the form which has remained unaltered for three centuries, and 'royal' pendulum was *de rigeur* for long-case clocks by 1675 or earlier.

Some of the earliest long-case pendulum clocks have 61in pendulums beating 1¼ seconds, and the cases for such movements generally have the front panel of the base hinged to give access to the pendulum bob and 'rating nut'. The great majority of long-case clocks have seconds pendulums (a very few, mostly of late eighteenth-century north-country origin, had ¾ second pendulums) and as soon as the new escapement and 'royal' pendulum became established, the clock dials were furnished with a slender 'finger' to indicate seconds on a comparably slender engraved and silvered ring below the XII. With a seconds pendulum, a thirty-tooth escape wheel revolves once a minute and it was consequently logical and easy to provide the seconds indicator merely by making the escapement wheel arbor long enough to reach just short of the dial plate, so that it could carry a 'pipe' or short tube to which the hand was attached.

Until the early years of the eighteenth century, the seconds hand invariably took the form of a small, slender, unbalanced pointer; larger and heavier seconds hands, with 'tails' to balance the operative parts, came into fashion about 1710 and at the same time the seconds rings became rather wider and more prominent. Although it cannot be proved, it is fairly certain that in the seventeenth century the 'minutes' of the clock were pronounced as 'my-newts' rather than as 'minnits', and the designation 'seconds' came from the fact that they were originally the 'second minutes' or subdivisions of the small or minute divisions of the hour.

The addition of the seconds hand and ring was not the only outward change in the long-case clock. To allow for the swing of the

Page 107 PLATE 16 Thomas Tompion *c*1685–90, in walnut case with parquetry inlays; the flat-topped hood has a convex moulding above the dial in place of the usual band of fretwork and this may not be original

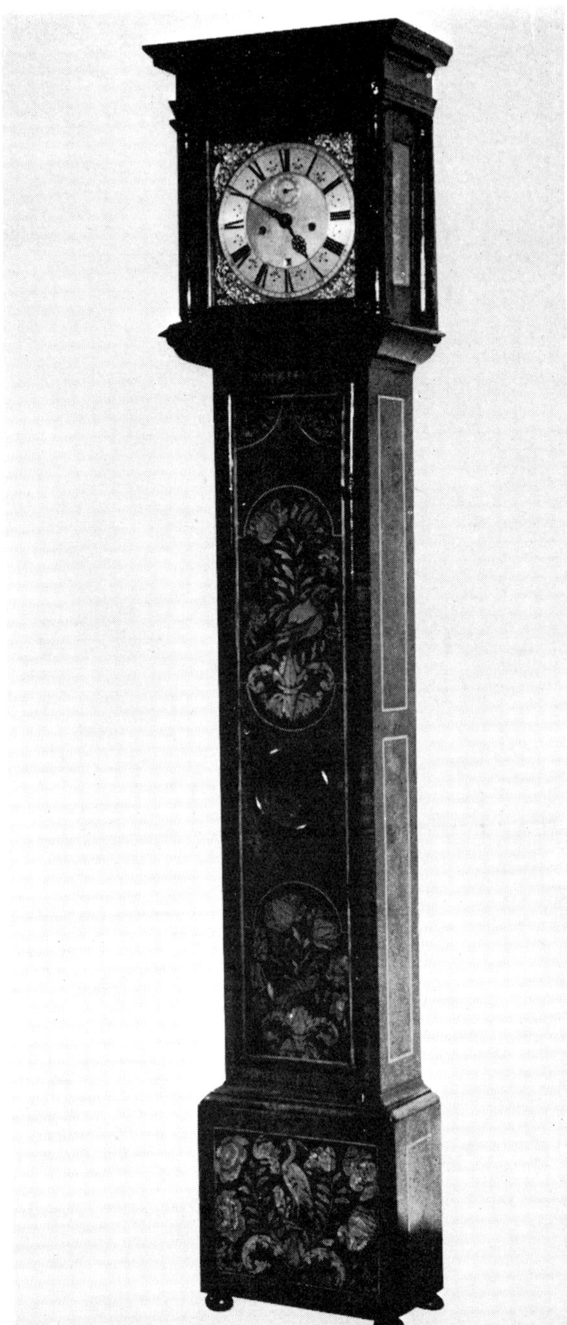

Page 108 PLATE 17 A fine example of Joseph Knibb's 'standard' late seventeenth-century long-case clock in bird-and-flower marquetry inlaid walnut case. PLATE 18 Rather similar to Plate 17, this marquetry clock by Richard Wise, London, *c*1695, has a 'lenticle' through which the pendulum may be seen. The box wood stringing on the sides of the case continue the tradition of the early panelled form royal pendulum, the trunk had to be a little wider than formerly, and some pre-1680 examples look a little stumpy in consequence. This was soon rectified by slightly increasing the height of the case with corresponding increases in the width across the base and hood; this in turn entailed increasing the dimensions of the dial, and during the last two decades of the seventeenth century the 'average' long-case clock stood about 6ft 3in high (exclusive of any carved 'cresting' or other superstructure which began to be fashionable), and had a 10in square dial.

The new-fangled pendulum, particularly the 'royal' variety, captured the public fancy and after 1675 it became common to put a circular or oval window in the door of the trunk, level with the bob of the pendulum, so that the latter could be seen in action. A bull's-eye glass was often used and this distorted the polished brass bob weight which appeared to flash behind it. The little window served the practical purpose that one could see at a glance if the clock had stopped.

Other outward changes followed in due course. Trunk sides and doors generally lost their divisions into three panels, although in many instances the sides were inlaid and veneered in such a fashion as to suggest the appearance of separate panels. The doors were surrounded by larger mouldings than formerly, generally half-round, which projected to cover the gaps between trunk and door when the latter was closed. This new fashion was perhaps less elegant than the flush-fitting doors, but probably experience had shown that the inevitable 'movement' of the oak carcases meant that the hazard of an occasionally jammed door could only be avoided by making the clearance large enough to be visible.

The architectural treatment of the hood, with its columns and triangular pediment, gave way to a flat-topped form with, most often, narrow bands of pierced fretwork, backed with silk, below the cornice moulding. These wooden frets served the functional purpose of letting the sound of the bell be clearly heard but, being very fragile, few originals have survived. Nor have most of the carved crestings which surmounted many of these flat-topped clocks. These were often carved in lime wood which, being fairly soft, came under attack from the furniture beetle; or, if they escaped such attack, they often had to be sacrificed if the clock passed into humbler surroundings where the ceilings were low. With the change from triangular pediment to flat or sometimes domed cornice, the side pillars of the hood ceased to be plain in most instances and gave way to the barley-sugar twist variety found on late Carolean and William and Mary chair backs. Plates 14 and 15 show typical examples.

The most notable change, though, was that the severe black cases, with their finely chiselled gilt metal mounts on pillars and in the tympanum, fell out of favour. Black cases continued fashionable for spring clocks for another 150 years, but as early as 1675 it began to be thought, no doubt, that as the long-case clock grew bigger it looked too sombre all in black. The change to lighter woods, amongst which figured walnut veneers predominated, also led to a lesser use of gilt metal mounts as the following letter shows. It was written in 1675 by Sir Richard Legh of Lyme Hall, Cheshire, to his wife:

> I went to the famous Pendulum maker Knibb, and have agreed for one, he having none ready but one dull stager which was at £19; for £5 more I have agreed for one finer than my father's, and it is to be better finished with carved capitalls gold, and gold pedestalls with figures of boys and cherubimes all brass gilt. I wold have had itt Olive Wood, (the Case I mean), but gold does not agree with that colour, soe took their advice to have it black Ebony which suits your Cabinett better than Walnut tree wood, of which they are mostly made. Lett me have thy advice herein by the next.

Sir Richard had only been married a few months but his young wife clearly knew her mind, as she replied decisively:

> My dearest Soule; as for the Pandolome Case I think Blacke suits anything.

As one of the most expensive commodities of the pre-railway age was transportation, it is probable that Sir Richard's London-made long-case clock cost him between £30 and £40 by the time he got it home to Cheshire. Allowing for the decline in the value of money, this represents the cost of a tolerably good, small, family car in today's terms; but the mere fact that the art of long-case clock making had not, apparently, reached Cheshire by 1675 indicates how much rarity value must be added to the money value of his Ebony Pandolome.

The change to walnut and other decoratively figured veneers in place of ebony was followed, or accompanied rather, by the new fashion for marquetry inlays of vari-coloured woods. The process of marquetry cutting and laying evolved from the highly-skilled inlaid *intarsia* work which developed in Italy during the sixteenth century; its elaboration into the marquetry technique took place in the Netherlands in the seventeenth. The process requires thinner veneers, and consequently more elaborate tools and skills than those which sufficed for earlier types of inlaid work, and the early English marquetry was very similar in style to the Dutch. It is very difficult, however, to sustain the belief that until at least 1700 all the marquetry clock cases and other objects made in England were decorated by immigrant Dutch workers. This used to be an article of faith in antique-dealing circles, but there is no evidence for it. No doubt some Dutch craftsmen brought the art to England and stayed to practise it, but English cabinet-maker's soon learnt the new technique.

The marquetry decoration was at first confined to relatively small areas, generally only on the fronts of the cases, defined by borders of box or other light coloured wood. The 'bird and flower' pattern with infinite variations, arranged in panels as shown in Plates 17 and 18 is typical of the first type of marquetry work; this particular style dates from about 1685–90 when rather more elaborate patterns were already coming into favour. These developed by the turn of the century into 'all-over' floral and arabesquerie designs, which are generally rather less pleasing, even though they must be admired for their technical excellence. Even more admirable technically but less pleasing to the English eye, is the fussy elaboration of the so-called 'seaweed' marquetry which originated on the continent and became briefly fashionable in England about 1720.

The taste for oriental lacquer decoration is also found in both long-case and spring clocks. Oriental lacquer, and its many European imitations, it much too large a subject for this book. It may be summarised by observing that pre-1695 lacquered long-case clocks (spring clocks were not similarly decorated until much later) are rare, and may occasionally have had their cases sent to China for decoration. A rather more common practice, apparently was to send only the trunk door and to have the rest of the case painted locally in imitation of the genuine lacquer work; though there is one school of thought which holds, on rather tenuous grounds, that a number of Chinese workmen settled either in Portugal or Holland and that the 'genuine Chinese' lacquer work was done there, rather than in the East. What is rather more certain is that after 1700 all, or nearly all, the so-called lacquer work on clock cases was executed in England. Rather confusingly the eighteenth century name for all such work, whether genuine or imitiation, was 'japanning'.

English 'japanned' work, although often very pleasing, was done by a much simpler series of processes than the real thing, and was consequently less brilliant and far less durable. Therefore lacquered clock cases, particularly the long-case ones, are apt to be either very shabby, much faded and crazed or chipped, or, if they are undamaged and effulgent, they are all too likely to be have been so enthusiastically 'restored' fairly recently as to be virtually newly done.

Mechanical developments in the long-case clock after the introduction of the 'royal' pendulum caused further modifications in appearance. The construction of the movements became rather heavier, though wheels and plates are often still relatively thin and light by comparison with eighteenth-century examples. Clocks 'to go a moneth' or more, as Fromanteel had promised, became an actuality, and the addition of the extra wheel, or wheels, to the trains involved altering the position of the winding holes. Those of the normal eight-day long-case clock are usually level and just below the horizontal centre line of the dial, but on a month clock they generally lie roughly on the line of the figures IIII and VIII, and are correspondingly nearer to the inner edge of the chapter ring.

Another distinguishing feature of a month clock, useful as a means of identification in a crowded antique shop or auction room, is that the addition of the extra wheel in each train means that the going train great wheel must revolve clockwise; consequently the winding operation has to be done anti-clockwise and the teeth of the ratchet mechanism on the barrel are inclined as shown in Figure 11. Although only the going train *must* be arranged in this way, with anti-clockwise winding, the strike train was usually, but not always, similarly arranged as a matter of convenience.

Three-month clocks are very much rarer than those of month duration and have their winding squares even lower in the dial plate; so much so that the holes may have to be pierced through the chapter ring. Year clocks, rarest of all, were generally time-pieces with no striking or quarter chiming work, as the space required for the extra wheels and the great mass of the driving weights, presented constructional difficulties; therefore there is but a single winding hole, generally placed just above the numeral VI. Spring clocks of more than eight-days duration are much rarer than long-duration weight clocks; the difficulty of providing the necessary extra power from springs was considerable, and one of the most remarkable of Thomas Tompion's productions was a spring clock which is not content with going for a year with one winding but strikes the hours and quarters as well. This astonishing piece of work, which was made for King William III, stands only 30in high inclusive of the silver figure of Britannia which surmounts the case. In passing, it may be remarked that the modern year-duration spring clocks, known in the trade as four-hundred-day clocks, or in America as anniversary clocks, achieve their results not by the addition of extra wheelwork to the train but by the use of a form of escapement, the ingenuity of which is not matched by any corresponding ability to keep time.

It may also be mentioned that from the mid-seventeenth century onwards, English clockmakers took pains to arrange the wheelwork so that the winding holes were symmetrically placed in the dial. This often called for some ingenuity and extra expense in laying-out the mechanism. There are a few exceptions to the rule, and most of these exceptions are clocks to which a quarter-chiming train has been added at a later date. Continental makers were much less scrupulous; throughout the eighteenth century many French, Austrian and Dutch clocks, often of the highest quality, sprout winding holes in unexpected places to the detriment of their appearance.

The 'bolt-and-shutter maintaining power', previously referred to, which was generally fitted to the very early long-case clocks with crown wheel escapements and short pendulums, was less often fitted to their long-pendulum successors. The mechanism may be understood by reference to Figure 16, and it was ingeniously contrived so that it was impossible to wind up the clock without engaging the auxiliary power. The action of moving a lever, generally by pulling a cord, simultaneously removed the 'shutters' from the winding holes and caused the spring-loaded 'bolt' to engage with, and press upon, a tooth of the penultimate wheel in the going train. This provided enough power at the escapement, for enough time, to keep the clock going whilst the main power supply was interrupted by the act of winding. As the appropriate wheel revolved sufficiently to release the 'bolt', it sprung clear of the mechanism and the shutters swung back again to close the winding holes.

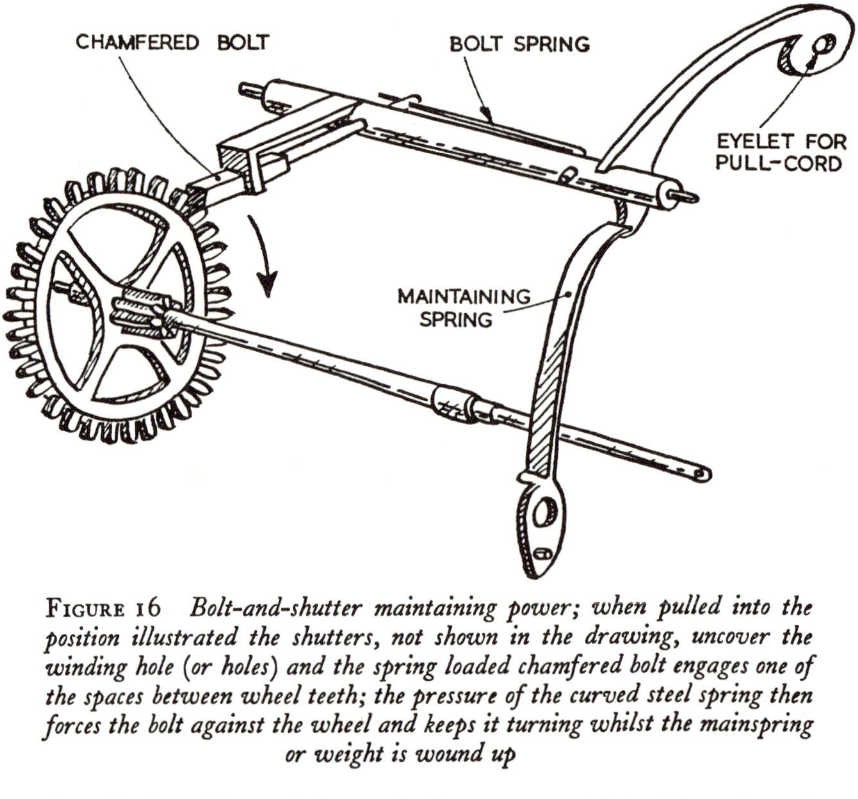

FIGURE 16 *Bolt-and-shutter maintaining power; when pulled into the position illustrated the shutters, not shown in the drawing, uncover the winding hole (or holes) and the spring loaded chamfered bolt engages one of the spaces between wheel teeth; the pressure of the curved steel spring then forces the bolt against the wheel and keeps it turning whilst the mainspring or weight is wound up*

As the 'royal' pendulum clock was capable of keeping time within less than a minute a week, against a possible error of three to five minutes for a verge clock with bob pendulum, the loss of the few seconds during winding would seem to be more important for the former than for the latter. Many writers on horology have expressed surprise that the maintaining power generally fitted to the less accurate types of clock was not always found on their more accurate successors. The logical explanation is that the early makers were not so much concerned with the loss of a few seconds as with the need to keep the clock going. The short, light pendulum of a verge clock might come to rest during the winding process, but the inertia of the long, heavy seconds pendulum was enough to keep it swinging through a wide enough arc to allow the clock to start again after as much as a couple of minutes interruption of its power supply.

Although it became less common, bolt-and-shutter maintaining power continued to be fitted to the finest clocks of the later seventeenth century. On the grounds, presumably, that it might jam and cause trouble nineteenth-century repairers often removed it, leaving tell-tale vacant holes in the plates where the various pieces had been pivoted or mounted. It would have been quite possible to avoid all risk of jamming merely by removing the chamfered operative end of the 'bolt', leaving the shutters and the rest of the maintaining work intact and restorable but, as the clock collector soon discovers, the Victorian professional repairers were never content with anything less than radical removal. This is why so many antique clocks have been bereft of their calendar work, repeating work, maintaining work, 'rise-and-fall' pendulum adjustments and many other refinements. It is not uncommon to find clocks from which the entire striking mechanism has been removed, though it could have been made inoperative, if that is what the owner wished, merely by removing one lifting-pin.

The introduction of the 'dead beat' escapement, temperature compensation and other refinements early in the eighteenth century led to the development of the sorts of precision long-case clocks known as regulators, and these were always fitted with maintaining work in the interests of accurate timekeeping. After about 1760, the old bolt-and-shutter mechanism gave way to a fully automatic variety, without the shutters, which needed no preliminary action before winding and which was originally devised by John Harrison in connection with his marine chronometers.

Being concerned with the main stream of progress, it is not possible, unfortunately, to give much space to the exceptional clocks of any period. Probably the best source of information about the rare, complicated, always interesting and sometimes fantastic special creations is *Some Outstanding Clocks over 700 Years* by H. Alan Lloyd. Even so, the improvement in timekeeping so stimulated progress in other directions that some of the side-results must be mentioned.

The foundation of the Royal Observatory in 1675 was partly the result of horological improvements and, in turn led to further precision in timekeeping. The *raison d'etre* for the observatory was, according to Charles II's charter, 'the finding of the Longitude of Places'; and one of the first tasks of the first Astronomer Royal, John Flamsteed, was to determine whether or not the earth rotated at a constant speed. Astronomers assumed this to be so, but they had no way of proving it until John Flamsteed's observations, reinforced by the accurate time measurements by Tompion's 'great clocks', which he installed, settled the question and proved the apparent isochronical rotation of the globe. 'Apparent' is a necessary qualification, as twentieth-century instruments and calculations have detected variations in the rotation which are, however, so trifling as not to invalidate Flamsteed's further deductions from his 'proof'.

Flamsteed referred to this investigation as the proof of the 'Equation of Natural Days', and he went on to provide the first accurate computation of what is rather confusingly known as the 'equation of time': that is, a table of the daily variations of solar time (*tempus apparans*) from that shown by a perfect timekeeper going at a constant rate and therefore showing 'mean' or 'equal' time, which seventeenth-century savants referred to as *tempus aequale*.

Now that domestic clocks could keep time within a minute a week, it was no longer enough to check and set them, should they have stopped, by an ordinary sundial as they might then be as much as a quarter of an hour ahead of or behind true mean time. The leading makers of long-case clocks began to provide printed equation tables, which were pasted behind the trunk doors, so that the owners could take advantage of a sunny day to set their pocket watches by the nearest accurate sundial, and then make the necessary addition or subtraction from the equation table in order to set their clocks to correct 'equal time'.

Thomas Tompion's equation table of 1685 is headed 'A Table of the Equation of Days, showing How much a good *Pendulum Watch* ought to be faster or slower than a true *Sun-Dial* every Day in the Year', and it is interesting that he still used the generic term 'watch'. At the same time that these equation tables came into use the leading makers, amongst whom the Knibbs, Thomas Tompion, Daniel Quare and Joseph Windmills were prominent, devised ways to make clocks show mean and solar time simultaneously. These were easily checked against a sundial, as setting the solar time correctly would automatically ensure the correct indication of mean time, and the usefulness of 'equation clocks', as they are called did not lessen until the mid-nineteenth century when the new-fangled electric telegraph brought the new-fangled 'railway time' to all parts of the country.

Various ways were adopted for showing the equation. One method, shown in Plate 21, used two concentric minute hands, one for mean and the other for solar time, the latter being distinguished by a little gilded 'sun in splendour' mounted near its tip. A more complex and ingenious system had only one minute hand but two minute circles, the inner one, fixed, for mean time, and the outer one for solar time. The outer minute circle was moved forwards or backwards, by the clock mechanism, in relation to the fixed chapter ring in accordance with the variations, and the solitary minute hand consequently gave an instant indication of the difference. Another plan was to have a subsidiary dial traversed by a hand revolving once a year, and this could serve to point to the date and to the minute degrees of 'Sun Slower' or 'Sun Faster' engraved with suitable spacing round the periphery; alternatively a revolving disc and fixed pointer could serve the same purpose. A fourth arrangement initiated by Tompion, partly for ease of reading and partly for aesthetic reasons to increase the height of the clock, was to add a 'broken arch' to the top of the dial plate and to have the essential calendar and equation of time notations engraved round the semicircle thus provided. The pointer, working over such a semicircle and having reached the end of its annual excursion, had to leap back to the beginning in one movement. This entailed some ingenious complication.

Even further complication was entailed in those clocks which showed the equation by an additional minute hand or an extra, moveable, ring carrying the minute markings for solar time, as these had to move irregularly being sometimes behind, sometimes in advance and only twice a year coincidental with the mean time indicator. The difficult business of making a machine which went at a constant pace move one of its indicators at varying speeds was achieved by means of a cam, known from its shape as the 'kidney piece'. This cam was mounted on that wheel of the extra motion work which was arranged to revolve once a year, and the varying curvature of the kidney piece, its humps and hollows, caused a spring-loaded arm—a cam follower in modern engineering terminology—to rise and fall; the necessary motion was transmitted to the indicator, the subsidiary hand or minute ring, by suitable links which often included a toothed sector and pinion.

The design of all these appurtenances, and particularly the calculation of the curvature of the kidney piece, was a matter of the utmost nicety which would set an advanced engineering designer of the 1970s on his mettle. As the equation work, whatever its form, required a subsidiary train of motion wheels, one of which had to revolve once a year, the equation clocks not infrequently also showed calendar and lunar movements and gave astronomical information of movements of the planets, times of sunrise and sunset throughout the year and so forth; as though all this were not enough these clocks were sometimes of three months or year duration. Where Sir Richard Legh's 'Ebony Pandolome' cost the equivalent of a middling sort of motor-car, these astronomical and equation clocks, housed in cases of suitable magnificence, represent the seventeenth-century equivalent of a 'Silver Shadow' Rolls-Royce. It is true that elaborate astronomical clocks had been made in previous centuries, but they were exercises in ingenuity rather than practicable machines. Those of the later seventeenth century and early eighteenth were useful as well as ingenious, as they were controlled by clockwork which at least knew the time of day.

Between the year 1670, when the 'royal' pendulum was introduced, and the end of the century, the art of clockmaking advanced more than it had done during the previous three centuries. The art of horology one should say, as watchmaking also made spectacular advances thanks in great part to the work of Thomas Tompion in giving pratical shape to the ideas of Hooke and Huyghens (arrived at independently) about applying a controlling spring to the old-style balance mechanism. This gave the portable timepiece a naturally synchronous controller—the vibrations of a given length and stiffness of spring being performed in equal time—and improved the performance of the verge watch (in conjunction with improvements in the workmanship) to nearly the same degree as the pendulum had improved the timekeeping of clocks. Because of this, the balance spring was often referred to as the pendulum spring, and until the novelty wore off the first of the new sorts of watches were called pendulum watches. This leads to great confusion as some watches were made with *mock* pendulums, and these are still called pendulum watches by collectors.

Until the mid-seventeenth century, horology had been an empirical business, but scientists, following Huyghens, increasingly worked at the fundamental and theoretical aspects. Dr Hooke, whose greatest contribution was an indirect one—his wheel-cutting engine—also investigated tooth formation, and although the ideal was not reached for some while it began to be appreciated that teeth of cycloidal form would give the best result by substituting rolling for sliding friction between wheel teeth and pinion leaves. Hooke's wheel-cutting machine, the direct ancestor of the modern method, improved the accuracy of clocks by removing the inevitable errors which arose when the correct spacing of the wheel teeth depended entirely on the sharp eye and skilled hand of the craftsman.

The period also saw the publication of the first books on clock-making in English. Probably the most famous is Dr William Derham's *The Artificial Clockmaker*, first published in 1696. Just as 'sophisticated' no longer means 'adulterated' or 'falsified' but has gone up in the world, 'artificial' has declined and become almost pejorative. Then, the word 'artificial' conveyed the idea of skill and inventiveness, best illustrated by the Duke of York's (King James II) remark on Wren's model for the new St Paul's Cathedral which he described as 'awful, artificial and amusing'. In our terms he meant 'awe-inspiring, ingenious and amazing', and in his sense the artificial work of the late seventeenth-century horologists is truly amusing.

Chapter Seven
Spring-driven Clocks

THERE is no reason why the new anchor escapement should not have been adapted to spring-driven clocks soon after it was evolved for the long-case, long-pendulum variety. The pendulums would necessarily have been shorter but advantage could have been taken of the small swing to increase their weight and consequently their 'dominion' over the clockwork. For reasons which will emerge, this was not done until after 1800, and with relatively few exceptions English spring-driven clocks were made with the old-type verge escapement and light, wide-swinging bob pendulum on a knife-edge suspension until the first years of the nineteenth century.

The principal change in the years between 1670 and 1680 was one of appearance. The first English spring pendulum clocks had been, as we have seen, almost exact copies of the type established by Salomon Coster, except that they had fusees instead of going barrels and no cycloidal cheeks. The Dutch prototypes were, at first, very plain in rectangular wooden cases with little or no embellishment. Although they could be placed on any convenient table or shelf, they were fitted with suitable hoops, or 'keyhole plates', and were normally used as hanging clocks. Although they could not keep going when they were carried (when the pendulums were hooked out of action) they were easily portable and usually fitted with carrying handles. This applied to both the Dutch and English examples, but the former were often equipped with grooves in the cases into which solid wooden panels could be slid in front of the glasses when the clocks were packed for travelling.

These plain rectangular Dutch cases soon developed in France, for example, into the type of clock known as a '*religieuse*'. In England they were at first given the same sort of architectural form as the long-case clocks. Therefore, the 'typical' English spring clock of, say, 1670–80, rather resembles the upper part of a long-case clock without the trunk. The example by William Clement in Plate 9 is of this type, which may either stand or hang on the wall. The pendent acorn finials serve as feet, but the proportions are such that the clock looks better hanging than standing.

The English makers of spring clocks soon broke away from the hanging clock concept, which lingered much longer on the continent, and concentrated on designs more suited to standing on a table, chimney-piece or cupboard—in the old sense of a two- or three-tier arrangement of open shelves for the display of plate and valuables. In the eighteenth century, particularly during the second half, the larger types of spring clock were often placed on elegant matching wall-brackets, a few of which survive, and consequently the generic name of 'bracket clock' has come into being. It is not a particularly accurate name, as bracket clocks on brackets were always in a minority, but it is widely understood. Some purists refer to these English spring clocks as 'table clocks', which leads to confusion with the metal-cased continental timepieces with horizontal dials.

The change from a hanging to a standing type of case was undoubtedly because these spring clocks were even more expensive luxuries than the contemporary long-case variety, and only the richest of owners would have more than one. Therefore, it was convenient to have it in a form which was easily carried about, used in the parlour by day and the bedroom by night, and placed on any suitable table or cupboard. This accounts for the fairly swift transformation from the William Clement type shown in Plate 9 to the fully developed 'bracket clock' in Plate 11. It also accounts for the fact that the majority of early bracket clocks are fairly small, with dials only six or seven inches square, and are always fitted with stout carrying handles. The triangular portico gave way to a lozenge-shaped top, or a flattened dome or 'caddy' which, in the richer examples of about 1680 onwards, was sometimes of pierced and gilded metal, backed with silk, instead of the solid wood top adorned, perhaps with metal mounts. These pierced metal affairs are known as 'basket tops'.

The most important result of the need for portability was its influence on the retention of the verge escapement and bob pendulum on a knife edge. Of all the forms of pendulum mechanism, this is the combination least affected by changes of angle. Very few surfaces in any house, and particularly in a seventeenth-century structure, are exactly horizontal and a bracket clock with an anchor escapement and short, heavy, pendulum (and to get the best results from the escapement the pendulum bob had to be as heavy as possible), swinging through an arc of about 10°, having been adjusted to be 'in beat' for one surface will be out of beat if it is moved to another place with only a 1°–2° difference in slope: it will then perform badly or possibly refuse to go at all. The wide-swinging pendulum of a verge clock is much more tolerant of slight changes of angle; having 45° to play with, as it were, it can afford to be 2°–3° out of plumb without becoming notably out of beat. Also if a clock with a heavy pendulum hanging from a spring suspension (for various reasons the knife-edge was used only with light pendulums) is moved carelessly without removing or locking the pendulum much damage may be done. This risk did not apply to the verge and bob pendulum clock; a hook or hold-fast of some kind was always provided to lock the pendulum to the back plate when travelling, but it was not really necessary to use this when merely moving the clock from room to room. In order to provide an alternative means of regulation, to be dealt with later, some bracket clocks with verge escapements do not have a knife-edge but a spring suspension. Although these need more careful handling than those with a knife-edge, they will still tolerate a change of angle sufficient to stop an anchor escapement.

Therefore the seventeenth- and eighteenth-century clockmakers were quite right to continue with the verge escapement after the superior anchor mechanism had been developed. Even when the bracket clock was no longer a rare luxury and quite ordinary households had clocks in most rooms, it still made sense to use the old type of mechanism. It might no longer be necessary to take the sitting-room clock up to the bedroom, but no amount of persuasion would deter the average householder, or rather his servants, from moving the clocks about when dusting the house. Every clock repairer and dealer is acquainted with the type of customer who is constantly complaining that a clock has stopped, but is apparently incapable of understanding that it stops only because it is incautiously moved about.

This aspect of the business was lost sight of during the second half of the nineteenth century, when seventeenth- and eighteenth-century clocks were merely old-fashioned and of no value. Until past the turn of the twentieth century, it was an article of faith amongst the top-flight repairers, and was stated in all the technical hand-books, that worn or maladjusted verge escapements were not worth repairing. It was implied that the earlier makers had been merely stupid or obscurantist; their reasons for continuing so long with the verge escapement were forgotten and old bracket clocks were converted wholesale, being fitted with new third and escapement wheels, anchor pallets, spring suspensions and heavy lenticular pendulums. No attempt was made to shape or engrave any of the new parts to match the old, and standard components of uncompromisingly Victorian type were used.

That any appreciable number of old bracket clocks have survived unaltered is fortunate, and may be attributed to the fact that many of them fell into the hands of the lesser repairers who lacked the facilities and the skill to finish and fit the new escapements. These practitioners were contemptuously dismissed as 'bodgers' by the top-class repairers, and indeed their work was often bodged with worn pivot holes not re-bushed but roughly punched into shape, scored and rutted pallet faces filled with solder, and, in some cases, loss of power at the escapement occasioned by general wear and neglect, dealt with by the crude expedient of putting in a more powerful mainspring so that the unhappy clock had no option but to go or bust. Even this uncivilised treatment was better than relegation to the scrap-heap or conversion. There is now a flourishing trade in re-converting to verge escapement antique clocks which Victorian or Edwardian craftsmen had converted to anchor: the ethics of this will be discussed later.

One significant result of the change from hanging to standing forms of clock was seen in the decoration of the movements. It is probable that the earliest long-case and spring-driven pendulum clocks had the brass parts of the movements gilded and the steel work blued by heat treatment after careful burnishing. Glass panels to the sides of the cases or hoods were usually fitted, and, as well as allowing the owner to 'watch the wheels go round', these served the purpose of letting him see the position of the catgut weight or fusee line so as to judge whether the clock required winding. Seen from the side in this way, the most decorative features of these early movements were the pillars separating the plates. These were elegantly turned into baluster or 'knopped' shapes, and were, at first, riveted into the front plates, with the ends filed and burnished flush with the plate and projecting through holes in the back plates which were secured by taper pins or, in all the better seventeenth-century specimens, pivoted latches. After approximately 1670, it became the practice to rivet the pillars to the back plate leaving the front one detachable. This also left the back plate completely plain except, in many instances, for the maker's signature beautifully engraved in faultless calligraphy. Additional decoration was sometimes applied to the locking plate of the striking mechanism, which was mounted outside the back plate and often engraved with a Tudor rose. Also exposed on the back plates of these early clocks were the winding squares, ratchet wheels and clicks concerned with the initial 'setting up' of the mainsprings. These, too, were handsomely treated, with concentric turning of the ratchets and elegant elaboration and shaping of the blued-steel clicks and springs. In common with the contemporary door latches, hinges, gun locks and other wrought-iron or steel objects, it seems that the seventeenth-century craftsmen were incapable of making these utilitarian objects anything but well-proportioned and attractive.

After about 1680 the locking plates disappeared from view, either because they were mounted between the main plates or were abolished in favour of the new rack mechanism, usually mounted on the front plate. The setting-up ratchets and clicks were also moved to the front plate, most probably to remove from the owner the temptation to meddle with them, with probably disastrous consequences. All these developments coincided with the establishment of the spring clock as a semi-portable table or shelf timepiece, and it became the practice to glaze the back door or panel of the case and to decorate the entire surface of the back plate with engraving. In addition, the 'apron' of the pendulum clock was enlarged and made a focal point for elaborate pierced and engraved decoration. The apron was not only decorative, but served a useful purpose as it

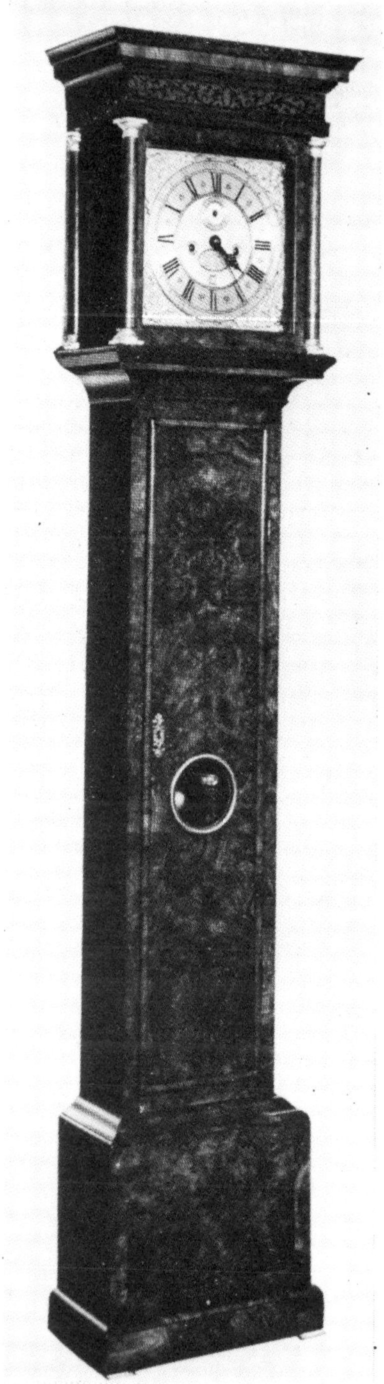

Page 125 PLATE 19 The walnut long-case clock of *c*1710 by Joseph Windmills has all the features of a 'best London-made' piece of that period, but the example by Windmills and Elkins, *c*1740 (PLATE 20) is curiously old-fashioned in many ways for its time and may have been made to special order in oak with none of the new-fangled nonsense of arched dials and walnut veneer

Page 126 PLATE 21 Precision timepiece by George Graham, showing the equation of time by means of a solar minute hand concentric with the mean-time hands. It has bolt-and-shutter maintaining power, Harrison gridiron pendulum, dead-beat escapement. Revolving disc in the arch provides perpetual calendar indications and the right-hand winding square is for adjusting these. There is no striking train carried and concealed a horizontal projection which formed a ledge over the 'V' of the knife-edge and prevented the pallets of the escapement being jerked upwards out of engagement with the wheel, if the clock was abruptly moved or jolted. By the end of the seventeenth century the aprons became very much smaller and were no longer pierced.

The style of the engraved decoration broadly reflected contemporary fashions and all manner of motifs were included, from those inspired by tulip-mania to chinoiserie, and from chinoiserie to neo-classical with Adam-style urns, cartouches and swags of flowers. Rather more care was lavished on the decoration in the seventeenth century than later, but the standard of engraving remained generally high until the end of the eighteenth century. Provincial spring clocks were quite often undecorated, and some of the leading London makers of the later eighteenth century, such as Leroux and Perigal, also seem to have thought the decoration unnecessary. By their time, they may well have been right; as the clocks were no longer taken from room to room there was less occasion for the engraving to be seen, but the public liked it and the tradition died hard.

It was originally the custom to burnish the engraved plate, heat it, run melted black wax into the engraved lines (the chapter rings were blacked in by a similar process), wipe off the surplus whilst it was still fluid, re-polish the plate and keep it from discolouring with a coat of gold lacquer. This threw the engraving into sharp contrast with the surrounding areas, in a similar fashion to niello work on silver, but repeated cleanings have usually removed the pigment and few repairers trouble to renew it.

By the second decade of the nineteenth century, the engraving degenerated to a mere border, usually of wheat-ear design, round the edge of the plate with, perhaps, an oval cartouche of flowers or *arabesquerie* for the maker's signature. There appears to be no particular rule about signatures. Very early spring clocks seem generally to have been signed on the back plate only, but from about 1670 the signature appeared on the bottom of the dial plate, then moved to the bottom edge of the chapter ring early in the eighteenth century. After mid-century, the maker's name and address were often engraved on a shaped silvered plate, fastened behind a suitable opening cut in the dial plate. With the signatures on the dial, most makers gradually gave up the practice of signing the back plate, but at all periods between about 1680 and 1860 one finds clocks which are signed in both places. It is always desirable, and adds slightly to the value, to have a signature on the movement as this lessens the possibility of a mixed marriage or faking.

Where famous names and great values are concerned, however, the determined faker will stop at nothing, and in his introduction to *The First Twelve Years of the English Pendulum Clock* Mr Ronald Lee includes this cautionary tale:

> There once existed a good table clock by Hilkiah Bedford, a very respectable maker from Fleet Street. The top of the case had been altered in the 18th century and in due course it was altered back to a portico top. It now looked as it should have done, very much like an early clock by Edward East. Some wretched fellow, obviously after some ill-gotten gains, decides to change the name and slightly to disguise the clock. A new back plate and a new dial are made, both signed East, also a pair of hands of different design. Ultimately auctioned the only recorded Bedford spring clock now graces a collection with a so-called snob name attached.
>
> Collectors to-day are very sensibly judging clocks on their individual merit or at least are tending to, with some wisdom. This judicious method brings other names to the top and makers whose output has been small but good are, at last, receiving their proper recognition. The case of the Bedford clock is a sad one . . .

Sad indeed, but it is at least some compensation that collector-dealer-authors of Mr Lee's stature are now bringing such impostures to public notice.

Another decorative feature of the early bracket clock, which came into fashion about 1680, was the 'mock pendulum'. A suitably curved slit was cut in the upper half of the dial centre and a gilt or silvered brass plate was mounted, on short pillars attached to the front plate, immediately behind it, leaving a gap of about $\frac{1}{8}$in in depth. In this space, a little engraved disc wagged to and fro like the bob of a pendulum. It received its motion from the pallet arbor, to which it was attached by a light strip of metal. The mock pendulum, like the visible bob weight behind glass on the contemporary long-case clocks, was primarily decorative, but it also allows one to see at a glance whether the clock has stopped, and an observant owner can also deduce from the declining vigour of the mock pendulum that the escapement needs cleaning or adjustment.

The mock pendulum was found on most bracket clocks up to about 1750, and was occasionally seen as late as 1790. Unfortunately, when a Victorian repairer converted an old clock to anchor escapement he generally abolished the mock pendulum as well. Not content with this he often removed, for no good reason, the little gilt or silvered backing plate behind the slot, so leaving an ugly vacant gash in the dial rather suggestive of a respectable elderly lady appearing at table without her teeth.

Seconds hands are very rarely found on bracket clocks, but very few are without a day-of-the-month indicator. As on the contemporary long-case clocks, this usually took the form of a rotating ring, engraved with the date numerals which showed through a 'window', generally rectangular but sometimes circular, in the dial plate. This date aperture was usually placed above the figure VI, but some early makers, particularly Joseph Knibb, preferred to have it immediately below the XII. More elaborate calendar and lunar work is occasionally found on bracket clocks, but it is rarer than similar complications on long-case clocks. Towards the end of the eighteenth century, the calendar ring and slot were often replaced by a subsidiary hand, rotating round a date circle engraved or painted in the lower half of the dial; more rarely a date hand is worked concentrically with the hour and minute hands, the day-of-the-month numerals being engraved around the inner edge of the chapter ring. Both these later arrangements are less pleasing to look at, but easier to adjust, than the original type. Calendar indicators are rare on bracket clocks after 1800, though they continued to be fitted to many long-case clocks until the middle of the nineteenth century.

Changes of style of hands, dials, spandrels, cases, mounts and so forth are best judged from illustrations, but a few general points may be mentioned. The design of clock hands could scarcely be faulted until the late nineteenth century. Whatever the chosen shape, the lines and proportions were nearly always good, and the differences in form and length were sufficiently marked to eliminate confusion between the hour and the minute indicators. This is where modern design nearly always fails. When the concentric arrangement came into use the clockmakers, understanding the public reluctance to come to terms with the new idea, took great trouble to design the hands so that it was as easy as possible to distinguish between them. To achieve this, the minute hands, until nearly the end of the eighteenth century, were decorated only at the root, leaving seven-eighths of the length as a plain tapering pointer; by contrast, the hour hands were plain at the root and shank but swelled to a boldly widened and pierced decorative tip, the shape of which was originally based on an arrow-head outline.

Of all the great names of the later seventeenth century that of Thomas Tompion ranks first, although in some respects he has been over-valued. Amongst his innovations were some affecting the appearance of clocks. Mention has already been made of the break-arch dials which became general for most top-grade long-case and bracket clocks after about 1710, but Tompion also inaugurated the fashion for wider chapter rings, with correspondingly shorter but heavier-looking and more ornate hour hands. It is probable that he introduced this new fashion with the intention of making clocks easier to read in dimly-lit rooms. Experience shows, though, that there is no real improvement in legibility and it is fairly generally agreed now that the earlier dials with their narrow chapters are much more pleasing. Joseph Knibb obviously thought so, for he kept the older fashion until past the end of the seventeenth century. Tompion also favoured a simpler shaped half-hour mark in place of the stylised fleur-de-lys, and his nephew-by-marriage and successor, George Graham, carried this simplicity to the extent of using a plain lozenge. With few exceptions, the quarter-hour divisions were still marked on the inner edges of chapter rings until about 1730, although the provision of the minute hand really made these markings unnecessary.

All English clock hands, with a few exceptions, before 1800, were of cut steel, highly burnished and blued by heat treatment. In the first flush of enthusiasm for the new-style clocks (approximately 1660 to 1690) the makers lavished a great deal of time on finishing the hands, which they bevelled or chamfered on all their visible surfaces. Thereafter, although the pierced work and finish were very delicate, the refinement of chamfering was given up. A similar decline may be noted in the amount of 'cleaning up' with the graving tool accorded to the spandrels and gilt metal case mounts.

At all times a few bracket clocks were cased in the fashionable woods of their period. Thus we find cases veneered with olive, walnut, yew, mulberry, laburnum, mahogany, satinwood, rosewood and amboyna in due season. Tortoiseshell veneers were occasionally used and lacquered decoration was applied to bracket clocks' cases in the eighteenth century, particularly on those intended for one of Britain's many export markets. At all times, though, black cases predominate and these were adorned with a greater or lesser number of gilt-metal mounts. The earlier cases were of oak veneered with ebony, but most later examples were made of, or veneered with, so-called fruit wood which made an excellent surface for 'ebonising' with one of a great number of staining and polishing processes evolved for the purpose. Although the relative numbers of mahogany and other cases increased towards the end of the eighteenth century, our forebears obviously still agreed with the seventeenth-century Lady Legh that black suits anything. Even with the plainest case, with no mounts but a carrying handle, the traditional gilt-and-silver dial was thought to look at its best when framed in black. Modern taste does not agree and, scarcity value apart, clocks in 'show wood' cases are more sought after than black ones.

The most important seventeenth-century innovation, after the application of the pendulum, was the rack striking mechanism which, in its turn, led to the invention of 'repeating work'. The invention came from the Rev Edward Booth, who later assumed his godfather's surname of Barlow; the original purpose of the invention was to avoid the nuisance of the striking getting out of sequence with the time shown on the dial. This can very easily happen with a locking-plate strike either when the hands are set forward without pausing sufficiently at each hour or if the striking train runs down before the going.

The number of blows struck by the old type of mechanism depended upon the 'locking plate' or 'count wheel' (Figure 17), which was a disc with notches cut in it at increasing intervals round its periphery. The count wheel detent which 'sensed' these notches was attached to an arbor which carried a second detent, between the plates of the movement, whose business it was to release or arrest the motion of the striking train. When the train was 'unlocked' for its preliminary 'warning' a few moments before striking, the count wheel detent was raised out of a notch. As the train began to run, the count wheel slowly rotated in due proportion to the turning of the wheel operating the bell-hammer, and consequently the count-wheel detent now rested on the edge of the count wheel and so held the locking detent clear of doing its duty until the next notch of the count wheel approached; the detent then fell into it and allowed the locking detent to drop into the 'hoop wheel' to stop the train. In other words, the piece of machinery which determined how many blows were to be struck was moved by that part of the machinery which did the striking and consequently could get out of phase with the going mechanism.

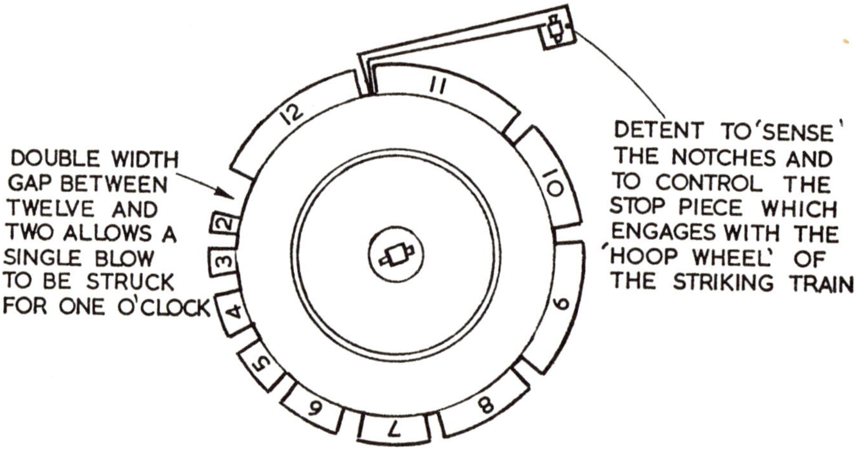

FIGURE 17 *Locking plate or count wheel of striking mechanism, with the detent which 'senses' the distance between gaps and controls the stop lever to check the striking train*

By contrast, the part of the rack striking mechanism which determined how many blows should be struck was attached to and turned with the motion work of the going train. This meant that, if all was in order, the number struck had to be the same as that indicated by the hour hand, and could not get out of sequence. Even if the clock hands were put forward several hours without waiting for the striking to operate fully, the mechanism would accommodate itself and count correctly when allowed to do so. Another great advantage of this was that it was very easy to arrange a 'strike/silent' device to shut the strike off at night and switch it on again in the morning without having to synchronise the strike with the going train.

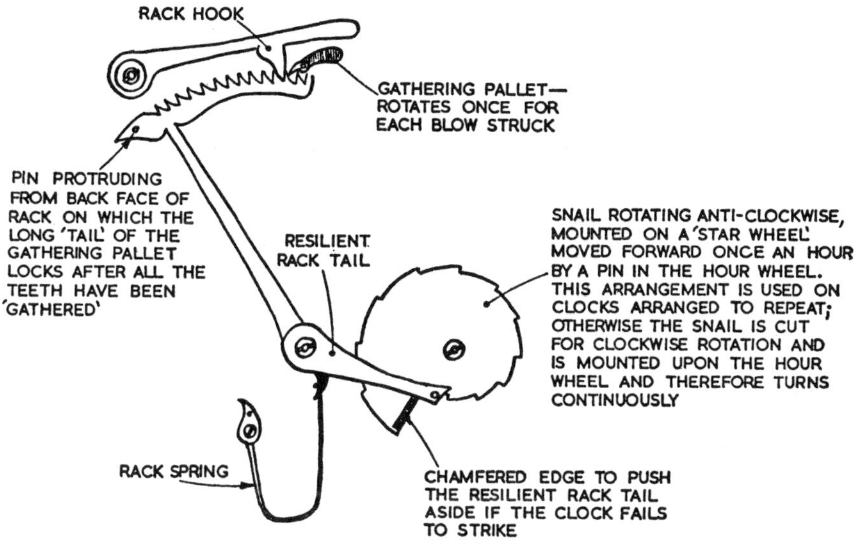

FIGURE 18 *The rack, snail and related parts which govern the number of blows struck, always in relation to the position of the hands rather than progressively*

The determining factor in the rack system was a cam, called 'the snail' for obvious reasons, which rotated with the wheel carrying the hour hand. The rack was shaped as shown in Figure 18 and was normally held stationary by the 'rack hook' engaging the last of twelve sloping teeth on the curved upper end of the rack. When the clock was preparing to strike, with the usual preparatory 'warning', the rack hook was lifted and the rack fell back under the impetus of a light spring; a flexible 'tail' at the bottom of the rack then came to rest on the snail, and the distance the rack fell was consequently determined by the position of the snail. If, for example, the hour hand pointed to IV, the tail of the rack would fall on the fourth step of the snail (counting from the highest) which would leave four teeth of the rack behind, or to the left of, the rack hook. On the strike train being allowed to run (by the release of the warning piece at the hour) a device called the 'gathering pallet' made one revolution for each blow of the hammer, and at each revolution it 'gathered' one tooth of the rack and moved it to the right, the rack hook automatically lifting (by reason of the slope of the teeth) and locking it in its new position, in readiness for the next turn of the gathering pallet. All the teeth having been gathered in this way, one of two things happened; on the earlier type of rack mechanism the last notch on the rack was cut more deeply than the others so that the rack hook fell far enough to allow an arm attached to its arbor, between the plates, to move into the path of a pin on the penultimate wheel of the striking train. The later and more usual arrangement was for the gathering pallet to have an elongated tail which, when all the teeth were gathered, locked on a pin protruding from the rack itself, so stopping the train.

As the count wheel rotates in proportion to the number of blows struck, it follows that it must make a complete rotation in twelve hours. In clocks of one-day duration, in which the great wheels revolve several times in twelve hours, the count wheel was mounted on a stud on the back plate or frame-bar, and was turned by a small pinion attached to a squared extension of the great wheel arbor; this pinion meshed with a suitably numbered gear wheel riveted to the underside of the count wheel itself. When the eight-day type of long-case or spring clock came into being, the great wheels of which revolve once every twelve hours, both on the going and striking sides, it was an obvious simplification to mount the count wheel on the squared extension of the great wheel arbor itself and to do away with the reducing gear. Early long-case and bracket clocks therefore still have the locking plate or count wheel visibly mounted on the back plate of the movement, but by about 1690 makers began to attach the count wheel beside the great wheel and it was therefore concealed from view between the plates. The distinction between 'outside' and 'inside' locking plate provides a 'dating feature', and one which must be considered with the usual allowance for the two arrangements having existed side by side.

The name 'locking plate' is more usual than 'count wheel', but it is misleading as it implies that the 'locking plate' is responsible for checking the motion of the striking train. As stated earlier, the actual locking is done by the 'hoop wheel' and the detent on the locking plate is only concerned with sensing the positions of the notches.

With both count wheel and rack mechanisms, it was easy to arrange for a single blow to be struck at each half hour. This was almost universal practice in France and other north European countries from the early eighteenth century onwards, but it was very rarely done in England until the nineteenth century was well advanced. The English makers doubtless thought that the man or woman who awoke during the dark hours to hear a single blow struck was not going to be particularly grateful for the information unless it unequivocally meant one o'clock.

In addition to being a more efficient mechanism which could not get out of phase, the rack striking was easily fitted with a trigger and pull-cord to lift the rack hook at will. Therefore the owner could take his clock to his bedroom at night and shut off the striking but still be able to tell the time within the nearest hour by pulling the cord. In order that the clock should sound the hour last past, and not anticipate the coming one, it was found necessary to remove the snail from the hour wheel, and mount it on a separate pivot, with a device known as a star wheel and 'flirt' actuated by a pin in the hour wheel: this ensured that the snail only started moving a few minutes before the hour and clicked swiftly into its next position. The next elaboration was to provide a small subsidiary chiming train, controlled by a four-toothed rack and a four-lobed snail, rotated once an hour by the motion wheels; this enabled a clock to sound the quarters as well as the hour at will. The subsidiary repeating train was powered by its own small mainspring, which was wound up every time the cord was pulled to set and release the mechanism. Having sounded the quarters, the quarter-repeating train unlocked the rack hook of the main striking work to sound the hour. The boon of being able to tell the time within fifteen minutes in the dark, merely by pulling a cord and without having to fumble with tinder-box and candle, is difficult to appreciate in our electrically-lit age. It was also possible to make a repeating mechanism to sound both quarters and hours from the subsidiary train and this type of repetition was not only fitted to 'timepieces' (clocks with no striking mechanism), but was scaled down and fitted to watches.

Repeating work on clocks falls, therefore, into three categories. First is the simple 'hour repeat' in which the normal striking mechanism is released by the pull-cord. Most striking bracket clocks were fitted to repeat hours in this way, and the striking train mainsprings and fusees were increased in size to cope with the demand for extra use. Secondly, were timepieces with full repetition work sounding hours and quarters; and lastly, striking clocks with quarter-repeat work which, having sounded the quarters, let off the main striking train to count the hour. These last were the most complicated and provided designers with several problems. The chief difficulty was to provide safety devices to ensure that the mechanism would not jam or miscount if the owner awoke and pulled the repeating cord just as the clock was about to strike of its own accord.

Thomas Tompion, in particular, went to great lengths to ensure reliability in the action of his repeating work, and the beautiful elaboration of his repeating clocks is justified by the results—and partly justifies their price. It was typical of him that his repeating work was arranged with two pull cords, one either side of the clock. Repeaters generally sounded the quarters on two bells in 'ting-tang' fashion, but as many as eight or even ten were sometimes used. Unfortunately, the complication of quarter-repeating work adds considerably to the labour of overhauling a clock and gave ample opportunity for the Victorian repairers to throw away the mechanism together with the verge escapement, the mock pendulum and the calendar mechanism. One is almost tempted to hope that when the hour of judgement strikes for them, they will receive no quarter.

Before the invention of repeating work, other methods of telling the time at night had been tried. Prince Rupert, that most inventive man, introduced an improvement upon a type of night clock occasionally made in Italy. This had a very large metal dial overlapping the body of the clock with the hour numerals cut out so that a candle, screened behind the clock, shone through them. This type of clock could only show the hour, and a rough approximation of the quarter, with the very wide tip of the single hand obscuring first one numeral and then the next. The tip was wide enough to start obscuring the next numeral before it had wholly exposed the previous one. The improved design attributed to Prince Rupert was executed by Joseph Knibb, amongst others, and allowed the time to be read easily to the nearest minute by a most ingenious arrangement of perforated discs, showing the hour numerals, revolving at suitable intervals upon a larger disc, two-thirds of which was obscured behind a painted panel, which itself revolved to expose the 'wandering hours' (as they are called) in juxtaposition to a fixed segment through which quarter-hour and minute indications were pierced.

These 'wandering hour' night clocks were spring-driven and outwardly similar to large contemporary portico-topped bracket clocks, with an oil lamp above the movement which shone through the perforations. One of the few surviving examples is from the collection of the Duke of Sussex, now in the British Museum.

This type of night clock was as ingenious as Prince Rupert's process of mezzotint engraving, but the presence of a hot lamp and the possibility of oil leaking into the mechanism were undesirable features, and the repeating clock was a much more satisfactory solution. To the average man of the late seventeenth century a repeating clock, or more particularly a repeating watch, must have seemed as wonderful and as incomprehensible as computers do to his counterparts today. Yet such are the inconsistencies of the human mind that a highly-placed computer expert, recently encountered, not only could not understand the mechanism of a quarter-repeating clock but was quite unable to comprehend its purpose.

Chapter Eight

Later Lantern and Thirty-hour Clocks

IN 1675, Sir Richard Legh had had to buy his new-fangled long-case pendulum clock from a London maker; there were doubtless local makers who could have supplied him with a good lantern clock, and ten or fifteen years later he could have bought an excellent clock of the new style from Liverpool or Chester. The provincial long-case clocks of the turn of the century were, many of them, comparable with the best that London could produce; but the lantern clock, and derivatives from it, was by no means dead even in London.

There is so much overlapping of trends and styles throughout the eighteenth century that it is unwise to be dogmatic about details which are supposed to indicate period. It used to be argued, for example, that lantern clocks could be 'dated' by the style of the frets. Firstly, came what is known as the heraldic pattern; secondly, a design in which stylised (and barely recognisable) tulips figure as the principal motif; whilst the commonest sort, with entwined dolphins as the dominant feature, came last of all. If these indicators are taken in isolation, they can be misleading. Dolphin frets were occasionally used as early as 1660 it appears, and the heraldic frets on the Peter Closon clock in Plate 3, which dates from about 1650, are almost identical with those recently seen on a Bristol-made clock of about 1710. Similarly the tulip frets on the Edward Burges clock of *c*1665, in Figure 4, differ only in size from those on a clock by Thomas Moore of Ipswich, recently examined, on which the tulip frets appeared to be original although the clock was probably no earlier than 1740. Quite apart from this overlapping, the frequency with which lantern clocks with one or more frets missing, have replacements of dubious antiquity married to them makes it most unwise to take the pattern of fret as an indication of date.

Another generalisation which should be treated with reserve is that very wide overlapping chapter rings, which gave rise to the name 'sheep's head' for the type of clock so fitted, were peculiar to East Anglia. They were certainly favoured there, but by no means exclusively, and the rather clumsy 'sheep's head' style is occasionally found on London-made clocks as well as on those from the various provincial centres. Sometimes, very wide chapter rings are later additions to quite early clocks.

Engraved dates must also be viewed with suspicion. Lantern clocks, and some others, were occasionally dated but it was not common practice and other features should be considered together with the date. Sometimes both name and date, if on the front fret, may indicate the original owner and the date of acquisition, not the maker; however, the date will be near enough to that of manufacture. The unrestored example in Plate 5 is dated 1669 and, as this corresponds to the character of the clock as a whole, it may be accepted; but the occasional unreliability of engraved dates was well demonstrated at a country-house auction in Hampshire in June 1971. One of the lots sold was a late provincial lantern clock, with long pendulum, suspicious frets and a chapter ring which was almost certainly older than the rest of the clock. It was indeed what the motor enthusiasts call a 'bitza', but it flaunted a London maker's name and the date 1661 in the *centre* of the dial plate. This unusual place for a signature had been chosen, no doubt to fill a blank space left by the alarum-setting disc which, together with the alarm mechanism, had been removed at some time. The engraving of the signature and date should not have fooled anyone; it appeared, indeed, to have been executed with a knife and fork, but the auctioneer's catalogue eulogised this 'seventeenth century' dated clock in the heaviest type the printer could command, and the clock sold for a sum one would have hesitated to ask for a genuine mid-seventeenth-century piece.

In very general terms, it is probably safe to say that the manufacture of lantern clocks in London dwindled to a trickle after 1700 and practically ceased by about 1725, with the exception of some made for export. These generally had no front fret, the place being taken by the arched part of a small break-arch dial similar to those of contemporary long-case and bracket clocks. These arched dials overlapped the frame of the clocks and obscured the side pillars from view. Lantern clocks in this form are less attractive than those of the conventional sort; nevertheless, a number seem to have been made in this way for the home market, although the majority appear to have been intended for the Middle East and were dis-

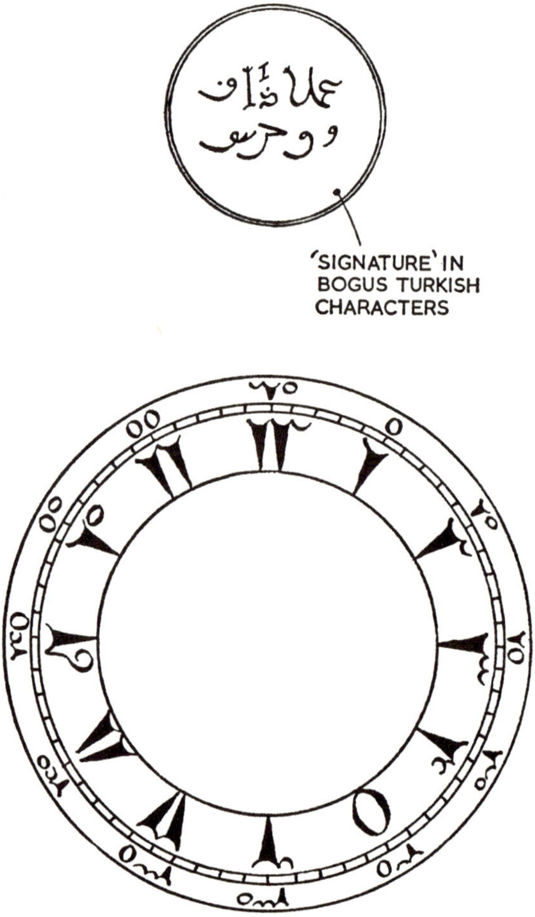

FIGURE 19 *'Turkish' numerals as written on clock dials for export to the Middle East*

tinguished by so-called Turkish numerals (which were not exclusive to Turkey) as in Figure 19. The 'Turkish market' comprised Persia, upper Egypt and what was then vaguely known as the Levant, which included the parts of the Balkans under Ottoman suzerainty. The production and export of these Turkish-market lantern clocks continued into the first quarter of the nineteenth century, and many of them were made with quarter-chiming trains. There is practically no difference between a 'Turkish' clock of 1720 and one of 1820.

As we have seen, lantern clocks began to be made with short bob pendulums on knife-edge suspensions not long after the appearance of Fromanteel's first-generation pendulum clocks. The old balance control lingered on sporadically for a surprisingly long time, particularly on country-made specimens. The latest example I have seen may well have been made as late as 1710 or thereabouts as the maker, Richard Greenhills of Maidstone, does not appear to have been in business before 1700. As he also made long-case, long-pendulum clocks of little less than London standards, this old-fashioned lantern clock probably represents a thrifty desire to use up old castings.

From about 1670 onwards, however, the majority of lantern clocks had the combination of verge escapement and short pendulum already described. There is no reason why they should not have been made at that time with the new anchor mechanism and heavy, long, spring-suspended pendulum; but this does not seem to have been done much before 1725, and even thereafter it was by no means universal. Once again there was a great deal of overlapping, and I have simultaneously owned a London-made lantern clock by George Clarke, about 1710, with an original anchor escapement and 61in second-and-a-quarter pendulum (a most unusual attribute for a lantern clock), and a 'Turkish market' lantern by George Prior, London, probably no earlier than 1810, with verge and bob pendulum. There is a tendency for non-specialist dealers to regard all bob-pendulum lantern clocks as necessarily earlier than those with long pendulums; but the situation is not so straightforward.

If the change, or partial change, to the anchor mechanism came rather late, the business of converting old lantern clocks was established before the end of the seventeenth century. It was not an easy matter to convert a balance-wheel clock to verge and bob pendulum, and this was seldom done; but it was very simple and cheap to convert to anchor and long pendulum. The change necessitated only one new wheel, the 'scape wheel, and this could be mounted on the old arbor and pinion and turn in the old bearings. The pallet arbor, balance wheel and upper cock, or potence, had to be removed but the lower pallet arbor cock and footstep could be left, unless the craftsman was tidy-minded and chose to file them down or remove them. It was then only necessary to widen the hammer slot, in the top plate, to make room for the anchor pallets, and to mount front and back pallet arbor bearings, or cocks, the rear one being combined, as usual, with the projecting bracket for the pendulum suspension spring.

As this conversion was so easy and the improvement in performance so great, very few balance-wheel lantern clocks remained unaltered; and as the reverse conversion is also not so difficult as to be ruinously expensive, many re-conversions have been done in recent years in the interest of authenticity. It is not usually difficult to see the traces of conversion and re-conversion. The Peter Closon clock in Plate 4 provides a good example and, in this view looking down upon the balance wheel, the circles of darker colour in the top plate show where screw holes, carrying parts for the anchor escapement, have been filled in by brazing with metal of different texture. The widening of the hammer slot for two-thirds of its length is also a tell-tale sign.

Most of these conversions from balance wheel to anchor escapement and long pendulum appear to have been done fairly early in the lives of the clocks concerned. Conversions from verge and bob pendulum to anchor and long pendulum are relatively less common, but are encountered. The change involved two new wheels and pinions of different 'count' to accommodate the change from a quick-beating escapement to a slower one. Judging by the shapes of the wheel collets, pallets and other parts, these changes seem mostly to have been done considerably later, and probably only when it was found that the old mechanism was so worn that a new escapement wheel and pallets were needed anyway.

So many lantern clocks have been so maltreated and mutilated, with

Page 143 PLATE 22 Long-pendulum hooded wall clock, or 'wag-at-the-wall', *c*1780, timepiece only with alarum (the alarum weight missing) by Elizabeth Hunte of Overton near Basingstoke

Page 144 PLATE 23 Typical oak-cased thirty-hour 'cottage grandfather', with handsomely engraved single-hand dial, *c*1775 by James Staples of Odiham.
PLATE 24 Imposing Queen Anne period clock by James Drury in mulberry-veneered case with ebony mouldings

amateur repair work, punch and file marks disfiguring everything, missing frets replaced with incongruous ones, missing side doors not replaced at all and with holes drilled willy-nilly, in the top plate to accommodate botched up repaired escapement parts that it takes an experienced eye to determine the original form of the mechanism. The most reliable indication that a clock was designed for balance-wheel control is that the great wheels revolve in opposite directions, each with its own weight, as described in Chapter 4. This means that the bell hammer must be pivoted on the three o'clock side of the frame, with the count wheel and locking detent arbors at nine o'clock. As the balance was 'self-starting' but the bob pendulum was not, it was found desirable with the latter to have some form of maintaining power; and the simple endless cord system Huyghens had devised for the purpose was adopted. This has the driving weight acting on one loop of the rope or cord which passes over both great wheel pulleys with a counterweight on the 'inactive' loop. The one weight consequently drove both trains, and as both great wheels have to revolve in the same direction this involved changing the relative positions of the bell hammer and detent arbors.

Reference to Huyghens' own drawing of his pendulum clock, Figure 7, shows the arrangement of his endless cord system, with the main driving weight marked with a triangle and a counterweight labelled 'Z'. As the clock shown has no striking mechanism, the winding ratchet is attached to an idler pulley with a suitable spring 'click' mounted on the front plate. When the counterweighted loop of cord is pulled down to wind the clock, half the mass of the main weight still exerts a downwards pull although it is rising upwards, and thus sufficient power is still applied to the great wheel to keep the escapement going for a few seconds.

For a striking clock, the endless cord system is arranged with the winding ratchet on the great wheel of the striking train; and the same half-power is still available on the going train whilst the weight is being wound up. This system of single weight and endless cord is found on nearly all post-pendulum striking lantern clocks and on their most important derivatives, the thirty-hour or 'cottage grandfather' long-case clocks. In place of Huyghens' second pulley for the counterweight, English makers provided the necessary counter-pull to keep the rope taut, very simply, by a stout lead ring encircling the idle loop of cord. Towards the end of the seventeenth century, some clocks had chain instead of rope drive, and a very great number were converted to chain at a later stage. The alteration meant having new pulleys on the great wheels, with deep grooves between the spikes to accommodate the links, but did away with the nuisance of the soft rope wearing and filling the clock with dust and fluff.

In addition to being the progenitor of new kinds of timekeeper, the lantern clock went through a metamorphosis. After the middle of the eighteenth century, it generally lost its striking mechanism but was almost invariably fitted with alarum work. This was set in the time-honoured way by a disc, engraved with the hours from one to twelve and with subdivisions, mounted below and rotating with the hour hand. The disc could be turned, independently of the hand, until the hour, or division thereof, at which the alarum was required to sound was in line with the 'tail' of the hour hand which served as a pointer.

Lantern-alarums of this type may occasionally have been taken by travellers for use in hotel bedrooms; they were usually quite small and invariably had verge escapements and bob pendulums, so they were not too difficult to move about and set up on any convenient hook. Principally, however, they were the poor man's clock, although it may be supposed that they found a place in the servants' quarters of wealthier households. As all appear to have been supplied by provincial makers, one associates them particularly with the rural poor; and this doubtless accounts for the fact that they have no minute hands, as it is obvious that rural resistance to the nasty, new-fangled London idea of having concentric hands, so puzzling to the semi-literate, lingered well into the nineteenth century. The frets and decorative engraving became less well executed as the century advanced, but on the whole the standard of finish was good. Some of these little lantern-alarums were given break-arch dials, with the arch taking the place of the front fret, as was done on the London-made lantern clocks for the Turkish market. These arched dials had all the traditional features of matted dial centre, silvered alarum disc and chapter ring and a silvered boss with the maker's name and town or village in the arch.

Despite some coarseness of detail, particularly about the spandrels which, though gilded, were often scarcely cleaned of the foundry 'rag', these little country-made clocks are very attractive and so robustly made that they survive almost unlimited neglect and abuse. By the end of the eighteenth century, the metamorphosis reached its final form, and the erstwhile lantern clock became a plain rectangular metal box, with flat instead of turned frame pillars, plain brass dial plate with silvered ring but no engraved decoration, iron side doors, no finials or frets and with the bell supported on a single curved stalk instead of being hung from the elegant interlaced brass strapwork. For no very clear reason, this final and degenerate form of lantern clock is known to the trade as a 'postman's alarm'. They may possibly have been used to arouse the 'horsekeepers' at posting houses and coaching inns, whose duty it was to turn out and help change horses as the coaches came in, simply because they were the common alarm clocks of their time, but they were not officially issued by the General Post Office (as the Mail Coach Guards' timepieces were) and they have no connection with postmen in the modern sense of the term.

Alongside these latter-day lantern clocks, country makers produced great numbers of 'hooded wall clocks'. These do not descend from the hooded clocks of the early pendulum era, with their side-by-side trains, eight-day duration, minute hands and other innovations, but they are true descendants of lantern clocks with posted frame movements, three-wheel one-day trains and a single hand. They were very much better protected from dust and kitchen fumes than the contemporary lantern-alarums described above, and they probably represent the next step up in the social scale of clock buyer. Once again, they almost never have striking mechanism but almost always are alarum clocks. The combined brackets and cases, or hoods, are often pleasing in an unpretentious way and are nearly always of oak; though other woods, or even lacquered decoration, are not unknown. It is also not unknown for hooded wall clocks to 'grow' trunks and bases, and consequently to become that most prized of rarities a 'grandmother', or miniature long-case clock.

These hooded alarum clocks were not infrequently made with anchor escapements and long pendulums, as in Plate 22. The uncased, and therefore presumably cheaper, lantern-alarums seem always to have been made with verge and bob pendulum, until they faded out of existence early in the nineteenth century. The long pendulum, with its spring suspension, was more difficult to 'set up' if a clock had to be moved and more vulnerable to accident and interference; it therefore made sense to retain the theoretically inferior, but practically less easily damaged, escapement and knife-edge suspension for the sorts of clocks most likely to fall into unskilled hands.

The hooded wall clock, or 'wag-at-the-wall' in Plate 22 is a fairly typical example of the breed. It probably dates from about 1770–80, and the only remarkable thing about it is that it is signed by a woman, Eliz: Hunte of Overton (near Basingstoke, Hampshire). This almost certainly indicates inheritance of a business by a daughter or widow. Women were extensively employed in making various clock and watch components, such as fusee chains, from the late seventeenth century onwards, but very few appear to have practised as makers or 'masters' in their own right. Judith Lycett and Rosetta Hess are other women's names which appear as the 'makers' signatures' on late eighteenth- and early nineteenth-century clocks and watches; and I have heard Jean Wady, an early eighteenth-century London maker of renown, described as a Scotswoman. This would doubtless have astonished 'her' contemporaries for 'she' was a man, a Huguenot refugee.

The most important offspring of the lantern clock is what is commonly known as the thirty-hour clock. The term has been current in the trade for nearly two centuries, but it is a little misleading, as the lantern clocks and other wall clocks previously described are also of one-day duration (or even less); but the alternative designation of 'cottage grandfather' is distressingly coy. Ignoring these semantic subtleties, the term thirty-hour clock, without further qualification, means a long-case clock, with a movement which requires winding once a day, which is generally fairly small, plain and unpretentious, generally cased in oak and of provincial manufacture.

Like the long-case clock proper (generically known as the eight-day clock although often of longer duration), the thirty-hour clock was London-born. It required little imagination to see that a lantern clock movement could easily be married to a larger square dial, and the result could then be housed in a long-case to make a 'tall clock' of the newly fashionable sort, at much less cost. The fact that such a marriage produced a long-case clock without a minute hand (in most instances) was still regarded as a positive advantage by many people; and the disadvantage of daily winding was obviously not thought to be as grave a drawback in the seventeenth century as it is now. Leading London makers of the calibre of Tompion, Knibb, Quare and Windmills did not disdain to supply these humbler long-case clocks alongside their grander productions. 'Supply' seems the appropriate word rather than 'make', as it may be supposed that the movements were bought ready finished from lesser makers and passed through the superior makers' shops for dialling, inspection, finishing and adjustment.

Obviously the lantern-clock movements cased in this way did not need side doors, frets, finials, bell-straps and the other ornamental-cum-functional components. By the end of the seventeenth century, indeed, the turned brass pillars, supporting the frame plates had been replaced by flat bars, usually of iron. The movements made for thirty-hour long-case clocks were made considerably larger, than the normal lantern clock size. Otherwise, the old form of lantern-clock construction remained unchanged, even down to the unnecessarily heavy 'fly'. These early London-made, thirty-hour clocks were often finely cased in walnut or other fashionable timber; but few are known of London make of a later date than about 1700, and in the next thirty years they gradually became part of the regular stock-in-trade of every country clockmaker. By the middle of the eighteenth century they were being made in relatively great numbers. They filled a convenient niche between the upper-labouring class lantern, or hooded wall clock, and the richer farmer's or tradesman's eight-day long-case clock, which the provincial makers also produced in considerable numbers from the early eighteenth century onwards.

A few of the early London-made, thirty-hour, long-case clocks had verge escapements and bob pendulums; but by the time the type was firmly established as a country cousin, or poor relation, of the eight-day clock, all appear to have been made with anchor escapements and long, heavy, spring-suspended pendulums. The use of a 39in seconds pendulum was almost universal, and only one exception has come to my notice in forty years.

The thirty-hour 'cottage grandfather', therefore, was a very accurate timekeeper. Indeed, as the single weight and Huyghens, endless cord (or chain) system of driving was universally employed, they enjoyed the benefits of the maintaining power which this form of drive provides and were, consequently, fractionally *better* timekeepers than the majority of their grander cousins which, being generally without maintaining power, tend to lose a few seconds whilst they are being wound.

Given a reasonable state of repair and a tolerably stable temperature, a thirty-hour long-case clock can keep time within half a minute a week or less. This is a much more accurate performance than that of comparable 'poor man's clocks' of other countries and, superficially, it seems surprising that so many of them were made without minute hands. During the second half of the eighteenth century, the numbers with and without minute hands are roughly equal; though of those without minute hands, a fair proportion have day-of-the-month indicators and a small minority show phases of the moon. Simple calendar indications were obviously more important to the countryman than the ability to tell time to the nearest minute. It is still widely believed that single-handed clocks must always be of greater age than those with two, or more, hands. Typical examples with and without minute hands are shown in Plates 23 and 34, but the styles of the cases, the dial engravings, spandrels, hands and the known dates of their respective makers show that the two clocks were made at the same time, in about 1775.

The construction of single-handed clocks survived well into the nineteenth century on the evidence, amongst others, of a deal-cased specimen with a painted iron dial; the four painted spandrel decorations showed crude representations of the royal lion, the unicorn, Britannia and a youthful Queen Victoria with crown and sceptre, from which it is proper to date the clock from, or after, 1837, the year of Victoria's accession.

That there was still sales resistance against the new-fangled concentric minute hand, which the less educated of our forbears found difficult to understand, seems less surprising when the converse is considered and it is discovered how many twentieth-century citizens find a single-handed clock not only incomprehensible, but inconceivable. It is so much taken for granted that all clocks must have minute hands, as though by divine ordination, that the majority of sightseers who level their cameras at the west front of Westminster Abbey never notice that the large dial in one of Hawksmoor's twin towers has but one hand. The point was forcibly brought home, some years ago, when I sold to a well-educated middle-aged woman a pretty little elm-cased thirty-hour, single-handed, clock by a Woodchurch maker. The buyer had recently settled in Woodchurch and was delighted to find a locally-made clock, very modestly priced, small enough to stand in a low-ceilinged eighteenth-century cottage parlour, where it might well have stood when it was new. The clock was very much admired when it was delivered and set in place, but rapture turned to rage when the lady's husband came home in the evening and pointed out that it had only one hand. An irate telephone call demanded the instant removal of so useless a thing and the refund of the money; or, at least, that the missing minute hand be replaced. It was useless to explain that the clock was supposed to have only one hand; and the couple firmly believed they were the innocent victims of one of the many swindles practised by antique dealers.

Because these thirty-hour clocks were intended for the cottage trade, they are generally fairly short, less than 6ft 6in high and they almost invariably have square dials. Exceptions to this general rule are mostly very late specimens. The break-arch dial which was generally adopted for eight-day long-case clocks about 1750 needed a hood arched to correspond; and this was often made even higher by more or less elaborate upperworks. All this demanded an increased length of trunk and base to keep the proportions in balance, and London long-case clocks grew to eight feet or more in height. The provincial makers followed suit, and although they did turn out some smallish, square dial, eight-day clocks, the majority were arched and stood around seven or more feet high. Extra cost apart, therefore, they are unsuitable for cottages; and small though most of the thirty-hour clocks are, some have obviously had to be cut down still further.

The need to keep the clocks as low as possible meant retaining the flat-topped hood of the 1680 style. A few had a very low 'crest rail' round the top of the hood which added an inch or so to the height; but of the few so fitted, fewer have survived with the crest rail still in place. The determining factor in deciding the height of the case was, obviously, the need to provide sufficient fall for the driving weight. With the pulley diameters and wheel ratios normally used, the minimum practicable height must be over six feet. The example by James Staples of Odiham in Plate 23 is smaller than most, though it appears never to have been altered, and has a 10in dial in place of the normal 11in square. It stands just under 6ft 2in, which allows it to clear the ceiling beams of the room in which these words are being written by seven-eighths of an inch; its duration of going is twenty-seven hours, which provides a tolerable margin of safety for daily winding. The Richard Comber clock in Plate 34 stands at the more common height of 6ft 5¼in (fortunately the kitchen is just high enough to accommodate it), and it has the more acceptable safety margin of 4½ hours. Very few 'thirty-hour' clocks have a duration of thirty hours.

In the last quarter of the eighteenth century, some thirty-hour clock movements were made on eight-day lines, with the going and striking trains side-by-side between large rectangular plates; but the older type of framed or posted movement, with back-to-back trains, did not disappear. Referring again to Plates 23 and 34, it is amusing, but by no means uncommon, to find that the 'modern' two-handed dial of the Richard Comber clock is attached to an old-style posted movement whilst the old-fashioned single-hand clock by James Staples has the movement between solid plates in the newer fashion. The very late single-handed clock referred to, bearing Queen Victoria's likeness, also had a posted movement in direct line of descent from the earliest known form of domestic mechanical clock.

Whether of posted or plated form, the movements of thirty-hour clocks were fairly stereotyped; but, given the circumstances of eighteenth-century production methods, no two are precisely alike. The parts bought 'in the rough' from various sources might be more or less identical in each batch, but every finisher would have his own ideas; for example, two men starting with similar basic pieces of material to make escapement pallets would finish with slightly different proportions and curvature according to their notions of the best form of the impulse faces, so the one pair of pallets would not be interchangeable with the other. Apart from these individual variations, there are local variations; and one occasionally comes across radical departures from the general plan with, perhaps, a form of rack striking in place of the locking-plate variety which was almost universal on thirty-hour clocks.

Because they were made for what modern jargon calls the lower income groups, it must not be assumed that thirty-hour clocks were poorly made. Even in their most degenerate early-Victorian form, with painted iron dials and deal cases which are both clumsy and flimsy (relatively), the movements were beautifully finished with heavy frames, well-cut wheels and pinions, and burnished steelwork. It was this high quality which eventually made them obsolete. American and German manufacturers of cheap clocks showed that a lifting piece to release the strike, for instance, could be made of bent wire at a tenth of the cost of a comparable English component, which would be filed from the solid, elegantly tapered, heat-treated and burnished. The clock by Richard Comber (Plate 34) even has some refinements which are not found in good London clocks. The calendar ring is supported on rollers of much better finish and proportions than are usually found; this entirely avoids the problem of wear causing a clock to stop, and giving cut-price repairers the excuse to abolish the calendar work. Also, both the fly and the hoop wheel of the striking train are very carefully balanced. Although good finishers used to see that the fly was poised, as a badly out-of-balance one might make the strike train reluctant to start from rest, most were content to leave the hoop wheel (the hoop of which only extends for three-quarters of the circumference) out of poise. Richard Comber, however, was one of those small-town craftsmen whose work was often superior to that of some quite famous London makers.

As with their aristocratic forbears, the cases of thirty-hour clocks were fairly narrow during the early part of the eighteenth century. On the evidence of chisel marks and slots cut in the sides, they were sometimes narrow enough to give trouble by allowing the pendulum to hit against the side panels; and after about 1730 they grew rather wider. With the necessary restriction of height, they sometimes tend to look a little squat; but until the general decline in proportion set in about 1840, they are mostly of agreeable appearance, and until the end of the eighteenth century, when painted iron dials came into use, the finish of the engraved dial plates, chapter rings, spandrels and hands was fully comparable with that of the best contemporary eight-day clocks. Engraved and silvered dial centres, rather than matt gilt, became fashionable for thirty-hour clocks, and the engravings not infrequently show land- or sea-scapes which are sometimes of local significance. As on the contemporary eight-day clocks, there was an intermediate phase between the painted iron dial and the traditional sort with its gilt brass plate, and separate chapter ring and spandrels. Therefore, between about 1785 and 1800, we find some thirty-hour clocks with one piece brass dial plates, with engraved numerals, corner decorations and centre piece. These one-piece engraved dials were originally silvered all over; but, as seen now, they are generally either blackened and corroded from neglect, or have been burnished to a brilliant brass with unfortunate effect. Thirty-hour clock dials were sometimes made with suitably placed holes through which dummy winding squares could be seen, to simulate the appearance of the 'richer' eight-day clocks. It is hoped one will not be accused of stirring up internecine faction by observing that this form of horological snobbery is most often seen on north country clocks.

Nearly all eighteenth-century country-made thirty-hour clocks were cased in oak. Towards the end of the century and after, it seems that the movements were bought ready finished from wholesale factories but the cases continued to be made by local joiners. Consequently there are fairly wide variations which not only reflect regional fashions but differences from village to village, and it is obvious that some craftsmen had a better 'eye' for proportion than others. Very small differences in the relationship between trunk, hood and base, and the curvature of the mouldings, can transform an undistinguished case into a handsome one.

Apart from the tendency to greater width as the century advanced, the cases show signs of cost-cutting in the use of thinner panels and lighter framing. At their cheapest, however, these provincial oak cases were made of good timber, free from flaws and shakes, and finished to standards which would put most modern furniture factories to shame. Early in the nineteenth century, oak became scarcer because the Napoleonic wars pre-empted home-grown timber for shipbuilding, and interrupted imports; consequently, deal began to be used. In conjunction with the new, cheap, painted iron dials, these deal cases make the clocks of *c*1810 to 1840 much less desirable than their predecessors; but the best of them are still not without merit.

The deal cases were generally grained and varnished to simulate oak or mahogany and these finishes became shabby and scratched, particularly if the clocks stood near open fires or cooking stoves, in cramped cottage rooms. They were then often overlaid with fresh coats of paint or varnish stain, lavishly applied by amateur hands over old dirt and blisters. Modern taste requires deal furniture to be stripped, waxed and sold as 'pine' in the trendier second-hand shops of Chelsea or the Portobello Road. Until the early years of this century, these deal-cased 'cottage grandfathers' were sometimes called 'club clocks', and the name referred to an early form of hire-purchase, financed by small savers contributing to village thrift clubs.

By the middle of the nineteenth century, importations of cheap 'Dutch' clocks from Germany (Dutch in this connection being a corruption of Deutsche), or 'shelf clocks' from the early mass-production factories in the United States drove the English thirty-hour clock off the market. The English makers refused to lower their standards, and would not see that the foreign clocks they despised were not only less than half the price of their cheapest products, but surprisingly good value for money. There is little point in arguing the merits of a Rolls-Royce to those who can barely afford a bicycle, and the niceties of heavy cast-brass plates and solid drawn-steel pinions were lost on a vast new market, in which the customers were quite content with stamped skeleton frames and soft iron wire lantern pinions, provided the result was a clock of some kind which they could buy new for a few shillings.

It may be thought that a disproportionate amount of space has been given to a type of clock which is of relatively little importance. Before the war, thirty-hour long-case clocks were almost unsaleable, as it was an article of faith in the antique trade that nobody would bother to wind a clock once a day; many were broken up, and of those which survived many were converted to eight-day duration, generally by marrying the old dial to an unwanted eight-day movement. This often resulted in dials engraved for single-hand operation, with no minute divisions, sprouting incongruous minute hands; this horological solecism gives the game away at once to those 'in the know'.

As little as ten years ago, it was still possible to buy very attractive thirty-hour clocks, such as the example by Richard Comber in Plate 34, for considerably less than £10, and the old antique trade dictum that they were only worth 'a bob an hour' (ie thirty shillings or £1.50) at auction was not far wide of the mark. As seen in the average second-hand shop or country auction, they usually appeared shabby and broken-down enough to justify this gloomy valuation; but if they were suitably cleaned, set in order and had their elegant dials properly restored, I found there was a ready, though scarcely profitable, market for them. The objection to the need for daily winding usually disappeared when it was seen to be a matter not of fumbling for a key but merely of pulling a cord or chain. Also, as both going and striking trains are driven by the one weight, a thirty-hour clock may easily be made to go for four or five days by preventing the strike from acting. This is useful if a house is to be left for a week-end, for example, and may easily be done temporarily by slipping a suitable wedge of folded paper or cardboard over the 'fly'. The belief that nobody will bother to wind a clock each day is still current, and the August and September 1971 numbers of the *Horological Journal* carry articles describing electrical apparatus to wind such clocks automatically.

Some antiquarian eyebrows may rise at the thought of such electrification, and it is true that some of the automatic winding devices used in the past have necessitated the removal of the striking mechanism and other parts from the clocks. It is possible, however, to do the job without taking anything from the original mechanism and adding only the switch-gear to the underside of the wooden seat board of the movement; the electric winding motors themselves act as driving weights and climb up the ropes on the 'monkey-on-a-stick' principle used in many modernised church clocks. Such an arrangement represents a good blend of eighteenth- and twentieth-century engineering, and is far better than the wholesale scrapping and alteration of thirty-hour movements which used to take place.

As with most other forms of antique furniture, the value of thirty-hour clocks has risen sharply in the last three or four years; and allowing for the depreciation of currency some now fetch approximately the same as they cost when new. The unfortunate fashion for pine furniture has put the highest prices on the least meritorious specimens, and practitioners in the 'ormolulu' school of interior decorating neither know nor care that the clocks they sell are usually mixed marriages, with dials which do not fit cases, movements belonging to neither, and in a state of decay beyond recall.

Disregarding the lunatic fringe of antique dealing, and despite the recent rise in prices, thirty-hour long-case clocks are still often undervalued; and the impoverished enthusiast may find a very rewarding field for starting a small clock collection in these often neglected but pleasing, simple country-made clocks.

Chapter Nine

Finding the Longitude

Good though the combination of anchor escapement and long heavy pendulum was—and is—for domestic clocks, increasing astronomical knowledge in the last quarter of the seventeenth century inspired demand for more and more accurate timekeeping. The principal weakness of the anchor escapement is that during the periods of recoil, following each impulse, the 'dominion' of the pendulum over the clock is reduced. Consequently variations in the force reaching the escapement wheel still affected the timekeeping, though to a much lesser extent than with the verge escapement. What was needed was a recoil-less or 'dead-beat' mechanism and there is some evidence that Townley, Tompion and others partly solved the problem in the last years of the century, and that some of the leading continental horologists were working towards the same end. A dead-beat escapement was also desirable for watches, and a joint patent was granted to Tompion, Booth and Houghton for a recoil-less watch escapement, known as the cylinder. It fell to George Graham, Tompion's nephew-by-marriage and successor, to perfect both mechanisms; his cylinder watches set a new standard and his dead-beat clock escapement remained in use unaltered for precision and observatory clocks until the end of the nineteenth century. Indeed, a number of eighteenth-century dead-beat timekeepers have been kept in use for some of the lesser purposes of the Royal Observatory to the present day.

As Figure 20 shows, the escape wheel and pallets of Graham's escapement are superficially similar to those of the anchor mechanism; but the essential difference is that the dead-beat 'anchor' provides four pallets instead of two. In the anchor mechanism, each pallet serves both for locking and impulse, and the need for each

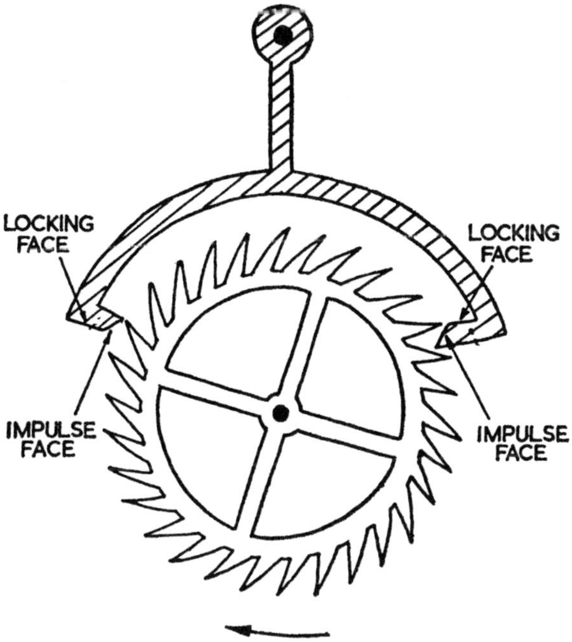

FIGURE 20 *George Graham's dead-beat escapement*

face to be so curved as to receive impulse resulted in that same curvature imparting contrary motion, or recoil, to the escape wheel during the residual or supplementary arc. In the Graham escapement, the locking faces are more gently curved, each describing the arc of a circle whose centre is the pivotal point of the pallet arbor. The acting faces of the tangentially-toothed escape wheel incline towards the direction of rotation; so that only the points of the teeth make contact with the locking faces, neither giving nor receiving motion from them, but resting 'dead' during the full course of the 'supplementary arc'. Only as the pendulum draws near the centre point of its swing and the resting tooth escapes from the locking face, does it then pass to the impulse face which is so radiused as to receive the necessary 'tiddley-wink' push from the passing wheel tooth.

To reduce the arc of the pendulum as far as possible, it is necessary for the pallets to span almost the full circumference of the wheel. This called for great nicety of calculation and execution, to make an accurate dead-beat escapement, despite its apparent simplicity. The advantages of the escapement are as follows:

1 Positive locking with no recoil, and consequently less by-the-clock interference with the naturally isochronous action of the pendulum.
2 Less friction, and therefore less wear and less effect from changes in the viscosity of the lubricant on the sliding faces.
3 Impulse given near the central point of the pendulum's excursion, with consequently greater effectiveness.
4 The greater effectiveness of impulse was matched by a corresponding reduction in the power needed, with consequently less stress and wear on all parts of the going train.
5 The dead-beat escapement can be constructed to work reliably with as little as 2° to 3° of pendulum arc, thus reducing 'circular error' to negligible proportions.

The dead-beat escapement can take other forms than that perfected by George Graham. Some thirty years after his mechanism took its final form, Amant of Paris produced a variant which had an escape wheel on which the teeth were replaced by a series of hardened steel pins, protruding at right angles from the periphery; these acted on pallets of suitable form. This pin-wheel escapement was improved by Jean Lepaute and, in one form or another, it was used by the leading French makers for their finest precision clocks. It performs admirably; but suffers the disadvantage that it is very difficult to persuade the necessary lubricant to stay where it is wanted, on the escapement wheel pins.

Because it could be made to work with so small an arc, the Graham escapement allowed the use in domestic clocks of large, heavy pendulum bobs, almost of turret-clock size, and these increased the control exerted by the pendulum over the clock. In many instances, these very heavy pendulums were hung from stout anchorage brackets bolted to the thick oak back-boards of the cases, in order that they might have a more rigid mounting than the usual pendulum cock attached to the movement. The improvement in timekeeping, by comparison with the best anchor escapement long-case clock, was sufficient to make the errors introduced by changes in temperature a nuisance. Hitherto, the chief nuisance of temperature changes had been their effects on the viscosity of the

Page 161 PLATE 25 Provincial bracket timepiece with alarum, signed behind the mock pendulum John Coleman, Ipswich. The left-hand winding square is a dummy, the wide chapter ring, large minute numerals and absence of quarter-hour divisions suggest a date *c*1740, although the style of the clock is basically seventeenth century

Page 162 PLATE 26 Small bracket clock signed Nathaniel Seddon behind the mock pendulum; calendar and strike/silent in arch, quarter repeating on two bells, *c*1730; (*right*) bracket clock by John Seddon, *c*1760, strike/silent and pendulum 'rise and fall' controls in arch, no quarter or half-hour marks; a less happily proportioned case than its companion oil, which resulted in more or less power reaching the escapement, but now the expansion and contraction of the pendulum rod itself had to be taken into account.

This problem was also solved by George Graham, in 1726, with the first compensated pendulum. Graham made the bob of the pendulum in the form of a stirrup, which supported the base of a tall cylindrical glass jar, three-quarters filled with mercury. If the height of the column of mercury was suitably proportioned to the length of the complete pendulum, the downwards expansion of the steel rod, when the temperature rose, was nullified by the upwards expansion of the mercury, which raised the effective centre of gravity of the 'bob', and vice versa. In practice, a jar of mercury about 10in high by 2–3in inside diameter, containing about a 9in depth of the heavy liquid metal (about 14lb) was used and gave perfect results. The only drawback to Graham's compensated pendulum was that it was extremely difficult to deal with if a clock had to be moved; and as it became the practice, during the second half of the eighteenth century, for observatory clocks to be taken by naval vessels to be set up at various shore stations and temporary observatories round the world, in connection with astronomical, navigational and cartographical purposes, other forms of temperature compensation were devised. The most notable were those of Harrison and Ellicott.

Because it was easier to make than the dead-beat, and because it was quite accurate enough for ordinary domestic purposes, the anchor escapement was not supplanted, for the run-of-the-mill long-case clocks, throughout the eighteenth century; but following Graham's example most of the top-flight makers, London and provincial, produced a particular type of long-case clock which was given the name of 'regulator'. The name reflects the fact that many of these clocks were kept by their makers as standard timekeepers, by which they regulated the other clocks they made or repaired. They were also used to check and correct the local church clocks which were relied upon by the local people to a much greater extent than now. They were also used by the Royal Observatory (and by amateur astronomers) and, as we have seen, quite a number were taken overseas by the Navy and set up in various temporary observatories. They also became popular as standard timekeepers in large households and, until the nineteenth century was well advanced, they were nearly all designed as handsome pieces of furniture, as well as being precision instruments. In addition to being rather shorter than the fashionably tall London long-case clocks, and with cases of the most rigid and heavy construction possible, they differed from ordinary long-case clocks in the shape of the hood and dial. Plain square or circular dials were often used, and Plate 35 shows a form of regulator dial, with hood and trunk door-top to correspond, which became fashionable about 1760. Whether of this elegant shape or not the regulator dial after mid-century was nearly always a plain engraved and silvered brass plate, sometimes in two pieces with the centre recessed as shown, but with no separate chapter ring, corner pieces or decoration. The seconds circle was made as large and clear as possible, and to simplify the motion work and reduce friction the hour indicator was not concentric with the minute hand but took the form either of a rotating disc, showing the hour numerals through a slot in the dial as in Plate 35, or, on later specimens, a short hour hand traversing a suitably inscribed hour circle balancing the seconds circle in the upper half of the dial. As the original function of the regulator type of clock, for astronomical use particularly, was to let the seconds and minutes be clearly read at a glance, it was of little consequence that the hours were less easily seen than on a conventional dial. The particular shape of the dial plate shown, by George Margetts, lent itself to an attractive form of case top and was sometimes used on conventional clocks of good quality: the small bracket clock by Allam and Clements in Plate 27 is a good example.

As the regulator was concerned only with showing the time with the greatest possible precision, striking work and calendar work were not fitted (with rare exceptions), in order to relieve the going train of the load of unlocking or moving them. The plates and pillars were very massive but the wheels were as light as possible; instead of the usual four spokes, or 'crossings' as clockmakers call them, the wheels had six- or eight-armed crossings of very slender form. Where pinions of six or eight leaves are found in ordinary movements, regulator trains had high numbered pinions of ten or twelve leaves. Although these high numbered pinions reduced the degree of multiplication between each wheel and the pinion it drove, they ran with less friction as there was less difference in 'pitch' between wheel teeth and pinion leaves.

Every other method of reducing friction was adopted. Pinions and pivots were hardened, ground and polished with meticulous care, anti-friction rollers were used in some instances; 'end-plates' or 'end-stones' were often fitted over pivot holes in order that the end float or thrust of the arbors would be taken on the ends of the pivots rather than the shoulders; finally, the acting faces of the pallets were often jewelled by being made of slips of agate, ruby or other hard stone to provide a hard-wearing surface offering the least possible friction.

Maintaining power was essential for a regulator, and the old style bolt and shutter mechanism was generally used until about 1770, when an automatic type began to be adopted. This had been devised by John Harrison in connection with his marine chronometers; and it could function equally well as part of the barrel of a weight clock, or in the fusee of a spring-driven timekeeper.

The result of all this attention to reducing friction was that a regulator of one month duration would need less power than the normal eight-day long-case clock, and it is not uncommon to find an eight-day regulator with a driving weight of 2–3lb keeping a 14–20lb pendulum swinging. As far as the timekeeping is concerned—the object of the whole business—a first-class regulator with Graham escapement and heavy, compensated seconds pendulum, maintained in proper order and securely anchored to a vibration-free wall or other surface, can keep time with an error of no more than a second a month. By using an escapement of his own invention, known as the 'grasshopper', which has the great merit of working without oil, John Harrison claimed to have kept one of his regulator clocks running in his own house for fourteen years, with an accumulated error of just under thirty seconds.

Such precision not only enlarged astronomical knowledge, by making more accurate observations possible, but had all manner of secondary results. For example, to make clocks capable of such performances the wheel-cutting techniques had to be improved; and improved wheel-cutting engines, such as those of Henry Hindley of York, allowed more accurate means of dividing the circle and this in turn brought about the construction of more accurate navigational and astronomical instruments. On what may be called the manufacturing side of horological history, we find the beginnings of modern precision engineering. At a time when Boulton and Watt had difficulty in getting an iron cylinder bored to the very modest standards of accuracy Watt required (he specified that clearance between piston and cylinder should not exceed the thickness of a worn sixpence), clock, watch and instrument makers were working to tolerances which a modern ball-bearing manufacturer would not despise. The twin pillars of precision engineering, the screw-cutting lathe and the micrometer, grew out of the work of clockmakers such as Graham, Hindley, Mudge, Ellicott and many more. The 'thermostats' which perform so many vital offices in industry and regulate our domestic cooking stoves, refrigerators and central heating systems are directly descended from Harrison's bimetallic compensating device and this must bring us to a look at the marine chronometer.

The Swiss watch industry officially gives the name 'chronometer' to any watch which performs within a certain standard of accuracy on stringent test; the watches so certified generally have lever escapements or, nowadays, electro-magnetic vibrator or tuning-fork controllers. In English horological language, a chronometer is specifically a marine timekeeper with the type of detached, single-impulse detent escapement originally devised by Pierre Le Roy and brought to practical utility by Arnold and Earnshaw, independently, in about 1780. Also, in English usage, a pocket chronometer is a watch with a detent escapement of the marine chronometer variety.

Because the marine chronometer is of necessity a portable timepiece, and in its final form, which remained fundamentally unaltered from about 1780 to the present day, its mechanism broadly resembles that of an overgrown watch, a detailed account of its development belongs to the history of watchmaking. Or, indeed, it has its own history, and in particular Lt-Cdr Rupert Gould's *The Marine Chronometer—Its History and Development*, which not only shows the author's mastery of his subject but of history in general and the English language in particular.

The development of the chronometer, however, is so intertwined with clockmaking that it must be briefly chronicled here. As stated earlier, the English government passed an Act in 1714 (12

Anne, c15) 'For providing a Publick Reward for such person or persons as shall discover the Longitude'. The test for any method or mechanism was to be performed on a voyage from Britain to the West Indies (which might well be a matter of six months in the eighteenth century): if the longitude was then determined within one degree, £10,000 would be paid; if within forty minutes (of arc, not of time) the prize would be £15,000; whilst the full prize of £20,000 would be paid if the position was determined within half a degree, or thirty minutes, of longitude. At the lowest estimate, this prize represents more than £150,000 in present values; and the largeness of the sum represents the importance Queen Anne's government attached to the question, and fully accounts for the large number of clockmakers and others who tried to solve the problem.

As the problem has been solved for more than two hundred years, it is difficult now to comprehend its magnitude. Although such startling results had been achieved with regulator clocks before mid-century, even the most up-to-date and well-made watches were not accurate enough to use for navigation. Graham's improved cylinder watches performed well enough when newly cleaned and kept in a stable temperature, but no way had been found of compensating the effects of expansion and contraction of a balance spring by heat and cold. Graham experimented with a large marine timepiece with a cylinder escapement, and carefully plotted its changes of rate with changes of temperature. It was proposed to send the watch to sea together with the table of temperature effects and an accurate thermometer, so that at each four-hourly change of watch the temperature could be noted and the timekeeper's current error estimated. It was obvious, though, that such a fallible compensating mechanism could not be relied upon at sea.

There were many squabbles between rival contenders for the 'finding of the Longitude', and it is tempting to say that if some of the partisans had devoted as much attention to solving the problem as they did to publishing vituperative attacks upon their rivals, the marine chronometer would have been born considerably earlier. One of the most heartening aspects of the business is that the first man to help John Harrison financially was George Graham, who was himself a contender for the award.

Harrison was a carpenter from Barrow in Yorkshire. On the evidence of a few letters and one short published pamphlet, he was barely literate; but on the evidence of his work he was a man of outstandingly original thought and perseverance. It is often said that his approach was purely a matter of trial and error, but this is too superficial a view, and in many ways he showed himself more aware of the principles of scientific experiment and logical deduction than his better educated contemporaries.

John Harrison was born in 1693 and turned his attention to horology, largely as a part-time occupation, as a young man. He made a number of long-case clocks, some with the help of his brother James, with wooden movements. Two of his guiding principles were the reduction of friction and the use of mechanisms and materials for escapements which could work with little or no oil. It is clear that the eighteenth-century horologists were at a loss to find suitable lubricants. Mineral oils, which are unsuitable for clockwork because of their low surface tension and consequent tendency to creep, were unknown; vegetable oils such as colza, rape or olive dry out quickly to form sticky gums or varnishes; and the chemistry of the day was not advanced enough to provide clockmakers with whale or porpoise oils of stable consistency and with the ability to resist thickening by age or fall in temperature.

Therefore in his early regulator clocks and his first marine timekeepers, Harrison did not object to a recoiling escapement provided it would work without oil; and by using anti-friction rollers (then a new development by Henry Sully, an English clockmaker working in Paris) he kept friction through the movement to a minimum, even though his wooden wheels and lantern pinions looked rather clumsy. When he began working in metal in a more orthodox horological fashion, he clung to his friction-reducing expedients. The 'grasshopper' escapement referred to was theoretically inferior to the dead-beat, as it required a fairly wide angle of swing, about 12°, and had to rely upon recoil to perform the unlocking; but there is no sliding movement between the escape wheel teeth and the pallets, which consequently work without oil. On his early examples with wooden train wheels, Harrison made the pallets of oak or lignum vitae; but later makers, with conventional metal wheels, used ivory. He also used a device known as a 'remontoire' in many of his timekeepers. This provides a way of keeping the force acting on the escapement as nearly constant as possible, and consists, in effect, of a subsidiary motor, a spring or weight according to circumstances, acting directly upon the escapement wheel or the one immediately before it. This subsidiary spring or weight is wound at appropriate intervals by the main train of wheels and a very great deal of ingenuity is required to design and make such a mechanism. Various forms of 'constant force' devices were tried by Harrison's contemporaries but his seem to have been particularly reliable. One of his surviving regulator clocks, owned by the Royal Astronomical Society, has a remontoire which is wound every thirty seconds, whilst his prize-winning chronometer has a beautifully delicate one which is wound every 7½ seconds.

At about the same time that Graham invented his mercurial pendulum, Harrison devised his 'gridiron' or bimetallic compensation which acted on the principle, discovered and assessed by Robert Hooke, that different metals expand by different amounts at given temperatures. Of the two metals most used in clocks, brass expands more than steel in the ratio of five to four; and Harrison's gridiron pendulum consists of a yoke or inverted T-piece with two steel rods anchored at its extremities. These two rods extend downwards to a distance appropriate for the overall length of the pendulum, and at their lower ends they carry and are united by a second cross-piece. Into this, two brass rods are anchored which extend upwards to a point just below the top yoke where they are joined by another cross-piece. From this again, two more steel rods depend, united at their lower ends by another bar carrying yet another two brass rods upwards; they in turn carry a final cross-piece from which the final steel rod depends, passing through both the lower cross-pieces and extended below them to carry the pendulum bob itself, as Figure 21 shows.

The ratio of expansion being five to four, Harrison always used five steel rods and four brass ones in his gridirons. This was not really necessary, and greater or lesser numbers would have done as well, provided the proportions were correct; but disregarding this blind spot in his reasoning, Harrison's arrangement provided as effective a method of temperature compensation as Graham's mercurial pendulum and was less expensive and fragile. Also, as Harri-

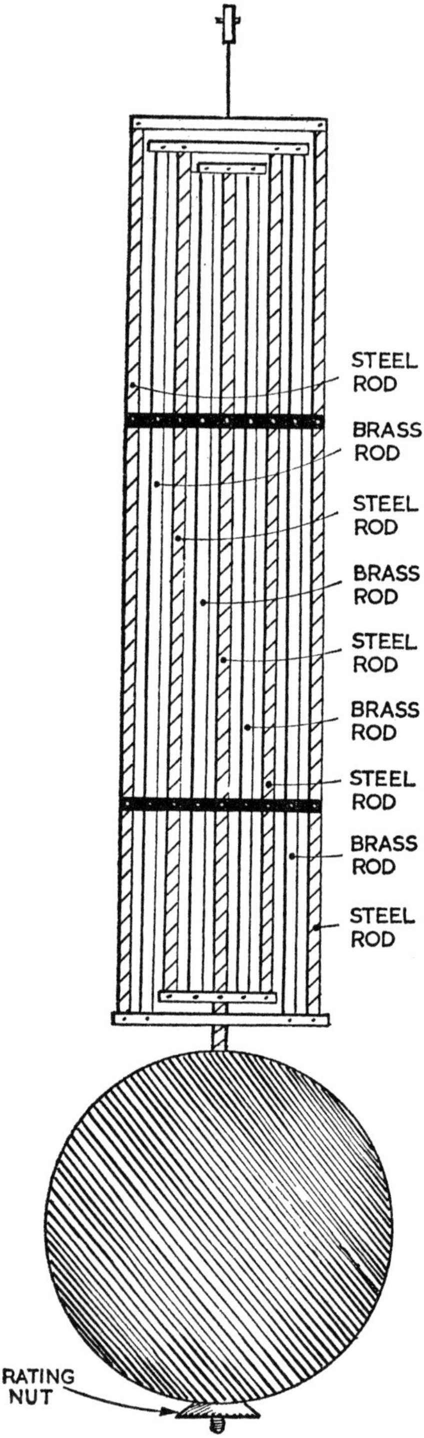

FIGURE 21 *Harrison's bi-metallic compensating or 'gridiron' pendulum*

son demonstrated, the bimetallic principle could be applied to correct the effects of temperature on a watch balance spring. On his first two marine timepieces, which had four helical balance springs, he used a variant of his gridiron arrangement; but he then evolved a form of 'thermometer curb' which consisted of a suitable strip of brass riveted (or, later fused) to a steel one of similar dimensions. Such a bimetallic strip, being firmly anchored at one end, would bend in one direction or the other by the differential expansion of the two metals with changes of temperature and this movement was used to alter the effective length of balance spring. After Harrison's time (as he had foreseen) it was found better to concentrate the compensating effect in the balance wheel itself, leaving the spring free; but the same bimetallic action was used and Harrison's 'thermometer curb' is the direct ancestor of the modern thermostat.

In 1728, Harrison came to London with his plans for a marine timepiece which he showed to George Graham. The latter unselfishly lent him, without security or interest, sufficient money, tradition says £200, to support himself whilst he made and tested a prototype and submitted it to the Board of Longitude, set up under the 1714 Act. He returned to Yorkshire and presumably encountered more difficulties than he had bargained for, as it was not until 1735 that his first chronometer, H1, was ready for trial. It was a large machine weighing about 75lb with frame and train wheels of oak, and lantern pinions with revolving trundles of lignum vitae. Nearly all the arbors turn on large anti-friction rollers and two large mainsprings drive a single fusee, which contains the first example of Harrison's automatic maintaining power. The escapement is a grass hopper acting on two large vertical cross-bar or dumb-bell balances working in contrary motion and kept in phase by a system of fine wires running over counterbalanced segments of such large radius, 10in, that the axial movements at their pivots are so slight as to be almost frictionless.

This amazing piece of apparatus, together with Harrison's other chronometers, were rescued by Commander Gould some forty years ago from the state of almost unbelievable neglect, decay and corrosion in which they had languished for more than a century. Deploying his charm and persuasive eloquence to the full during long-drawn negotiations, Commander Gould contrived to extract from the government department concerned rather grudging permission to restore, at his own expense, these priceless public treasures which the State had so shamefully neglected. Entirely as a labour of love, he completed the work in fifteen years; as the restorations entailed woodworking as well as watchmaking techniques, and involved replacing broken or missing pieces the original shapes and functions of which were often unknown, the extent of Gould's unpaid skill may be assessed. Thanks to him, the four Harrison timekeepers may be seen in action (except when withdrawn for cleaning) at the National Maritime Museum at Greenwich.

Because of the risk of capture, as Great Britain and Spain were at war, Harrison's No1 was not sent to the West Indies but was tried on a voyage to Lisbon and back. It performed well enough for the Board of Longitude to pay Harrison £500 so that he could continue his work, and according to Gould it might just have qualified for the £10,000 award. Harrison did not claim this and spent the next four years on No2. This was a refined, but even larger, version of No1, made all of metal and with a most ingenious remontoire which was wound by the main train sixteen times an hour. Complete with its case and gimbals (which have not survived) it weighed more than a hundredweight, and although it showed great promise on land, and on a barge on the river Humber, it was never tried at sea. Harrison preferred to submit a third chronometer, on which he pinned his hopes, and the board advanced another small sum to keep the work going.

For reasons which have never been satisfactorily explained, the making, testing, altering, re-testing and again altering of No3 took seventeen years. It was another large machine with two contra-oscillating wheel balances controlled by a single spiral spring, which was compensated for temperature changes by the first example of Harrison's thermometer curb. Although he was not fully satisfied with the compensation, Harrison thought more highly of this chronometer than of its predecessors, but when he reported it ready for trial in 1757, he asked for it to be held back until he had finished a much smaller timepiece which would serve as a 'deck watch' to the main chronometer. This smaller instrument, No4, was finished by the end of 1759, and Harrison reported that it went as well as No3. The board agreed to test Nos 3 and 4 together, but by the time a suitable vessel was available and all arrangements had been made, Harrison decided to send No4 alone. As he was nearly sixty-eight and growing frail, he sent his son William to take charge of the timepiece and watch his interests on board HMS *Deptford.*

No4 was made on the lines of a very large silver pair-cased pocket watch of the period; it was just under 5½in in diameter and had a centre-seconds hand. The workmanship is exceptionally fine and the escapement outwardly resembles that of an ordinary verge watch of the period, but the pallets, which are made of diamond, are of quite different form and function and receive impulse both on their flat faces and on cycloidally curved backs. Other distinctive features of this watch, which is signed 'John Harrison and Son', include Harrison's maintaining power, thermometer curb and a 7½ second remontoire. No attempt was made to fix it in gimbals and it made the voyage in a cushioned box in William Harrison's cabin. It seems that the captain of the *Deptford* was not very enthusiastic about the chronometer, but the ship's log makes reference to William Harrison as a 'Civil and Obliging Man'.

The trial voyage started on 18 November 1761 and on arrival at Jamaica the timepiece determined the position with an error of only 1¼ minutes of longitude, which was handsomely within the thirty minutes specified in the Act to qualify for the full award. This ended the official trial, but unofficial tests were continued on the homeward journey and at one point there was a discrepancy of more than thirty nautical miles between chronometer reckoning and dead reckoning. The former was proved right and at the end of the journey, after nearly six months in all, the total error of the chronometer still did not exceed 28½ minutes of longitude.

It will occasion no surprise in those accustomed to the ways of official bodies and government departments that, having taken more than thirty years to produce an instrument to comply with the government's stipulations, Harrison was obliged to spend the next ten years trying to make the government honour its commitment. Small sums were doled out which, together with those already advanced amounted to less than half the prize so fairly won. The root of the trouble was that the then Astronomer Royal was firmly wedded to the Lunar Table system, and most of the experts on, or called in by, the Board of Longitude were watchmakers who favoured other methods than Harrison's. The 'official' reason put forward was that the true merit of Harrison's chronometer could not be assessed until it was proved that other makers could make similar machines of equal merit, at reasonable cost.

Such conditions had formed no part of the original stipulations and were monstrously unjust. When he was nearly eighty and going blind, Harrison contrived to finish No5, which was almost identical with No4, and put his case before King George III. That much maligned monarch was the right man to ask: he took No5 into his well-equipped private observatory at Kew and gave it as severe a test as could be done on land, with frequent changes of position and temperature. After ten weeks, its error on mean time was less than five seconds and the king asserted his authority. A special Act of Parliament was passed at his behest, and Harrison received the money due to him whilst he still had nearly three years in which to enjoy it.

The rest of the chronometer story can only be summarised here. Larcum Kendall was commissioned by the Board of Longitude to make a replica of H4 and this instrument, known as K1, performed splendidly throughout Captain Cook's second voyage, proving such instruments able to keep their 'rate' over long periods, and contributing greatly to the proper charting of hitherto unknown places. Kendall also made two chronometers of his own design, closely resembling Harrison's, which were accurate enough for navigational purposes but never such consistently close performers as H4 or his own copy of it. One of these Kendall chronometers was with Captain Bligh on the *Bounty* at the time of the mutiny; it went with the mutineers to Pitcairn and only returned to England, after many vicissitudes, in 1843.

Other contenders for the prize included John Ellicott, the second of that name, whose chronometer experiments never reached the trial stage, but who nevertheless did valuable work on temperature compensation. He used Harrison's bimetallic principle and devised a pendulum in which the bob alone was raised or lowered by bimetallic expansion pieces acting on pivoted levers. This pendulum is said to have been unsatisfactory as it worked jerkily, but another form of Ellicott compensation worked to a nicety. This took the form of a massive steel and brass expansion piece, or 'thermometer curb', mounted on the front plate of the movement and acting upon a counterbalanced rocking lever to move sliding 'chops' up or down the pendulum suspension spring, so as to vary its effective length. Personal experience of a five-month-duration regulator, with this form of compensation, showed it to be accurate and still sensitive to small temperature changes after two centuries of use.

Another aspirant for the finding of the longitude, who devoted almost as many years to the problem as Harrison, was Thomas Mudge. On his way, he invented the detached lever escapement and included it in a fine watch which that knowledgeable connoisseur, George III, bought for Queen Charlotte. One is tempted to say it was rather too good for that formidable lady. The 'invention' is also claimed on behalf of the Abbé Hautefeuille; but it seems probable that the abbé's escapement was a forerunner of the rack-lever, which had a certain popularity about 1820. The detached lever escapement of the present day stems directly from the type Mudge used, and it is one of the oddities of horological history that although the escapement was invented before 1770, it did not come into common use until after 1830.

Although Mudge thought his lever watch could equal or better the performance of H4 he also thought it was too difficult to make, which is ironical in view of its successful mass-production in recent years. He chose instead to devote many years to his peculiar constant-force escapement which was so difficult to make that even the twenty or so chronometers his son made to his designs after his death failed to measure up to the three made by Mudge himself. Commander Gould has calculated that if the trial formula adopted by the Admiralty in 1840 had been in use when Mudge submitted his chronometer, it might have done better than H4; but it was certainly a more complex and fragile instrument.

Seven years after the trial of H4, Pierre Le Roy of Paris made a prototype of the 'modern' form of detached detent chronometer escapement, but for various reasons this was not developed into a practicable marine timekeeper. Working without knowledge of Le Roy's escapement, John Arnold produced the first of several chronometers with escapements of similar principles in 1773. Thomas Earnshaw also produced rather similar instruments but there were such quarrels, accusations of plagiarism and counter-accusations between Arnold and Earnshaw that the exact order of priority will probably never be known.

What came to be known as the Earnshaw type of spring-detent chronometer escapement prevailed and remained in production, with only minor modifications, from about 1785 until the present day. Apart from the superiority of the escapement, the merit of Arnold's and Earnshaw's contributions is that they made it possible to produce reliable marine chronometers, of more-or-less standard design, at about £40 apiece before the end of the eighteenth century. In present-day terms this is less than the cost of fairly simple radar equipment. Useful though radar is, one could still venture to sea without it, but it would be a foolhardy man who attempted a long voyage without a chronometer or its present-day equivalent of a radio set for receiving time signals.

Chapter Ten

Long-case Clock Development from Queen Anne to Queen Victoria

After the maritime excursion of the previous chapter, a return must be made to the domestic scene to consider the development of the eight-day type of long-case clock after 1700. Disregarding the change from locking plate to rack striking which took place fairly early in the century (it is rare to find an eight-day long-case clock made after 1720 with a locking plate), there were no fundamental changes in the mechanism. This does not mean that the eighteenth-century craftsmen were reactionary, but that their seventeeth-century forbears had brought this type of clock to a state which was admirably suited to its purpose and could only be improved upon by developing it into the regulator type of precision instrument already described.

This is not to say that individual mechanical parts did not change. There were slight but continuous alterations to the shapes of such items as the escapement pallets, which grew wider and heavier, movement pillars, pendulum cocks, hammer springs and stops and the various studs, posts and cocks on the front plate which supported the motion work, calendar wheel, and various parts of the striking mechanism. The 'collets', or brass collars, hard soldered to the wheel arbors, on which the wheels themselves were in turn hard soldered, went through a slow metamorphosis; they started in the seventeenth century as small rounded objects, rather like halved doughnuts, to become very much larger, rectangular in section, with protruding shanks or sleeves which, by the early nineteenth century, often extended for half an inch or more. Figure 22 shows an early type.

Study of details such as these enables one to 'date' a movement with tolerable accuracy, or to detect alterations. Allowance must be made for the inevitable overlapping of these details, and it is most unwise to be dogmatic in assertions to the effect that such-and-such a form of so-and-so 'proves' a clock to have been made before a particular date. It is important for a collector to be able to recognise, or, as it were, to sense the approximate date of the significant parts of a movement, as these things can be valuable clues to marriages of dials, movements and cases of different periods. It is often also useful to be able to recognise what parts of a clock have been renewed.

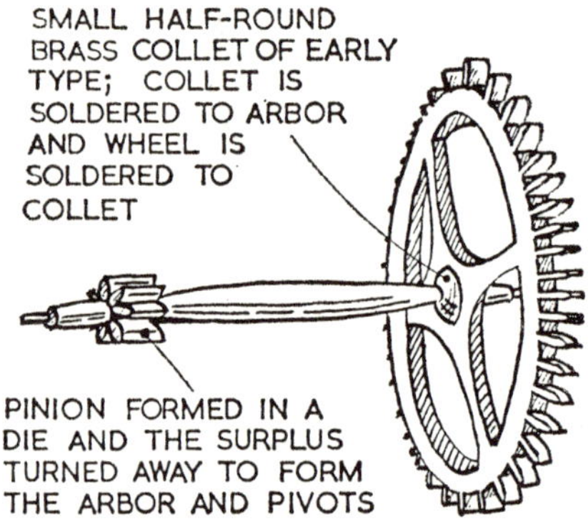

FIGURE 22 *Assembly of wheel, arbor and pinion as fashioned, with the arbor turned from solid-drawn 'pinion wire', from seventeenth century onwards*

The length of the pinions, for example, is significant. In the seventeenth century the pinions were generally not much longer than the width of wheels which meshed with them. By approximately mid-eighteenth century, it was realised to be an advantage to make the pinions wider than the wheels so that if the former became worn the latter could be shifted along their arbors to mesh with the unworn part of the pinion. Not all the wheels could be shifted, because of their relationship with other parts of the movement; but where it was possible, it became a recognised repairer's 'trick of the trade', and the pinions were made about twice the width of the wheels. In the nineteenth century they grew even longer, sometimes extending for four or five times the width of the wheels, which was not only ugly but served no purpose whatever. A

Page 179 PLATE 27 (*left*) Small bracket clock with verge escapement, rise-and-fall pendulum adjustment, calendar unusually placed and 'regulator' shape of dial, by Allam and Clements, *c*1785; (*centre*) travelling clock in rosewood brass inlaid case, with lever escapement, maintaining power, hour strike and repeat by James McCabe *c*1825; (*right*) early balloon or 'waisted' case clock with dead-beat escapement, strike/silent and plain silvered and engraved dial by John Leroux *c*1765. Height of the smallest clock $9\frac{3}{4}$in

Page 180 PLATE 28 Engraved movement of Allam and Clements clock, showing anchorage straps, oil sinks, suspension spring of rise-and-fall pendulum passing through fixed 'chops' and pendulum rod locked for travelling in swivelling holdfast present-day repairer who understands the restoration of antique clocks and who finds an old pinion worn beyond recall will take care to turn down the new one to match the original; but Victorian and later repairers never bothered to do this and were quite happy to leave incongruously long pinions, or typically Victorian-pattern heavy rectangular collets as evidence of the new wheels and other parts they had fitted.

Without a great number of extra illustrations and much rather boring matter, it is not possible to describe all the changes of detail. The best way to learn is by handling and examining as many clocks and parts of clocks as possible; and one of the first things the novice collector must do, if he can, is to cultivate the acquaintance of a knowledgeable repairer who specialises in the restoration of antique clocks. Sitting in a workshop examining bits of clocks and talking about them with an expert will be more useful than reading any number of books.

As we have seen, the fashionable London long-case clocks began to grow taller towards the end of the seventeenth century, and this meant enlarging the square dials from ten to eleven, twelve or sometimes thirteen inches, in order to keep the proportions correct. The 'break-arch' type of dial, which had originally been designed to make room for calendar or equation work, was found useful as a means of adding height, because the new shape of the dial demanded a hood shaped to correspond and made more lofty still by the addition of top-hamper. These additional mouldings, domes and double domes, themselves surmounted by finials, were occasionally overdone; but in general the cases were kept in proportion, and after about 1725 it became usual to shape the top of the trunk door to match the lines of the broken-arch dial and hood. This added to the impression of height and had a slimming effect.

Apart from some regulator clocks, square dials were obsolete in London by about 1720. There were exceptions, of which Plate 20 is an example. This clock was made by Windmills and Elkins: the Windmills in question was a son of the famous seventeenth-century maker and as his partnership with Elkins was apparently formed about 1728, this clock may well have been made as late as 1740; but apart from its size (7ft high with a 12in dial) it has many features characteristic of the 1690s. The panelled door is curiously old-fashioned and the use of plain oak for so late a London clock of such good quality is most unusual. On the other hand, the large minute numerals are similar to, but even more prominent than, those of about 1750. It could be that all these oddities were insisted upon by a provincial customer of old-fashioned habit and short sight who wanted a 'best London-made' clock but who would have none of the new-fangled arched dials and the Frenchified walnut veneers and other fan-tods.

A few, a very few, early break-arch dials for long-case clocks were made in two pieces, and the most probable reason was that the makers concerned had a few square dial plates in stock 'in the rough' and wanted to adapt them to the new mode. An example recently through my hands is on a fine walnut clock of about 1725, by James Reith, London, on which the arch was separate from the square part of the dial plate. The joint uniting the two pieces was of the type known to carpenters as lapped, scarcely visible, and held together by stout riveted straps; the line of the join was concealed by the cast ornamental pieces flanking the strike/silent ring and index mounted in the arch. There was no doubt that the movement, with its strike/silent action, belonged to the dial and that the dial had been planned as a whole and gilded after the two pieces had been united. As a general rule though, an arched dial made in two pieces must be regarded with suspicion as such a thing usually indicates a marriage. What seems to be the usual sequence of events is that an old square-dial movement (often a good, early London-made example) loses its case because of rot, warping, fire or some other accident, and comes into the hands of a dealer with an arch-dial type of case on his hands for which he has no movement; or perhaps the movement in it has a painted iron dial in poor condition. An arched piece is then tacked on to the old square dial, often very crudely, by screwed straps with daylight showing through the join, and some sort of central feature, and ornaments, usually out of period, are then mounted on the new arch. These marriages are often so incongruous as to be more in the nature of shotgun weddings, and the result is certainly a bastard which should deceive nobody but often succeeds in doing so.

At this stage it is useful to consider what filled the arches of break-arch dials both of long-case and of bracket clocks—for the break-arch style soon spread to spring timepieces. One of the advantages of the rack-striking system was that it was easy to provide a switch to shut the strike off at will, because the counting device kept in phase, as we have seen, and the clock would automatically strike correctly when switched on again. The strike/silent control on early clocks was usually worked by a little lever moving about half an inch from end to end of a slot, near the edge of the dial plate; and the extremities of the slot were marked 'S' and 'N' for 'Strike' and 'Not'. This arrangement never disappeared entirely; but many arch-dial clocks had the strike controller made in the form of an index or pointer which could be moved around a circle, inscribed 'Strike' at the top and 'Silent' at the bottom, and this made a convenient feature with which to fill the arch.

By no means all long-case and bracket clocks were fitted with this type of strike/silent control, many indeed, had none; and on some of the more costly examples the arch was filled with subsidiary dials for calendar and astronomical indications. Musical clocks, with carillons of bells worked by a pinned barrel, often had a selector hand and circle or sector in the arch, engraved with the names of the tunes available.

At the other end of the scale from these uncommon and expensive clocks, one often finds the centre of the arch occupied merely by a slightly convex silvered boss, with the maker's name and town engraved on it. Alternatively the boss might carry a decorative engraving (a bird, or a ship perhaps) and although it is not common, it is not unknown for the boss to bear the coat-of-arms of the clock's original owner. The legend *Tempus Fugit* which is so often found on modern reproduction antique clocks was very rarely used in the eighteenth century, and should consequently be viewed with suspicion. On country-made clocks the boss, or perhaps the whole arch, was occasionally used for the display of some exhortation such as: 'Keep Mee Clean and Use Mee well and I will Strive the Truth to Tell.' All these engraved bosses or discs (for on poorer quality clocks they were flat) are readily detachable, and so provide a way for the unscrupulous dealer to substitute the name of a famous maker for a lesser one.

The arch was often used as a place for a phases-of-the-moon indicator. This was particularly true of country-made long-case clocks of about 1750 onwards; and the value of the information to country dwellers needs no stressing, when it is remembered that the decision to take a night-time journey would be decided by the amount of moonlight available to show the way. On earlier London-made clocks (or those of the best provincial make) the lunar indicators were fairly elaborate and of two main types. The more elaborate took the form of a circular opening in the dial arch, through which a ball about two inches in diameter protruded; one half of the ball was painted black or dark blue and the other was white and as it rotated at a speed appropriate to the lunar cycle the alternating areas of light and dark simulated the waxing and waning of the moon. Alternatively, the moon might be represented by a circle cut in a rotating disc, generally gilded but sometimes enamelled dark blue and spangled with stars. This disc rotated against a silvered background on which was engraved a suitable crescent shape made dark by black pigment; this hatched or shaped area showed through the hole in the disc, as the latter rotated, in greater or lesser areas of light and dark, again representing the waxing and waning of the moon. The disc usually carried a 'pip' or pointer, which indicated the age of the moon in days on a series of numerals suitably engraved about it. A variant on this form of lunar indicator had the outer disc with the hole in it fixed and the rotating disc behind it.

The commoner sort of lunation work found on the country clocks referred to (and on some of London make) was simpler both in appearance and operation. The greater part of the arch was cut away in the manner shown in Figure 23, leaving a narrow segment across the top and two protruding semi-circular 'humps' at the bottom. Behind the dial plate, a large disc rotated with half its circumference visible through the cut-away portion, and on this disc were painted two representations of a full moon, usually with a rather simpering face, so placed at 180° that as one moon began to rise above the 'hump' on the left its fellow disappeared behind the 'hump' on the right. The 'humps' were usually painted or engraved to resemble halves of terrestrial globes.

In the space outside the moons on the rotating disc, divisions and numerals were inscribed up to 29½ to indicate the age of the moon in days, against a projection forming part of the fixed segment above the lunation disc. Alternatively, the figures for the moon's age were inscribed round the fixed segment and a 'pip' projecting from the top of each moon pointed to the appropriate division. The moon's age figures were written in Arabic numerals; and on many clocks made in or near seaports, it was often customary to add another row of figures and divisions, using Roman numerals, and by noting these in relation to the 'pip' on the moon it was possible to read the time of high water at the particular place. The words 'High Water at Bristol Key', or 'High Tyde at Leverpool', or what-

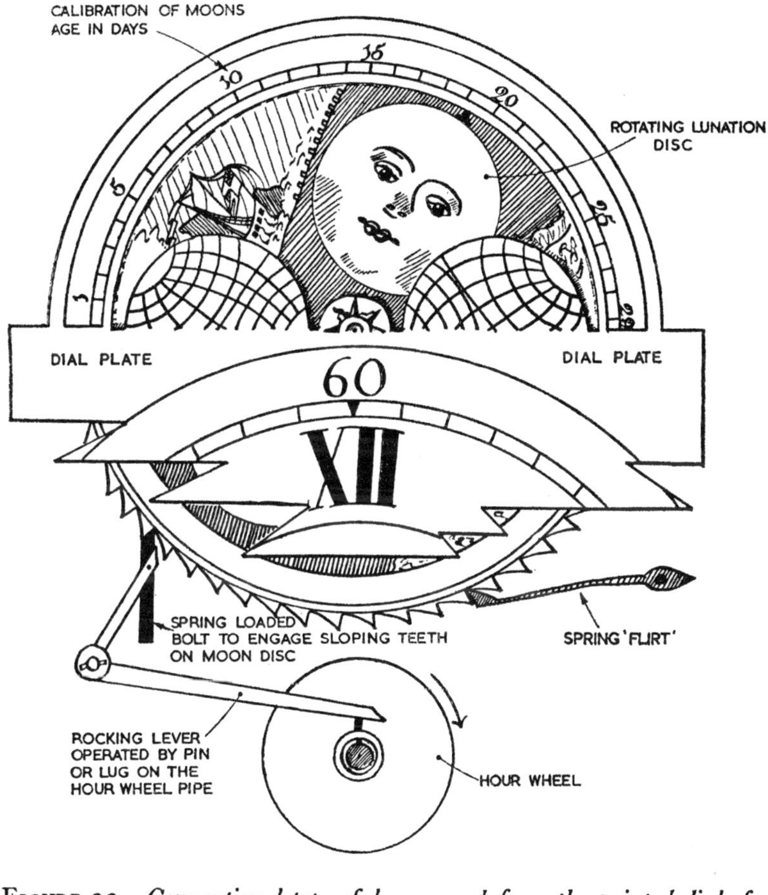

FIGURE 23 *Conventional type of lunar work from the painted dial of a long-case clock by Bartley and Eggert of Bristol*

ever was appropriate, would be engraved above the row of Roman numerals.

These rotating moon discs had 118 sloping or ratchet teeth cut round their peripheries; and a simple spring-loaded latch or trigger, known as a 'bolt', was operated by a pin or lug in the hour wheel pipe to jerk the disc forward one tooth every twelve hours. A curved piece of metal, attached to a light spring tail, rested in the tooth spaces and acted as a 'flirt' to prevent the disc moving too far, by clicking over each tooth as the disc moved.

This simple mechanism made each moon face traverse its journey in 29½ days, with negligible load on the clock, but this resulted in an error of half a day in every sixteen lunations as the real lunar cycle represents 29 days, 12 hours, 44 minutes and 2·87 seconds. This trifling discrepancy was of no consequence for ordinary domestic purposes, and the moon disc would occasionally have to be corrected by reference to an almanac. On a few of the more elaborate lunar indicators the mechanism was more complex, and by using a suitable train of subsidiary wheels and pinions the ratio of lunar day to solar day could be more nearly expressed. The late Courtney Ilbert calculated that the moon work on the Thomas Mudge lever escapement clock, now in the British Museum, was so correctly geared that the discrepancy was only one lunar day in 4,000 years.

The final solution to the problem of filling the arch was found by using it as a background for automaton figures usually moved by the escapement. The automata included such things as a cut-out figure of Father Time busily doing the grim reaper business or, less often, pairs of painted figures with moveable arms and racquets playing battledore and shuttlecock with the shuttlecock moving unnaturally slowly (being linked to the seconds-beating pendulum) between them in a curved slot. A lion or some other creature rolling its eyes in a sort of slow motion horological nystagmus is occasionally seen; but the most popular automaton was a ship forever pitching or rolling against a recessed and painted seascape. Although most often found on provincial clocks, the rolling ships also appear on some late London specimens of lower-than-best quality; many of the ships, cut out of sheet brass and painted, were inscribed with the name of the *Royal George* after the public imagination had been stirred by the disaster when a stiff-necked officer of the watch had quite needlessly caused that warship to sink, with the loss of nearly all on board, whilst she lay at moorings on a calm day in a safe harbour. A very late example, *c*1830, of the rocking ship automaton is shown in Plate 37; but here the original flat, one-dimensional sheet-metal ship was removed by a Victorian repairer-vandal and replaced by me with a 'half-round' wooden model.

Nearly all long-case clocks, other than regulators, had two trains of wheels and struck the hours only. The continental practice of sounding a single blow at the half-hours was occasionally followed after 1830. Quarter-chiming work on four, six or eight bells is sometimes found but is not very common, and should always be closely examined as a proportion of the quarter-chiming clocks have had the third train of wheels and the necessary under-dial work added in the nineteenth century. At one time the addition of a quarter-chiming train was regarded as a test of skill for an apprentice, and late Victorian repairers' handbooks published various plans for doing the job. Some of these plans entailed 're-planting' the existing wheels so that all three winding holes were symmetrically placed in the dial (as they are in a clock designed originally to have a chiming train); but less expensive ways of making the addition entailed adding the extra train to the three o'clock side of the existing mechanism, in extensions riveted to the plates, with the consequence that the new winding square protrudes through the chapter ring. A clock which sounds 'Westminster' quarter chimes must either be a Victorian specimen or have been modernised, as the familiar four-bell signal was virtually unknown before Lord Grimthorpe's great clock began work in 1859.

As we have seen, one of the earliest English, or crypto-English, domestic clocks, by Nicholas Vallin, has a carillon of thirteen bells on which rather implausible music is played. Musical clocks, long-case or bracket, were made throughout the eighteenth century and into the nineteenth, but they were never common. Extremely elaborate, costly, and sometimes rather gaudy musical spring-driven clocks, were made for export to the Middle East and to China. A few of these played small pipe organs in place of the usual bells. James Cox, who was in business *c*1760–88 and who had a 'museum' of automata in London, held a dominant position in the

China trade (just as 'Diego' Evans had a near-monopoly of the Spanish market), and his most remarkable invention was a 'perpetual' clock, wound by changes in atmospheric pressure acting upon a gargantuan mercury barometer. The principle was re-invented in Switzerland about fifty years ago, without acknowledgement to Mr Cox, and is used in the modern 'Atmos' self-winding clocks.

The majority of musical clocks played their tunes automatically, sometimes twice or thrice over, every four hours, at three, six, nine and twelve o'clock, and at will by pulling a cord. Many examples made do with only eight bells, on which only simple airs could be played; but the more bells the greater the range, obviously, and in order to be able to sound individual notes in quick succession the best musical movements have two hammers to each bell. On very late examples, the pin barrel and the bells and hammers are arranged transversely across the back plate of the movement, with the barrel driven by contrate or bevel wheels. This allowed a greater length of barrel, and more bells and hammers, than when the mechanism had to be contained between the plates. The most elaborate musical long-case clock I have seen was made about 1810 by Andrews of Bristol although the dial was signed 'Jackson, Bath'; it had thirty-two bells and sixty-four hammers. It played seven tunes which were changed automatically each day and automaton musicians and dancers moved in the arch of the dial, except on the seventh day when they were obscured by a shutter on which was engraved 'Remember the Lord's Day to Keep it Holy', in accordance with which the mechanism obliged with a solemn rendering of the 'Old Hundredth'.

Many experts consider the works of some of the most famous makers grossly over-valued; and it can be argued that there is no justification for paying £15,000 for a clock by Thomas Tompion, when an equally good specimen by the little-known Thomas Tomkins can be had for £1,500. How much should be paid for the name, beyond the merit of the clock itself, both as a piece of interesting antique machinery and as a piece of aesthetically pleasing antique furniture, is a question which each collector must answer for himself. Chance and fortuitous circumstances, as always, play a large part in deciding which 'name' will attract the most money and it is a tenable proposition, for example, that the reputation which

Tompion won in his own day because of the superiority of his watches unduly enhances the value of his clocks in our day, although it can be demonstrated that those of some of his contemporaries are certainly as good and sometimes better.

In addition to the handful of great names, from Fromanteel in the seventeenth century to Jump who took over Vulliamy's business in the nineteenth and whose own business survived into the 1920s, the collecting and big-money emphases have been upon London-made clocks. Now that antiques in general have multiplied in price tenfold in the last decade, provincial examples are also being valued more highly. This belated recognition is welcome. Country makers obviously produced much run-of-the-mill stuff, but nearly every part of the United Kingdom, including the off-shore islands, appears to have fostered at least one clockmaker of outstanding ability and inventiveness.

The merits of some of these countrymen, such as Cockey of Warminster or Hindley of York, have been known for some years; but now that a very long pocket is needed to buy 'best London-made' the field of provincial horology gives the modest collector a chance to find something outstanding at a price which is still well below that of a comparable London piece.

The long-case clock by John Calldwell in Plate 31 is a case in point. On the evidence of the engraving, calligraphy and other features, the clock was probably made about 1760. It is housed in a plain but handsome oak case, the movement and dial are far from ordinary, but little is known of the maker except that he worked in Appleton, in Yorkshire, in the third quarter of the eighteenth century.

The photographs shows three winding holes in the dial and this indicates the presence of a quarter-chiming train, which functions on six bells. There are two calendar apertures, so that the name of the month is shown as well as the date. The place normally occupied by the seconds hand and ring is taken by an unusual form of lunar indicator, whilst the arch of the dial is occupied by a double-twelve hour chapter ring surrounding a rotating disc which shows the movement of the sun above the horizon. The horizon is represented by the upper edge of a painted landscape which rises and falls throughout the year, so that the times of sunrise and sunset may be judged by the relationship between the moving landscape and the fixed ring of numerals. The calibration is appropriate to the latitude of northern England and the indication of sunrise and sunset has the unusual merit of being visible at a quick glance. This offsets the drawback that it is not possible to judge the indication more closely than to the nearest quarter hour, but for ordinary domestic or farming purposes this is precise enough.

The mechanism is ingenious; and involves a fairly elaborate train of subsidiary wheel work under the dial. The standard of workmanship, particularly the engraving of the dial and its subsidiaries, is up to 'best London' standards. The design of the complications owes nothing to known sources, and the clock may have been made to the specification of a particular customer.

Nearly all eighteenth- and early nineteenth-century long-case clocks have the seconds dial as shown in the various photographs. Occasionally the seconds indicator occupied the arch, being driven by a vertical shaft and contrate or mitre wheels; and a few long-case clocks were made with centre-seconds hands in the modern fashion. Agreeable though these are to watch in action, they are a source of trouble. In order to have a centre-seconds hand, the going train must either be arranged with the escapement wheel in the middle of the clock, with extra wheels in the motion work, or with two idler wheels to convey the motion from the escape wheel arbor to the centre. In either case, there is extra friction and relatively slight wear often causes the big sweep hand to run out-of-true and foul the minute hand. The centre-seconds hand is also a nuisance when the clock has to be wound unless, as was sometimes the case, extra mechanism has been added under the dial to bring the winding squares outside the chapter ring.

The changes in hands and spandrels are reflected in the illustrations, but in very general terms the sequence of spandrel design was as follows:

1	Winged cherub's head in high relief	1660–1690
2	Winged cherub's head in less high relief, with the area of spandrel extended by interlaced foliage	1690–1715
3	Two cherubs holding sceptres flanking a central crown, in low relief	1695–1710

4 Woman's head mask surrounded by rococo foliage in low relief — 1710–1760
5 Interlaced arabesquerie or strapwork, low relief — 1760–1785
6 Cast female figures representing the four seasons, country-made clocks at various dates throughout the eighteenth century

These dates are only approximate and the inevitable overlapping of styles must be taken into account, particularly when considering provincial makers' work.

The central features in the arches were at first generally flanked by rather attractive dolphins with their tails raised; but, from about the middle of the century, the dolphins were replaced by arabesquerie or strapwork designs matching the corner pieces. The 'ringed' winding holes seen on the clock by Benjamin Merriman, Plate 33, about 1700, were once held to be exclusive to clocks made between about 1695 and 1710, though the feature did not appear on all clocks of that period and examples of considerably later date are occasionally seen.

The practice of engraving quarter-hour divisions on the inner edge of the chapter ring was not really necessary when the concentric minute hand came into use, but it was only gradually given up. Here again there is a great deal of overlapping. The clock by Richard Wise in Plate 18 dates from about 1695 and has no quarter divisions, whilst the Windmills and Elkins of much later date, in Plate 20, still has them. The half-hour marks lingered on after the quarter divisions had generally disappeared, and the simple lozenge favoured by George Graham ousted the more elaborate fleur-de-lys pattern. In general terms both quarter divisions and half-hour marks had gone by 1750, and the Arabic numerals marking each fifth minute, which grew steadily larger between about 1700 and 1740, began to grow smaller again. By the end of the century, the minute numerals began to disappear, or in some instances to be marked at fifteen-minute intervals only, particularly on the smaller clocks. Arabic instead of Roman numerals for the hours crop up occasionally at all times, but they became rather more fashionable between about 1810 and 1830 although they never ousted the old-style Roman 'chapters' and never looked so well.

The traditional rectangular calendar aperture, sometimes replaced by a circular one, particularly post-1750, with the date numerals on a large ring moved forwards once every twenty-four hours, began to be replaced by a simpler and cheaper device about 1780, particularly on country-made long-case clocks. The new arrangement took the form of a fairly large semi-circular slot in the lower part of the dial, behind which was a disc, with the date numerals on it, and with sixty-two ratchet teeth cut around its periphery. The disc was held in place by a 'flirt' and spring, and moved forwards one half-division every twelve hours by a pin in the hour wheel, which passed into the path of the teeth on the disc. The same pin actuated the lunar disc, if one were fitted, and the arrangement did away with the need for the twenty-four-hour wheel of the older type of calendar. The upper part of the slot had a projecting tongue or 'pip' which served as a fixed pointer against which the date numerals could be read, as shown in Plate 37. After 1800, particularly on bracket clocks, the slot and visible disc were sometimes replaced by a hand attached to the disc and traversing a circle marked on the dial with the date numerals.

As we have seen, the regulator type of clock, from about 1740 onwards, was usually furnished with a plain one-piece dial of silvered brass; and some of the leading London makers began fitting rather similar one-piece dials to their standard long-case and spring clocks, after about 1760. An example of about 1770, by Charles Cabrier, is shown in Plate 36; but the fashion did not become general until after about 1780, and the traditional type of dial with its gilded, or gold-lacquered plate, separate chapter rings and spandrels lingered on beside the newer fashion. The one-piece silvered dial had the advantage of being more legible as well as being cheaper to make; and many of them have very attractive engraved corner decorations and signatures. Unfortunately, as the chemical silvering process used is not permanent and needs renewal at intervals of about fifty years (or less in a corrosive atmosphere), these dials often appear in badly neglected and corroded state or have been scrubbed down to the brass and burnished, which looks garish. Their proper restoration will be dealt with in Chapter 14.

The last stage in the development of the English clock dial marked a sad fall from former glory. A few eighteenth-century clocks were made with enamelled dials; the enamelling being mostly done at the Battersea or Bilston works on copper plates. The French developed one-piece vitreous-enamelled dials extensively from about 1750 onwards, and very fine they are too; but they were not similarly developed in Britain and, towards the end of the eighteenth century they, and the traditional sorts, were elbowed aside by one of the first fruits of the industrial revolution—sheet iron from the new rolling mills of Pontypool and Wolverhampton. This new material, which brought a host of new industries into being, was cheaper than brass or copper but it could not satisfactorily be gilded, silvered or enamelled; and although many beautiful clocks were still made, the coming of the painted iron dial marked the beginning of the end.

Some of the paintings in the arches and corners of the new-style dials are competent and attractive; but the majority, particularly on country long-case clocks, tend to be rather crude and amateurish. They may have a certain bucolic charm, but are seldom of artistic merit. The numerals, divisions, signatures, seconds and calendar markings are usually nicely proportioned and elegantly 'written', provided they are in good condition. Unfortunately, they are often illegible or have been re-done, either by amateur hands or by professional 'dial writers' who have ruined the proportions by using the heavy, elongated numerals, fashionable from about 1880 onwards on office clock dials, instead of reproducing the original forms.

The reason why relatively few painted iron dials, particularly of long-case clocks, have survived with their original numerals in good condition is that, although the backgrounds and ornamental paintings on the iron plates were executed in oil paints, often hardened by gentle baking, the numerals, divisions, circles and signatures were done in a water-soluble medium chiefly composed of lamp-black. The reason for this maddening practice is obscure but has had disastrous consequences, as so many owners have been understandably tempted to clean a filthy, streaked, smoke-stained dial with soap and water, only to have the mortification of seeing the corner pieces and arch spring to life again whilst all the black markings blotch and smear.

Almost from the beginning, English clockmaking was a business involving specialist suppliers of different components, some in the rough, some part-finished, and 'out-workers' in such processes as gilding and engraving, all combining to supply the 'master clock-makers' who, with their apprentices and improvers, saw to the finishing, assembling, casing and testing of the complete clocks to which they put their names. It is no more reasonable to suppose that Thomas Tompion 'made' his clocks from start to finish (though he was capable of doing so) from lumps of raw metal than that Messrs Rolls and Royce personally cast, forged, turned, filed and fitted every piece of their motor-cars. Nevertheless every Tompion clock was the brain child of Tompion, even those few for which he 'bought out' complete movements; just as the 'Silver Ghost' model was Henry Royce's masterpiece, even though he was no draughtsman and relied on various suppliers for the component parts.

Eighteenth-century advertisements often throw light on the extent of the components industry; and the way in which many clock and watchmakers could have lived happily in that famous colony of washerwomen who lived by taking in each other's washing. Typical of many is the following from the *Norwich Mercury* of 9 December 1773, in which one Thomas Harland listed the different sorts of watches, turret and domestic clocks, and regulators he made and sold, and to which he added this postscript:

> N.B. Clock faces engraved and finished for the trade. . . wheels and fuzees of all sorts and dimensions, cut and finished upon the shortest notice, neat as in London and at the same price.

The possession of a fusee engine or wheel-cutting engine of known superiority would guarantee its owner a steady income and would be eagerly sought by trade rivals, when he died or gave up his business. It also seems that country makers in remote districts depended, to some extent, on itinerant craftsmen, particularly engravers.

Towards the end of the century although the leading makers, both London and provincial, continued to design and finish their best quality pieces in their own shops, the ordinary run-of-the-mill products were increasingly fitted with movements turned out, fully finished and tested, from factories in Clerkenwell, Birmingham, Prescot, Ormskirk and lesser centres. This development coincided to a great extent with the introduction of the painted iron dials;

and the word 'factory' in this context often meant a two-men-and-a-boy concern working in a tiny back-street shop, and themselves heavily dependent on outworkers. A number of those who supplied finished movements to the trade in this way rose to prominence, and also sold complete clocks under their own names. One of the best-known London suppliers in this category, still in business, were Thwaites & Reed who supplied movements to many of the most famous London makers of the 1790 to 1840 period. Men of the eminence of the royal clockmaker, Benjamin Vulliamy, Samuel French, James McCabe, or Dwerrihouse and Carter bought movements from Thwaites & Reed, whilst still designing and finishing their best pieces on their own premises.

The dependence of most provincial makers of long-case clocks, after about 1790, on the factory-made movements is underlined by the practice of supplying the movement complete with a 'skeleton' dial plate, or iron frame, which was attached to the front plate by four short pillars. This could easily be removed and drilled to take the feet of the dial plate proper (the drillings could not be standardised as the positions and sizes of the feet were not standardised), so that there was no need to dismantle the movement and drill the frontplate. These dial sub-frames were often stamped with the name of the firm responsible for the movement. The clock in Plate 37, for example, is signed 'J.S. Shortman' on the dial but the sub-frame makes it clear that this Kentish maker bought the movement from Messrs Walker of Birmingham. Although these ready-finished movements, and the painted dials, brought prices down, there was no reduction in the quality of the mechanism which continued to be well made of heavy brass and burnished and hardened steel.

The only evidence of price-cutting in the mechanism, which did not affect performance, is to be found in the weights and pendulums. Early long-case clocks have lead weights encased in brass, and the lenticular pendulum bobs were also of lead faced with brass. After about 1740, the brass casings were omitted from the weights; and early in the nineteenth century, both the driving weights and the pendulum bobs were often made of cast iron. The iron pendulum bobs were often decorated with stencilled designs in 'Dutch gold', a form of imitation gold leaf, and the pendulum rod itself, formerly of soft iron wire about $\frac{1}{16}$in in diameter, was made of strip brass about half-an-inch in width. Theoretically, the brass pendulum rod was less accurate than the iron wire variety, as brass alters more than iron with changes in temperature; but the change had no effect in practice.

One other mechanical innovation is worth mentioning, and this is the use of 'oil sinks'. On early clocks the ends of the pivots protruded slightly through their bearings and oil placed upon them quickly drained away down the plates, as the contact between the pivot and the hole broke the surface tension, unless the oil were so thick as to be more hindrance than help. As we have seen, finding a suitable lubricant was one of the problems facing the craftsmen of two and a half or more centuries ago; and persuading it to stay where it was needed was another. About 1715, Henry Sully showed that a small semi-circular basin, formed around each pivot hole to about a quarter of the thickness of the plate, tended to keep a drop of oil in place (provided the pivot did not protrude beyond the upper edge of the basin) as the surface tension, being now unbroken, made it reluctant to go round the corner. Except for lantern clocks, very few movements are found without oil sinks, even though they may antedate Sully's innovation, as their benefits were so marked and their addition so easy. The back plate of the Allam and Clements movement in Plate 28 shows the oil sinks fairly clearly.

To deal adequately with long-case clocks as pieces of furniture, with all the changes of style made between the reigns of Queen Anne and Queen Victoria, would require this book to be doubled in length, and to contain far more photographs. Numerous books have been published on antique furniture in general, or long-case clock design in particular, which will be found useful; Cescinsky and Webster's *English Domestic Clocks*, R. W. Symonds' *Masterpieces of English Furniture and Clocks* and Ernest L. Edwardes' *The Grandfather Clock* must be particularly commended.

Disregarding the late deal-cased clocks described in Chapter 8, the majority of thirty-hour clocks were cased in oak; but the country-town makers offered their eight-day clocks in walnut (before about 1760) mahogany or oak according to quality. Other woods such as laburnum, yew, pollard, oak, elm and birch are occasionally seen and many late eighteenth-century country-made

Page 197 PLATE 29 London simplicity, a small, plain, elegant bracket clock by Grimalde and Johnson, Strand, *c*1800

PLATE 30 London exuberance, conventional verge escapement bracket clock profusely adorned with fine quality gilt metal mounts, by Charles Penton, *c*1790

Page 198 PLATE 31 Elaborate and decorative dial by John Calldwell, showing month and date, moon phase, declination of the sun and times of sunrise and sunset; the hour hand probably not original, *c*1750–60

clocks were of oak, cross-banded with mahogany. Contrary to some authorities, a few London makers continued to supply very plain oak long-case clocks, in the second half of the century. The belief that long-case clocks went out of fashion almost completely in London is expressed by C. Clutton in the seventh edition of *Britten's Old Clocks and Watches and their Makers* in which he writes: 'Long-case clocks by London makers after 1760 are very rare, except for the occasional complicated astronomical clock, and for the perfectly plain type of regulator.'

The other aspect of this is summed up by R. W. Symonds in *A Book of English Clocks*:

> Provincial clock-makers, unlike the London clock-makers, did not always make spring- as well as weight-driven clocks. Judging by the scarcity of Spring clocks of provincial make, and by the survival of the large numbers of provincial-made weight-clocks, it would seem that most country makers confined their clock-making to the latter.

Exceptions to these rules are rather commoner than the bare statements suggest, and in considering the alleged scarcity of London long-case clocks after mid-century one must consider what is meant by London. There may be a relative scarcity of run-of-the-mill grandfather clocks signed 'Snooks—London', but there are relatively many signed 'Smith—Greenwich', 'Brown—Camberwell', 'Robinson—Southwark' or 'Tompkins—Holborn', and even in the eighteenth century the inhabitants of these places thought of themselves as Londoners, or quasi-Londoners at least.

There are wide differences, naturally, both in style and quality of the provincial oak cases; these were dictated not only by the individual quirks both of clockmaker and casemaker but by the availability of suitable timber. The tendency to use lighter framing and thinner panels as the century advanced was more apparent in some districts than others. Clocks made in Cornwall where oak was scarce, the roads execrable and transport correspondingly costly, were flimsier and less well made than those of Nottinghamshire or Leicestershire. Some of the country-town clockmakers had the services of casemakers whose work was every bit as good, both in design and execution, as anything made by the best London cabinetmakers. The family of Lee of Leicester produced some clocks in truly admirable oak cases which to judge from the appearance, may well have been designed by Batty Langley. The very finest mahogany case I have seen enclosed a clock by Andrew Veitch of Haddington; as both clock and case were of unusual design, the latter was almost certainly also made locally. Although their cases assumed some extraordinary proportions after about 1790, casemakers supplying the extensive Liverpool and Prescot trade also did work of the finest quality.

Walnut veneered cases became rarer after 1740, as supplies of suitable walnut became scarce. Mahogany did not really come into its own much before 1750; and where oak would not do, the gap was filled, principally in London but in many provincial towns as well, by the use of japanned decoration. Many of the japanned cases have grown very shabby or have been over-restored; many more, we may suppose, have been broken up, which partly accounts for the fact that there are more long-case clock movements and dials searching for suitable cases than there are cases advertising for tenants. Also, some japanned cases which grew unendurably shabby have been stripped and painted black, or dealt with in some other way.

Some of the last of the walnut cases were veneered on soft wood instead of the oak, as used earlier. This was not done just to cut cost but because it had been found that oak is not the best foundation for veneers; no matter how well seasoned it is, English oak continues to 'move' with changes of humidity even three centuries or more after it has been sawn into planks and made into furniture, and the movements, though slight, are enough to crack veneers. Early mahogany cases were generally made 'in the solid' and were not veneered, as the hardness of the wood defeated the veneer-cutting techniques of the time. The mahogany first imported was rather dull, dark-toned, straight-grained wood; but more finely-figured timbers became available later and as the difficulties of cutting veneers had been overcome the trunk doors, bases and other large areas could be faced with matched panels of 'feather' mahogany. The best quality mahogany-veneered cases, those for regulators particularly, were of 'feather' mahogany, laid on a Cuban mahogany carcass. This expensive method was followed to ensure that the carcass should expand and contract in the same ratio as the 'show wood', in order to obviate all risk of cracking the veneers.

Applied decoration is nearly always restrained on English long-case clock cases, in marked contrast with those of other countries, France and Austria for example, which often suffered from a surfeit of ormolu mounts, applied over intricate inlays on cases of rather ill-balanced 'fiddle' or 'bombé' forms. In England, marquetry inlays seem to have gone out of fashion for clock cases by 1725, and the later work was often fussy and insipid by comparison with the bold, simple designs of 1680–1700. Japanned decoration, as we have seen, filled a gap between the age of walnut and the coming of mahogany, and 'lacquered' long-case clocks were rarely made after 1760, although bracket clock cases decorated in red japan continued to be made, principally for export, until 1800. Oak cases carved within an inch of their lives, all over the surfaces of base, sides, trunk-door and hood, are not infrequently seen but are most infrequently genuine. A very few late seventeenth- to early eighteenth-century oak clocks were carved all over, but the majority are fakes dating from the end of the nineteenth century when antique dealing and collecting as we now know it began in earnest, and when the more bulbous and riotously ugly forms of 'Jacobethan' oak furniture were highly prized. These elaborately carved cases were either built up out of panels and mouldings from genuine old furniture, or were plain eighteenth-century oak cases of heavy quality, ornamented by those Victorian woodcarvers who similarly 'improved' so many plain coffers, chests and cupboards with an unnatural rash of mock-Tudor decoration. These faked cases were not infrequently prominently dated, and the practitioners of the art were not abashed that the date was anything up to a century earlier than that of the clock mechanism and dial.

Flat-topped hoods in the fashion of the late seventeenth century were retained on most thirty-hour clocks as we have seen, but the superstructures of the grander long-case clocks went through many changes. Apart from the pierced cresting of late Carolean clocks, one way of adding height to a flat-topped hood was by a dome, or, indeed, a series of domes, which often became rather top-heavy in appearance, particularly when they were topped by carved wood or gilt-metal finials. Naturally, as so many have had to be adapted for lower-ceilinged rooms, relatively few very tall clocks have survived unaltered and many have had all or part of the superstructure removed. Plate 20, the Windmills and Elkins clock, shows an unusually flattened dome, which seems never to have been altered, rising from a concave architrave and topped by another concave moulding supporting a flat platform.

The general adoption of the break-arch dial with a correspondingly arched hood gave ample scope for designers to add height without making the result top-heavy; naturally some casemakers succeeded better than others. With relatively few exceptions the clock hood kept its link with its architectural past in that the upperworks, however elaborate they became, consisted in effect of architrave, frieze and cornice apparently supported by pillars. Domes and 'bell-tops' rose from or were recessed slightly behind the cornice, and the pillars were sometimes free-standing as in Plates 39 and 31 but were more often half, three-quarter or quarter pillars moulded into the structure.

The bases and capitals of the pillars were often of gilt (or gold-lacquered) brass, usually plain Doric but sometimes elaborately cast and tooled in the Corinthian style. The pillars were sometimes reeded or fluted and the lower halves of the flutes were sometimes adorned with gilt brass 'spurs'. At about the same time that these became fashionable, *c*1780, the better quality cases were frequently made with 'canted corners' to the trunks; and these recessed faces were often adorned with half-round pillars, metal-adorned to match those of the hood. One also finds cases with the canted corners left plain.

Early cases often had a band of pierced fretwork in the frieze which was backed with coloured silk, in order to let the sound of the bell be heard; similarly pierced panels of fretwork were sometimes let into the sides of the hood in place of the more familiar glass panes. Indeed, as these side frets were even more vulnerable than those in the frieze and were easily damaged when the hood was put on or off, many have been replaced by glass anyway and it is difficult to know whether the clock started life with glazed or pierced side panels. Pierced metal side frets, similar to those found on many bracket clocks, appear on late long-case clocks occasionally.

As it was soon realised that the clock bells were audible enough without pierced frets, some seventeenth-century clocks have 'blind frets' to simulate the real thing. Blind-fret carving on long-case clocks re-appeared towards the end of the eighteenth century, particularly on clocks made in or near Liverpool. On these clocks the blind frets, and other shallow carvings, which were often incongruous but always well executed, were often combined with a form of 'broken pediment' with curved or swan's-neck horns flanking a central ornament. The twin spaces between the horned pediment and the architrave were often filled by shaped glass panels decorated with gold and blue tracery. The pillars of hoods so finished were sometimes of the Gothic cluster form.

For no apparent reason, clocks of this Yorkshire style are usually referred to as 'Chippendale' by the antique trade, although they bear little resemblance to any of the drawings in *The Gentleman and Cabinet Maker's Director*. Indeed, Thomas Chippendale had little influence on clock design, and his drawings for long-cases are mostly over-decorated or of quite impractical form. His drawings did, indirectly, inspire a few very elegant long-case clocks with tapering trunks; and the clock by Andrew Veitch of Haddington in Plate 39 is one of the few which closely resembles one of the simpler *Director* drawings. The spendidly carved free-standing columns of the hood are complemented by two more free-standing pillars which form the main structure of the trunk; these pillars are hollow and the driving weights of the movement rise and fall in them, whilst the pendulum swings in the shallow 'cupboard' forming the back panel. Unlike most 'freak' long-case designs which are encountered, from time to time, this clock is as handsome as it is unusual.

At the turn of the eighteenth century, there was a return to inlaid decoration, very restrained and often including shell and other motifs associated with Sheraton. It is not really correct, though, to refer to such inlaid long-cases as 'Sheraton', as the antique trade generally does, for Thomas Sheraton's first book, *The Cabinet Directory* of 1803, makes his position clear:

> *Clock Case*; a tall piece of furniture, adapted to a pendulum clock, and is always proportioned from the figure and size of the dial, together with the length and motion of the pendulum. But as these pieces are almost obsolete in London I have given no design of any; but intend to do it in my large book to serve my country friends.

The 'large work' referred to was Sheraton's *Cabinet Maker's, Upholsterer's and General Artist's Encyclopaedia* of which only one

FIGURE 24 *A fine 'Yorkshire' Chippendale clock, c* 1790, *showing the local tendency to be over-decorated and too broad in the beam*

volume was published, in 1805, as Thomas Sheraton died before finishing the work. There are some long-case designs shown but they are surprisingly ugly and impractical, and as far as is known no cabinetmaker tried to work to these plans.

At a time when provincial long-case clock design still followed traditional forms, and in spite of Sheraton's view that such clocks were only for country bumpkins, a very refined 'new' style of London long-case emerged about 1810. Figure 25 shows the form of these Regency clocks, which seldom exceeded 6ft 5in in height and were nearly always of finely-figured mahogany veneers, often on a mahogany carcass. The arrangement of the hood door with a circular window in it, surrounded by a narrow gilt brass bezel, derived from a similar arrangement which became fashionable on bracket clocks rather earlier. Both dial and glass were convex, and the former was occasionally of engraved and silvered brass but more often painted. If such a dial plate has had to be re-painted, it is usually done dead white with elongated numerals; but the original form was with numerals no longer than the width of the figure IIII, almost square, on a creamy ivory background which is found to have a hint of green in it on close examination.

Some of these clocks have dead beat escapements and wood-rod pendulums, with elongated cylindrical lead bobs, which give almost as good results as a mercurial pendulum in adapting themselves to changes of temperature. A variant on this type of clock has a pointed-arch hood of Gothic form and the trunk door arched to correspond; restrained brass line inlays emphasise the Gothic line, and rosewood was sometimes used for these very attractive cases.

Clocks of these types, which were made as late as 1840 or thereabouts, are as elegant in a nineteenth-century idiom as those of the first great period; but the same cannot be said of most provincial long-case clocks of the 1810–40 period. Many of them are pleasant enough, though undistinguished; some well-proportioned cases were made in the south of England, and many of the Glasgow and Edinburgh neighbourhood clocks of the time are also housed in handsome cases which avoided the fault, apparent in so many localities, of growing too broad in the beam.

The worst excesses in this direction were perpetrated in Yorkshire and Lancashire; both in the 'rural' clocks in oak, or oak and

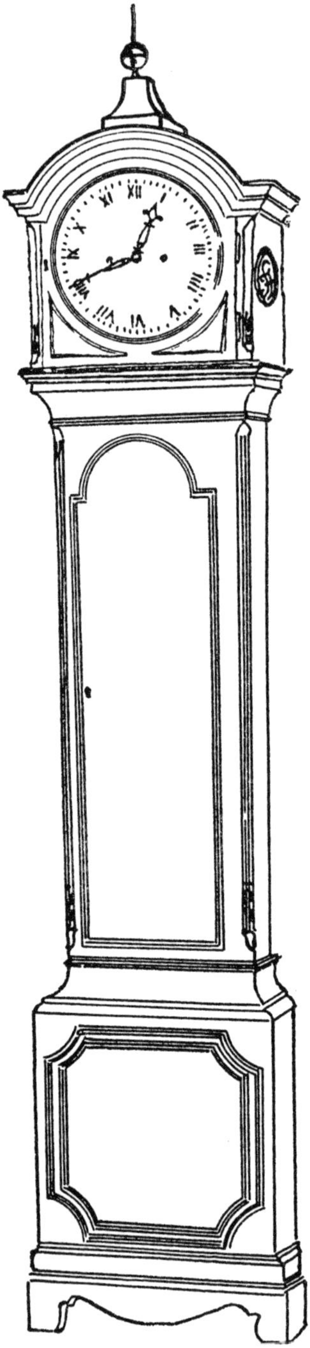

FIGURE 25 *Restrained London-made Regency long-case clock as sold by Dwerrihouse and Carter and other leading makers*

mahogany banded cases, and in the 'town' clocks mostly made in Liverpool or Prescot. The sad thing is that so many of these mahogany cases are of splendid quality, whilst also being of ludicrous proportions. The newly-rich cotton magnates and other industrialists wanted the best and were prepared to pay for it, but they also wanted to see plenty of richly-figured wood for their money. The result was a form of clock which grew ever wider and squatter. Trunks grew to as much as a yard in width with a ludicrous little 9 or 10in door in the middle. A trunk so wide had also to be very short, to keep the overall height of the clock within reasonable bounds, as the width demanded base and hood of correspondingly exaggerated dimensions. It is not unknown for the combined heights of base and hood to be twice or more the length of the trunk.

It is surprising that a nation which could produce the handsome and restrained types of London clock just described could simultaneously produce these dropsical north country monstrosities. The only thing to be said in their favour is that they rob the contemporary French provincial makers, particularly those of the Morbier district, of the distinction of making the ugliest long-case clocks in the world.

Chapter Eleven

From Bracket to Mantel

Many of the changes of appearance in details such as collets and pinions, spandrels and hands, dimensions of minute numerals and disappearance of quarter-hour marks apply equally to spring-driven as to long-case clocks. Because the spring clock is so much more easily portable than the weight-driven machine the variations in shape and size of case are, or can be, much wider; but with certain notable exceptions the English makers did not indulge themselves with the sorts of fanciful designs which were wrought to such perfection in France, Austria and elsewhere.

Where the French might have a clock dial and mechanism, contained in a cylindrical box, perched on the back of a fine bronze elephant, slung below the belly of an ormolu lion or precariously sharing the branches of an implausible gilt-metal tree with some wildy improbable Meissen porcelain flowers, the English makers preferred their clocks to look like clocks. Although many of the French creations were beautiful and superbly made, there is little doubt that there was a tendency for the time-telling function to take second place to the decorative function. C. Clutton summed up this aspect of the matter when he wrote:

> A favourite later type was a chariot or vehicle drawn by some animal, with a clock face in the wheel, where, the hands being indistinguishable from the spokes, it is practically impossible to read the time.

Because the English makers put the emphasis on function first and decoration second, it may seem surprising that the seventeenth-century combination of fusee, verge escapement, light 'bob pendulum' and knife-edge suspension survived in general use until the dawn of the nineteenth century; but there is little doubt that in ordinary hands the combination gave better results than the French makers obtained with the combination they used, from about 1750 onwards, of 'going barrel' (without fusee), anchor escapement and pendulum swinging on a loop of silk or linen thread. Given that each type was in good, clean condition, there might not be much to choose between them for accuracy of timekeeping; but the French spring-driven clock is much less tolerant of being jerked or moved than the English clock, and needs to be carefully set in beat.

By no means all verge escapement bracket clocks had the knife-edge suspension, and a substantial minority, perhaps one in twenty, combined the old escapement with the long-case type suspension by a strip of flexible spring steel. Disregarding those which are conversions, the spring suspension was fitted to allow for a system of regulation known as 'rise-and-fall pendulum adjustment'. This had been devised, in the seventeenth century, by the Rev William Derham as a means of regulating long-case clocks without stopping the pendulum to adjust the usual rating nut below the bob. Derham's arrangement provided a screwed extension to the upper block of the suspension spring, and a suitable threaded anchorage and nut or screw-collar, with which the whole pendulum could be raised or lowered by turning the screw. Below the anchorage, the suspension spring passed between fixed 'chops' or jaws consisting in effect of a brass block with a fine saw-cut in it, just wide enough for the suspension spring to slide up and down without buckling. Therefore, as the upper anchorage block moved up or down, the effective length of the spring, and hence of the pendulum, was varied without stopping the clock.

Although rise-and-fall mechanism is found on a few of the finest seventeenth-century long-case clocks, it was soon seen to be an unnecessary refinement; but similar devices were fitted to some of the finest spring clocks, particularly to those of the smaller sizes on which it is sometimes difficult to get at the bottom of the pendulum rod without taking the clock out of the case. Consequently the rise-and-fall adjustment on bracket clocks was always arranged to be worked from the dial, and the most usual way of doing so was by a subsidiary dial ring, usually numbered in tens from zero to sixty, traversed by an index. In Plate 27, the subsidiary dial on the right-hand side of the small bracket clock by Allam and Clements is for the 'rise-and-fall', flanked on the other side by a similar dial and index for the strike/silent. The actual mechanism usually consisted of a cam on the back of the dial plate, connected to the visible index hand, which gave motion to the rise-and-fall device by means of a rocking lever, pivoted at its centre and mounted on a plate sitting across the top of the movement. The presence of a rise-and-fall always adds to the interest and value of a bracket clock, and it scarcely needs to be said that Victorian repairers often removed the mechanism and threw it in the scrap box together with the repeating work.

Quarter-repeating work became relatively less common as the eighteenth century advanced, and it is rarely found on clocks made after about 1770. Before this time, many more spring clocks were being made each year than had been in the late seventeenth century; and the proportionate numbers of repeaters declined as bracket clocks ceased to be very rare luxuries made regardless of expense for rich customers.

As spring clocks became less rare and expensive, the need to carry one from living-room to bedroom and back each day lessened. Even the lesser gentry and middle class could afford to have more than one; and the simple-hour repeat, which could easily be arranged at practically no cost with any rack-striking mechanism, sufficed for most people. For the richer folk, who might once have bought a quarter-repeating clock, a quarter-repeating watch was doubtless found to be even more useful by the bedside.

Any rack-striking clock can be made to repeat the hours at will by extending the 'warning piece', normally lifted once an hour by a pin in one of the motion wheels, beyond its pivotal point and attaching a fine pull-cord to a hole drilled in the extension. It could happen, particularly if the string was a little too thick to move freely in the hole cut for it in the side of the case, that the warning piece would fail to drop back into place after being pulled to make the mechanism repeat. The clock would then go on striking until it ran down, or the infuriated owner threw it out of the window. On all good-quality clocks this difficulty was avoided by attaching the pull-cord to a separate lever, below the lifting piece, which was snapped back into place by a stiff spring. Even this inoffensive and trouble-free device has often been removed by repairers.

Another refinement which is encountered from time to time, and clearly designed with bedroom use in mind, is the 'silent escapement'. The most usual arrangement comprised a normal verge escapement in which the solid steel pallets were replaced by a 'skeleton' form in which a strand of catgut formed the acting face. The jaws or side members of the skeleton pallets were spring-loaded to keep the catgut at constant tension despite changes of humidity, and the arrangement worked admirably. The silent catgut pallets naturally did not last as long as steel ones; but the rate of wear is slower than might be expected and it was neither difficult nor expensive to replace the catgut. The same principles were applied to making silent anchor or dead-beat escapements in the early nineteenth century.

Quite early in the development of the bracket clock, some of the leading makers tried to combine the trouble-free bob pendulum and knife-edge suspension with a recoil-less escapement. Joseph Knibb devised a mechanism with an anchor-type escapement wheel, acting upon pallets shaped rather like an elongated comma which spanned only two or three tooth-spaces: as a rule, the normal anchor pallets span at least a third of the escape wheel teeth. The pallet faces were so contrived that impulse was given only to the elongated one, the tail of the comma, the other serving only for locking. The result was an escapement with a fairly widely swinging pendulum, which did not require careful levelling, receiving an impulse only in one direction, and acting with very little recoil. Some of Knibb's contemporaries, such as Daniel Quare, Thomas Tompion and Percival Mann, used this escapement with success; but it is very rarely seen and it was very seldom made after 1730. Not, that is, until it was revived towards the end of the nineteenth century in France, in connection with a cheap type of small, mass-produced clock known in the trade as a 'tic-tac'. This name is also given to the Knibb-type of escapement, which is unfortunate, as the little cut-price clocks were not very long-lived, scarcely worth repairing when worn, and some of their ill-repute has been transferred to their seventeenth-century ancestors.

The merit of the Graham escapement for precision work was that it could work with a long, heavy pendulum moving in a very small arc; but it was soon found that it was also possible to alter the impulse angles, so as to make it work a short pendulum through a wide arc, with no loss of its 'dead-beat' function. After about 1760, some of the leading London craftsmen made bracket clocks with modified Graham, or 'half-dead-beat', escapements working with a pendulum arc of about 10° to 15°. Most clocks of this type had spring-suspended pendulums with lenticular bobs weighing roughly twice as much as the pear-shaped bob traditionally used with knife-edge suspension. The 'balloon' clock by John Leroux, *c*1770, in Plate 27 is an exception to this general rule and has a dead-beat escapement with knife-edge suspension. The arrangement combines the best of three worlds, as the clock can be moved with impunity, is tolerant of different levels and performs with a remarkable degree of accuracy for a two hundred years old spring clock. John Leroux was on a par with the Ellicotts, Francis Perigal, William Dutton, Andrew Dickie, Benjamin Lewis Vulliamy and William Allam in the top flight of late eighteenth-century makers. Like George Graham before him, he disdained fancy work and his finely made movements do not have the usual decorative engraving on the back plates.

Another famous maker of dead-beat spring clocks was Weekes of Coventry Street. He was in business from about 1785 to 1820, and the oddest thing about him is that nobody appears to know his first name. He was well known as the proprietor of the much-advertised 'Weekes's Museum', in which for a fee, visitors could see and hear various elaborate clockwork barrel organs and musical automata; but he signed all his known clocks without forename or initial, and a contemporary street directory shows him as '— Weekes, Clock and Watch Maker'.

Weekes made a number of very fine, small clocks, many of which were 'in the French taste', as the language of the time has it, for which he evolved a distinctive form of timepiece movement with centre-seconds hand (often missing), and the dead-beat escapement wheel and pallets centrally mounted outside the back plate. Most of his clocks have enamel dials, on which he sometimes used gold numerals and divisions; and in order to avoid the nuisance of the centre-seconds hand fouling the winding key, some of his small clocks were arranged to be wound from the back, with the pendulum rod looped or cranked to clear the winding square.

Other forms of bracket clocks with dead-beat escapements were in the nature of spring-driven regulators, and mostly date from the early years of the nineteenth century. They were usually fairly large, plainly handsome, with large seconds dials, or sometimes a true regulator-type dial plate, and very heavy half-seconds pendulums.

All these were exceptions to the general rule that the great majority of eighteenth-century bracket clocks had verge escapements and knife-edge suspensions, which differed from their seventeenth-century forebears only in such details as the shape of the pendulum cock feet, the upper potence bracket or the wheel collets. At the turn of the century or a little before, the majority of clocks were made with anchor escapements and spring-suspended pendulums with the largest and heaviest bob-weights which could be accommodated in the space available. Though they are excellent timekeepers, such clocks do not take kindly to being jerked or incautiously moved about and, as always, the older variety did not immediately disappear. On the evidence of an example by John Ham, the verge escapement may have been dead by 1800, but it did not lie down until the reign of William IV.

It is very easy to distinguish between a clock which was originally made with an anchor escapement and one which has been converted. The conversion involved removing the pendulum cock, with its V-notch for the knife-edge and its shaped decorative 'apron', and replacing it with a new one drilled to take the back pivot of the new escapement arbor and with a projecting anchorage for the new spring-suspended pendulum. The old knife-edge pendulum cocks were usually made with prettily curved feet and were engraved to match the back plate; the new pendulum cocks were almost invariably made with rectangular feet, very few were engraved to match their surroundings and the colour of the brass is often significantly different from that of the older parts. The old pallet staff with its attached 'bob pendulum' was removed, together with the top and bottom 'potences' or pivot-brackets, for the verge escapement wheel: removal of these left tell-tale vacant screw holes and 'steady-pin' holes in the back plate. With the departure of the verge escapement wheel, the contrate, or right-angled, wheel which drove it also had to go and new third and escapement wheels, complete with new arbors and pinions, were fitted. These almost always have elongated pinions and clumsy-looking Victorian square-shouldered collets, in place of the eighteenth-century rounded variety.

As explained earlier, the workmen who did these conversions seldom bothered suitably to alter and re-fit the mock pendulum found on so many early bracket clocks. It is true that a mock pendulum attached to an anchor escapement, and therefore moving less than 10°, looks less engaging than one connected to a verge and vigorously wagging a 45° arc; but anything is better than the vacant toothless grin so many Victorian craftsmen, if such they can be called, were content to leave.

A number of vacant pivot and screw holes in the back and front plates of a movement, on the three o'clock side, usually indicate that the clock originally had quarter-repeating work. In the case of very valuable early clocks, restorers of a later date than those who removed the repetition mechanism have sometimes tried to hide the vandalism by filling all the vacant holes with molten brass, after which the plates have been suitably re-engraved and burnished. This may pass muster at first glance, but often leaves a suspiciously large vacant area which may lead one to look further and find small circles of metal of slightly different colour or texture.

Bracket clocks were occasionally fitted with alarum work in addition to, or in place of, the striking mechanism. The alarum mechanism consisted of a small mainspring, usually mounted in a fixed barrel on the back plate, wound up by a pull-cord and pulley similar to that used for repeating work. The alarum spring drove a 'great wheel' which in turn rotated a verge-type escapement wheel, and caused the bell-hammer to vibrate. The device to unlock the alarum consisted of a pivoted lever, one end of which stood in the path of a pin projecting from the edge of the alarum escape wheel and the other end of which rested upon a notched disc behind a visible disc in the centre of the dial plate. This disc rotated with the hour hand but could also be moved in relation to it, using the tail of the hour hand as a pointer to set it in the required position; at the appropriate moment the lever dropped into the notch and released the alarum. The pull-string arrangement was very convenient and it was only necessary to pull the cord before going to bed for the

Page 215 PLATE 32 Edward East, London, long-case clock, narrow chapter ring, finely proportioned simple hands giving great legibility, *c*1665

Page 216 PLATE 33 Benjamin Merriman, London. The chapter ring has grown wider, the minute numerals are no longer inside the circle. It has wider cherub spandrels with decorative engraving between them, ringed winding holes, original slender seconds hand, the hour hand about seventy years later, *c*1700 alarum to ring, as set, the following morning. Plate 25 shows an East Anglian bracket clock, by John Coleman of Ipswich, with such an alarum mechanism. It has no striking train, and the left-hand winding square is a dummy. The very wide chapter ring and the coarse case mouldings are clues to its rustic origin and a date possibly as late as 1740, although the general style of the clock with its 7in square dial and cherub spandrels, is in the manner of the 1690s.

A day-of-the-month indicator is to be found on most bracket clocks, and it was usually placed, as on long-case clocks, just above the numeral VI; but there are many exceptions. As noted earlier, both Joseph and John Knibb favoured a position below the XII; in the clock by Nathaniel Seddon in Plate 26, it shares the arch with the strike/silent dial, and on the Allam and Clements clock in Plate 27 it is most unusually situated just below the centre of the dial plate. Circular, rather than rectangular, calendar 'windows' are occasionally found on early eighteenth-century long-case clocks, and they re-appear on late eighteenth-century bracket clocks. Examples may be seen on the elaborate London clock by Charles Penton, Plate 30, and the elegantly simple provincial clock by Moore in Plate 43, both of which were made about 1785. Both clocks have the serpentine form of minute hand which came into fashion towards the end of the century, in place of the earlier straight 'poker' variety.

A concentric day-of-the-month hand, rotating below the hour hand, is occasionally seen, and the presence of divisions and numerals from 1 to 31, engraved on the inner edge of the chapter ring, often indicate that such a calendar hand *ought* to be there. A subsidiary day-of-the-month dial, usually in the arch, traversed by a suitable hand crops up at various times, and a similar arrangement in the lower half of the main dial became fairly common after 1800.

More elaborate calendar, lunar or astronomical indicators are sometimes seen on bracket clocks, but such complications are relatively less common than on long-case clocks. Very elaborate musical, or music-cum-automaton, clocks were made; those made for export were not infrequently cased in materials (such as Boulle metal marquetry) and styles far more elaborate than those made for the home market. Although they were spring-driven, these elaborate pieces were sometimes very large, and one of the largest, finest and most extravagant creations of this sort, made by James Cox, is to be seen at the Royal Military Academy at Sandhurst. As the music plays, mimic waterfalls flow and fountains play, whilst jewelled and enamelled flowers open and brilliant-set designs in the side panels change in kaleidoscopic fashion. This magnificent folly was 'liberated' from the Imperial Palace in Pekin when the Forbidden City was sacked during the Boxer Rising; that it was officially taken by the army at least saved it from destruction but it is sad that the authorities now responsible for it no longer allow it occasionally to be wound up and seen in action.

Although the need to carry one's bracket clock from room to room lessened, the original intention that it should be a semi-portable piece influenced design in one direction for 150 years. The fact that the clock no longer had to be moved frequently led to an increase in size, particularly after the break-arch dial came into fashion, but carrying handles remained an integral part of the design. On the larger clocks, towards the end of the eighteenth century, they were sometimes fitted at the sides of the case instead of on top, as in Plate 30; and after the traditional bracket clock had been transformed into what may conveniently be called the mantel clock, carrying handles were still fitted. It will be seen from Plate 41 that even the small inlaid mahogany alarum clock by John Ham, which was made about 1830, has vestigial handles which are, incidentally, of 'Brummagem' hollow-ware.

Today, a bracket clock should never be carried by its handles, since the glued joints of the case may not be as reliable as they were two hundred or more years ago, and it is wise always to carry a clock from the base. Some of the best casemakers, it is true, put iron strengthening straps in strategic places but it is best to take no chances.

Black wood, ebony veneer or 'ebonised' fruit wood, remained fashionable for bracket clocks long after it had gone out of use for long cases. The amounts of gilt-metal ornament varied from the severity of the two clocks by Nathaniel (left) and John Seddon in Plate 26, to the lavish opulence of the example by Charles Penton in Plate 30. Of the Seddon clocks, which are separated by about thirty years, the older one above and on the left almost certainly had wooden frets in the arch of the front door, in place of the metal ones now seen, but the metal frets in the John Seddon clock are original. Because of its fragility, wooden fretwork was seldom used after 1750 and most clocks of an earlier period, which may once have had pierced wood panels in the sides of their cases, have had replacements of glass or metal. On post-1750 clocks, metal side frets may be assumed to be original; and the commonest form is the so-called 'fish-scale fret' seen in the mahogany clock by Moore of Ipswich, Plate 43; the elaborately cast and chased 'sun in splendour' frets of the Penton clock are relatively uncommon. Such elaborate mounts as these, incidentally, disprove the contentions of some authorities on antique furniture to the effect that good quality ormolu mounts were not made in England. Ormolu, as a generic term for furniture mounts of cast, chased and gilded brass is an apparently French word which is only used in English. The French refer to ormolu mounts as *bronzes* and to the artisans who made them as *bronziers*.

Towards the end of the eighteenth century, the long-lived popularity of black-and-gold cases began to wane; mahogany took first place but one also sees clock cases of satin wood, rosewood, amboyna and other 'show' woods fashionable under the Regency. One of the last strongholds of the combination of burnished black wood and gilt brass was in the Gothic-style clocks which became fashionable about 1810. A miniature example, less than 7in high, by Comber of Lewes, is seen in Plate 44. The antique trade name for this style is 'lancet clock', and they appear nearly always to have been black and mahogany or rosewood examples are seldom seen.

As stated in Chapter 4, some early bracket clocks were made with domes or upperworks of pierced metal in place of wood. Sometimes these 'basket-tops' became elaborated into 'double-baskets' with superimposed domes, accompanied by a wealth of similarly pierced metal work elsewhere on the case. Seventeenth-century examples have cast and chased 'baskets'; but early eighteenth-century examples are sometimes seen on which the castings are cleverly simulated by thin sheet brass decorated by embossing or *repoussé* work. This technique was employed particularly by Claude (or Claudius) Du Chesne; it is sometimes said that rolled sheet brass was not used before about 1780, but these clocks seem to disprove the general rule. The metal needed to be very thin to be ductile enough for such elaborate high-relief work. Various members of the Du Chesne family worked as clockmakers in London, Paris and Amsterdam, and the 'English' Claudius obviously did a good business in France as many of his clocks, although wholly English in style and mechanism, have the calendar and other markings written in French.

The application of the arched dial to bracket clocks, which became almost universal after about 1715, led to a necessary modification of the case; the old domed or 'caddy' top gave way to new forms of which the commonest was the 'bell-top'. With variations in proportions and types of mouldings the bell-top remained in use for some eighty years and was also to be found on long-case clocks. The supposed resemblance to the cross-sectional shape of a bell is sometimes more fanciful than real. The combination of an old-fashioned square dial (though in the new one-piece style) with a bell-topped case in the clock by Moore, Plate 43, is uncommon and far from unpleasing. By contrast, on the Allam and Clements clock, Plate 27, we see a truncated-arch dial, similar in shape to that of the Margetts regulator, Plate 35, combined with a flattened dome of essentially seventeenth-century form, composed of relatively small areas of black wood sandwiched between plain, heavy mouldings of gilded metal.

There were, indeed, many more variations upon the original theme than can be shown, and the theme was that all the 'traditional' bracket clocks derived, however remotely, from a form suggested in the seventeenth century by the hood and dial portion of the 'traditional' long-case clock. Perhaps the first real break with this tradition, the first 'sport' in the biological sense, came when John Ellicott and his casemaker abandoned the idea of a square, or rectangular-with-arch-dial plate, and made the front of the clock, below the architrave and bell-top, in the form of a plain, square wooden door with a large circular, brass-framed window recessed into it through which a plain circular dial could be seen. Bracket clocks of this type first appeared about 1770, and are occasionally seen with ornamental pierced gilded brass corner ornaments, analogous to the spandrels of traditional dials, mounted on the front door panel. Although they did not oust the traditional type of spring clock, this new form provided a link between the seventeenth-century bracket clock and the nineteenth-century mantel clock.

Once the concept of the plain round dial, of engraved and silvered brass, or enamelled on copper, or painted upon iron, seen through a plain round window set in a narrow gilded or gold-lacquered bezel, was established there was no longer any need for the clock case to be essentially a rectangular box standing on a plinth and surmounted by a domed or pedimented superstructure. The combination of plinth, rectangle and superstructure was never entirely superseded but many alternative forms were developed; such as, for example, shapes based on Gothic or Roman arches. The chief structural change came when the front of the clock ceased to be a hinged wooden door with a fixed circular window in it, and became a fixed wooden front panel with a hinged circular bezel and glass attached to it. Except in the smaller sizes, this was not always an improvement, as the weight of a large cast bezel, and the domed glass it framed, was enough to cause a single, central hinge to sag and pull away from its screwed anchorage in time. As always, the two methods of construction existed side by side. The small travelling clock by McCabe, centrally placed in Plate 27, has its handsome 'snake' bezel and glass fixed in a hinged front, whilst the large mantel clock by Bagshaw, Plate 41, has a hinged bezel in a solid front panel, although both clocks were made about 1825. The example by Bagshaw shows an interesting adaptation of the 'Egyptian taste', promulgated by Thomas Hope, married to some rather incongruous elements which still continue to present a harmonious effect. The reeded 'roof' to the case has made a distant bow towards 'Chinese Chippendale', whilst the gilt metal pineapple finial is an old-established favourite which bears no more relationship to the Egyptian caryatids than to the brass side frets, scarcely visible in the picture, which are pure Regency 'Gothick'.

One of the first results of the break from the traditional shapes of dial was the form of clock seen on the right of Plate 27. The angle at which it was photographed makes this clock, which dates from about 1775, look rather clumsily proportioned. The style was known in the eighteenth century as 'waisted', and by the end of the century the form was greatly simplified with the sides flowing in smooth curves into the base; at the same time, the arcaded moulding disappeared and the plinth assumed a shaped 'apron' with outward curved feet in the Sheraton style. Weekes made some particularly elegant small clocks of this form, some of them in satinwood cases inset with painted cartouches and medallions in the Angelica Kauffman manner. From a fancied resemblance to the shape of a hot-air balloon, with its suspended 'gondola', the antique trade persists in calling these timepieces 'balloon clocks', although the type originated some fifteen years before the Montgolfier brothers sent their first balloon aloft.

Although the case-designer was given more freedom once the shape of a clock was no longer dictated largely by the shape and size of the dial, the functional aspect of English clocks was still paramount. The English makers at the end of the eighteenth century still enjoyed a large export trade to Turkey, Spain, Portugal, Russia and elsewhere; but it is obvious from contemporary descriptions and illustrations that the fashionable English gentry also bought French clocks in fairly large numbers. The decorative nature of the French timepieces filled a want the British makers were reluctant to supply. We see the beginnings of the ossification of English clockmaking which virtually killed the trade by the end of the nineteenth century. Nevertheless, a number of English makers did produce clocks 'in the French taste', particularly during and immediately after the Napoleonic wars had disrupted trade. B. L. Vulliamy had indeed married English movements and dials of superb quality to equally superbly designed and modelled ornamental cases of unglazed Derby porcelain, with ormolu mounts by Boulton, before the end of the eighteenth century; but although they had nothing in common with the traditional wooden-cased clock, these Vulliamy clocks were inescapably English rather than French in style.

From about 1805 onwards, such prominent makers as French of the Royal Exchange, Ogston and Bell, Robert Viner, Desbois and Wheeler of Gray's Inn Passage and others made small mantel clocks in bronze and ormolu cases, as nearly like the contemporary French fashions as they could manage. The resemblance is near enough for many antique trade experts to say that the cases were French, only fitted with movements by the English importers; this view conflicts with the known disruption of trade during the war and with the fact that the chiselling of the ormolu is slightly inferior to the best French work, but the colour of the gilding is superior. England never equalled the best the French *bronziers* could do, and they never quite achieved the colour and silky texture of the best English gilding. Weekes of Coventry Street also made clocks in marble, bronze, ormolu and porcelain cases which, at first glance, would certainly pass as French. Indeed, they have deceived many at second and third glance because in executing these French-style clocks Weekes carried his Gallic masquerade to the point of signing the dials '*Semaine*' instead of 'Weekes'.

The small bronze and ormolu Atlas clock by Desbois and Wheeler in Plate 45 is typical of its kind. Clocks such as these were made, as their French counterparts were, with no glass over the dials and it is consequently rare to find one with undamaged dial and hands. Also, the position of the external pendulum makes it difficult to enclose the back of the case to keep dust out of the movement; there is little doubt that when they were new such clocks as these, both French and English, were supplied with suitable wooden bases and glass domes. It will be seen from the single winding hole in the enamelled dial that this Desbois and Wheeler example is a timepiece with no striking mechanism. This is true of all similar English-made French clocks, if they may be so called; but all, or nearly all, comparable French clocks would have had a striking train. This difference gives a clue to one of the causes of the decline of English clockmaking.

From about 1750 onwards French spring-driven clocks had been made with circular movements, which was logical as they mostly lived behind circular dials, and, as stated earlier, without fusees. By using long, carefully tempered and rather weak mainsprings, which had relatively little variation in the power they delivered over a week's run, in conjunction with light, accurately formed wheels and very highly polished pinions, pivots and anchor escapement pallets, the French makers found they could achieve quite accurate enough timekeeping for ordinary domestic purposes, without the fusee. Their use of the locking-plate striking mechanism and silk-thread suspension until about 1860 made their clocks seem theoretically inferior to the British; but the abolition of the fusees saved so much space that it was possible, by careful attention to detail, to make reliable, long-lived and reasonably accurate eight-day striking movements as small as 2½ in in diameter. Fusee cutting and finishing was an expensive business, as the correct matching of spring to fusee could take a lot of time; by saving this cost, the French makers were able to produce very finely made movements at less cost than those of their British counterparts.

It was these small movements which made it possible for the French *bronziers* to produce the amusing and often beautiful mantel clocks of *c*1780 to 1840. This was a period which saw some remarkably inventive clock-case designs including, for example, a finely modelled bronze negro carrying on his back a gilded bale of cotton containing the clock dial and movement; or a dolphin with a clock embraced by the curve of his tail. The possibilities were almost endless, and all but a tiny minority of these elegant creations had movements which went for eight days or more, and struck the hours and half-hours on small but beautifully-toned bells. The English makers would not give up their fusees and insisted, moreover, on fitting them to the striking side, where they served little purpose, as well as to the going train. Consequently, if they made movements of three to four inches diameter for their French style clocks, they could not put striking mechanism into them for want of space, and the buyers had to be content with a silent timepiece costing as much as a French striking clock.

This insistence of retaining the fusee mechanism may be praised as a manifestation of the English horologists' adherence to the highest possible standards, and simultaneously deplored as a manifestation of the obstinacy which finally did their trade incalculable harm.

Chapter Twelve

Tavern and Travelling Clocks

It must not be supposed that lantern clocks (and their many derivatives), long-case clocks and bracket clocks exhausted the repertoire of the English school of horology. A relatively large number of special clocks for special purposes or particular clients were produced. These ranged from complex astronomical clocks and clock-orrerys, to simple 'journeyman' clocks whose function was to sound a single blow on a bell at regular intervals of thirty seconds, a minute, five minutes etc, so that an astronomer could mark the passage of time during an observation, without removing his eye from his telescope. Clocks built into panelling or pieces of furniture were not uncommon; and a popular conceit in some parts of the country was to have the dial and movement of long-case clock type built into the upper works of a dresser which would then in turn be attached more or less permanently to a kitchen or dining-room wall.

By no means all the most elaborate and ingenious astronomical or special clocks were made in London, as we have seen. Early in the eighteenth century, Edward Cockey (or Cockney, or Cocky, or Cokey) of Warminster made some fine astronomical clocks of monumental proportions. One of these stands in the great hall at Longleat House, in Wiltshire, but Cockey's fame extended beyond the five miles which separate Warminster from Longleat, and a very similar clock was sold to Queen Anne. At opposite ends of England, Thomas Lister of Halifax and Richard Comber of Lewes produced some outstanding clocks; whilst Henry Hindley of York, Moore of Ipswich, Whitehurst of Derby, Reid of Edinburgh, Andrews of Bristol and many more showed that the larger provincial towns could match London standards. Also, many eighteenth-century inventors either started adult life as clockmakers or took up horology 'on the side'. Amongst them was Jethro Tull who produced some fine clocks in Newbury before earning his place in industrial history, by making the first practicable reaping machine.

It is obvious that many makers were still concerned throughout the eighteenth century to find an acceptable alternative to the arrangement of concentric hour and minute hands, which so many of our forbears found incomprehensible. The six-hour dial, popular in Italy in the sixteenth and seventeenth centuries, appears on some English watches of the late seventeenth century and on a few clocks made at various times thereafter. With only six hour-numerals round the dial (usually with Arabic numerals from seven to twelve, superimposed on larger Roman numbers one to six), the spaces between them were large enough for each minute to be marked and each fifth minute to be numbered. The single hand rotated four times in twenty-four hours, and its elongated slender tip could indicate both hours and minutes with tolerable clarity.

An alternative arrangement which crops up from time to time was to have a large counterbalanced minute hand traversing a suitably inscribed and numbered circle, inside which was a disc with the hour numerals marked upon it. The hour disc rotated in the same direction as the minute hand, and at 11/12ths of its speed; consequently the single pointer indicates hours and minutes simultaneously. Ingenious though this system is, it suffers the disadvantage that the user must read the numerals (and the hour numerals are changing position and angle constantly if slowly) instead of merely noting the relative positions of a pair of hands. Once it was realised that the use of two concentric hands makes it unnecessary to read any numerals, it was also realised that the alternative arrangements were inferior. The fact that the numerals are not required has long been recognised and many clock and watch dials are made with 'batons', blobs, dots or other markings in place of numbers. Having recognised the essential simplicity of the two-handed system in this way, modern designers have then, very often, thrown the baby away with the bath-water by making the two-hand dial into a three-handed one. The centre-seconds hand, now common on domestic clocks and almost universal on watches, is often a source of trouble, particularly in the smaller sizes, as it involves extra friction and also makes the dial more difficult to read at a quick glance or in a poor light, as it is easy to mistake the seconds hand for the minute indicator. The current vogue for jumping-numeral timepieces, or 'digital clocks', gets rid of this confusion at the expense of putting the user back to the necessity of reading the numbers.

The growing number of church clocks with concentric minute hands undoubtedly helped to make the new system acceptable; and this also led to the development of what may be called a type of semi-public clock with two hands, which came into being in the first quarter of the eighteenth century. It took the form of a very large weight-driven wall clock which was well established by about 1735, continued with variations for 150 years, and on the way gave birth to a type of spring-driven clock, known in the trade as a 'dial', 'kitchen dial' or 'office dial', which is still being made.

The original form of wall timekeeper is shown in Plate 38. Clocks such as these were used in the kitchens of great houses, the larger inns and posting-houses, in government offices, assembly rooms and other places of public resort. The very large dials, which became in turn hexagonal or octagonal and finally circular, merged into a short trunk, and the distance from the top of the movement, some eight or nine inches above the centre of the dial, to the bottom of the trunk was sufficient to accommodate a seconds pendulum. The movement was weight-driven, but the distance from the great wheel and barrel to the bottom of the trunk only provided a drop of about four feet. Consequently to provide for eight days', or slightly less, duration of going, the train had five wheels instead of the usual four and a correspondingly heavier weight was needed. The lead weight was rectangular, with a chamfered lower edge, and nearly as wide as the trunk. There was usually no room for two such weights and these clocks generally have no striking mechanism; to save metal the plates of the movement, having only five wheels to accommodate, are of truncated triangular shape instead of rectangular. With a well-made mechanism and heavy seconds-beating pendulum, these clocks are accurate timekeepers and robust enough to stand the neglect they usually suffered; but many have been damaged by the gut line breaking; whereupon, unless the clock is almost run down, the heavy driving weight may break through the bottom of the trunk.

Black dials with gold numerals and bold counterbalanced hands of gold-lacquered brass, with gold-on-black japanned decoration on the trunks seem to have been *de rigueur* for these handsome, early 'tavern' clocks: though dark blue or red-japanned examples are sometimes seen. As the century advanced, the dials became relatively smaller and the trunks, in consequence, relatively longer. White-painted dials, nearly always circular, appeared about 1775, but many earlier clocks have been repainted and now appear with white dials and black numerals in place of the more pleasing gold and black. By the last decade of the century, the japanned decoration also disappeared and most of the clocks were given dial surrounds and trunks of figured mahogany; waisted or fiddle pattern trunks are sometimes seen on good-quality specimens. The very large all-wooden dials of the early tavern clocks were too large to be protected by glass; but by the end of the century, metal began to replace wood for the dial plate, and a protective glass in a hinged bezel was fitted. A west country clock of about 1795 in my possession has a 15in circular dial in a wide octagonal bezel which, like the trunk, is of figured mahogany with boxwood stringing.

A clock such as the one just described is the direct ancestor of the Victorian 'railway timekeeper' which was usually heavily cased in oak and had a long enough trunk to manage an eight-day duration, with a four-wheel train. Similar clocks were used in post-offices and other public buildings; they were often fitted with dead-beat escapements and had wood-rod pendulums with long cylindrical lead bobs. It had been found that this combination of wood and lead gave almost as good results in temperature compensation as the more expensive and fragile Graham, Harrison or Ellicott pendulums.

With its genius for inventing implausible names, the antique trade gives the generic name of 'Act of Parliament clock' to these eighteenth-century wall timekeepers, although they were well established some seventy years before the passing of the Act which is supposed to have brought them into being. The Act in question was the Finance Act of 1797 by which William Pitt, providing for the costs of the Napoleonic War, imposed an annual tax on all clocks and watches. The tax ranged from 2s 6d (12½p) on an ordinary house clock to 10s (50p) on a gold watch, and proved so unpopular and uncollectable that it was rescinded after only nine months; the old antique trade explanation that people refused to use or own clocks or watches and tavern and shop-keepers helped them dodge the tax-collector by putting large 'Act of Parliament' clocks in prominent positions cannot be sustained. Specialist dealers sometimes use the name 'tavern clock' which is much more appropriate; but the fancy names, once established, cannot be dislodged.

A smaller type of spring-driven wall clock appeared about 1770 and may have had its roots in the French-type carved and gilded 'cartel' clocks which were occasionally made in England. The simpler, no-nonsense varieties were perfectly plain circular dials, with occasionally a little carving round the bezel, with the eight-day spring movements concealed in a suitable casing behind the overlapping dial. Like the tavern clock proper, early examples are occasionally found with black and gold-figured wooden dials with no protective glass. As the movements, before 1800, almost always have the crown-wheel escapement with short pendulum and knife-edge suspension, there was no need for a trunk; but nineteenth-century examples with anchor escapements were not infrequently made with half-second pendulums which protruded beyond the diameter of the dial. The cases for these, like those of the tavern clocks, would then need a short trunk to accommodate the pendulum and a prettily-shaped and brass-framed window would often be let into this so that the motion of the large burnished pendulum bob could be seen. This type of clock, which was often cased in finely matched and figured mahogany veneer and handsomely proportioned, is known in the trade as a 'drop dial'.

Apart from the early ones with unprotected wooden dials, eighteenth-century spring wall-clocks have nicely engraved and silvered brass dial plates (often now scrubbed down to the raw metal and burnished), well-proportioned hands, turned mahogany bezels and domed glasses. Early in the nineteenth century the engraved and silvered dials were replaced by painted ones, occasionally convex and painted on wood but generally flat and of iron, and the wooden bezels gave way to narrow ones of brass. These changes corresponded with the change from verge to anchor escapement and the 'modern' office clock was born. Variations of the plain circular theme are seen, either in carved cases or with the circular dials set in octagonal mahogany or rosewood boxes with brass inlays in the Regency style.

Even the plainest of early nineteenth-century eight-day dials have that indefinable air of good breeding which stems from good proportions. The relationship between the visible wood framing and the narrow brass bezel, the size and shape of the numerals in relation to the hands and the elegant script of the maker's name and town all add up to a satisfactory whole. Unfortunately the painted dials have often been repainted, and the professional dial writers nearly always use the heavy exaggerated numerals fashionable from 1880 onwards which immediately throws all the other proportions out of gear. A display of twenty or thirty 'office dials' made between 1800 and, say, 1930, would say all that needs to be said about what went wrong with the design of commonplace objects during that time.

English bracket clocks with their knife-edge suspensions were portable in the sense that they could be moved gently from room to room without suffering. All were fitted with some form of hook or hold-fast to keep the pendulum from thrashing to and fro on longer journeys; but there was also a need for truly portable or 'travelling' clocks, with watch-type balance wheel and hairspring control, which could keep going as they were jolted over rough roads in carriages or tossed and rolled on board ship.

With typical ingenuity, Thomas Tompion made a number of small bracket-type clocks, the most splendid being cased in silver, designed for travelling. As the verge watch escapement, with balance-wheel and hairspring, kept time less well than the verge clock escapement with a pendulum, Tompion provided his travelling clocks with both. By moving subsidiary hands, or switches, on the dial plate it was possible to lock the pendulum out of action, and to put the balance-wheel escapement into action when going on a journey; on reaching his destination the user would switch back to pendulum control, for the sake of its steadier timekeeping.

Clocks such as these are very rare, and most travelling clocks of the late seventeenth century onwards were made in the form of very large pair-cased watches about five inches diameter and two or three inches thick. These travelling pieces were usually 'clock watches', that is they had a striking mechanism and sounded the hours on a bell shaped to the back of the inner case, and many had quarter-repeating and alarum work as well. Like the pocket watches on which they were modelled, they required winding daily. When not in use as travelling clocks they served as useful bedroom time-keepers. They are often referred to as 'coach' or 'chaise' clocks, but it is unlikely that they were hung up in the carriage whilst it was on the move. The motion of a wheeled vehicle over eighteenth-century roads would almost certainly have broken the delicate balance staff of such a timekeeper if it were allowed to bang to and fro as it hung from its pendent ring. The portmanteau would have been a safer place, and it seems that most of these watches had padded leather outer cases for use when travelling.

The name 'carriage clock' is also given to them, but this is generally taken to mean the familiar, small, rectangular gilt-metal-and-glass portable clocks made in vast numbers, mostly in France, in the nineteenth and twentieth centuries. These most useful and pleasing clocks were not, like the 'dashboard clocks' of horseless carriages, intended to be used *in* carriages, as the name suggests and as dealers often proclaim; a mistake which arises from a misinterpretation of *pendule à carriage* which was in itself an incorrect English trade term for what the French call a *pendule portatif*, or *pendule de voyage*. These French travelling clocks, to give them a more apt name, range in value from those of Breguet in silver cases with grand-sonnerie quarter strike, quarter-repeat, alarum and calendar work which would command some £15,000 at 1972 values, down to the simplest 'cylinder timepieces' of the lowest grade which were sold retail in England, complete with 'morocco' travelling cases, at the beginning of this century for 25s (£1·25). Even these very humble specimens, cleaned, re-gilded and fitted with new escapements, now fetch as much as £50, which represents a less justifiable inflation than the rise in value of the Breguet specimens.

English makers did make travelling clocks of rather similar type to the French before about 1850; this means they never competed in the mass-produced end of the trade which came later. Amongst the famous London makers of travelling clocks were Richard Jump,

James Ferguson Cole, whose work was influenced by and comparable to Breguet's, Charles Viner and James McCabe. Both the last named made travelling clocks in wooden cases, as well as the more familiar gilt-brass. An example of McCabe's work is shown in Plate 27, and is unusual in having an Egyptian style top to the rosewood case, into which the carrying handle folds out of sight, and in having an eight-day chain-and-fusee striking movement of unusually small size for its period, *c*1825. Most English 'carriage' clocks were timepieces only. The escapement is a lever which, although invented before 1760, only began to be widely used after 1810. As the lever mechanism, unlike the old verge watch escapement, is not always self-starting, Harrison's maintaining power is fitted to prevent the clock stopping whilst it is being wound. The case is 9in high and is clearly intended to stand the battering of long sea voyages (McCabe had extensive trade with Indian Army and civilian officers), as it is exceptionally stoutly made and strengthened with concealed flitch plates; it can be further protected in a very strong, baize-lined outer case of teak.

English travelling clocks of this sort, or in the more usual glazed metal cases, are very rare. A combination of bronze and parcel gilt was sometimes used to good effect, and decorative engraving and 'engine turning', both of the cases and the metal dials, is of very high standard. The mechanism represents the smallest size of eight-day movement (except for special purposes) normally produced by British makers. In common with contemporary small bracket or mantel clocks of the first quality, 'Vaucanson link' steel chains were used on the fusees in place of the familiar catgut. Similar but even smaller chains had been used in watches since the seventeenth century, as it had been discovered that catgut fine enough for the very small fusees and barrels was unreliable.

The 'small' collector or non-specialist antique dealer is not likely to see English travelling clocks of the McCabe, Viner or Cole calibre very often; but they will be familiar with another variety of small English portable timepiece known as a 'sedan-chair clock'. The exact origin and purpose of this type of clock is in dispute; and the only thing which is tolerably certain about them is that they were not used in sedan chairs.

The sedan-chair clock, for such we must unfortunately call it,

Page 233 PLATE 34 Very high standards of engraving and good proportions were not exclusive to expensive eight-day or month clocks, as this typical thirty-hour 'cottage grandfather' shows. The quarter and half hour divisions have at last disappeared, *c*1775

Page 234 PLATE 35 Dial of month regulator long-case clock by George Margetts, made in two pieces with a sunk centre. With the curves reversed the dial shape is reflected in the top of the trunk door. Compare Allam and Clements clock in Plate 27, *c*1780

PLATE 36 An early example of the plain engraved and silvered dial, often miscalled 'steel', on a large mahogany bracket clock with contemporary bracket by Charles Cabrier, *c*1770

had a 3–4in diameter dial, occasionally engraved and silvered but more often enamelled, set in a moulded circular wood frame which was generally ebonised and very similar to contemporary miniature or circular silhouette frames. The periphery of the frame was occasionally enclosed in a brass rim and there was always a nicely shaped brass pendant by which to hang the clock from any convenient nail. A hinged brass bezel and domed glass protected the dial, and a small hinged plate at the back opened to reveal, originally, a verge pocket watch movement which was not infrequently as much as a hundred years older than the rest of the affair. As the watch movement was being asked to carry and rotate a larger and heavier pair of hands than that for which it had been designed, the minute hand had a counterbalancing tail. Because of the twentieth-century objection to winding a clock daily, many of these little timepieces have been fitted with modern eight-day lever movements. A large number of reproductions have also been made in recent years and wily, or perhaps ignorant, dealers are able to say of them, with disarming candour: 'It has a modern movement of course—but then so many of them have been converted you know', which carries the implication that the rest is genuine.

These little timepieces were sometimes originally known as 'bed-post clocks', and they are certainly useful as bedroom or spare-room pieces. As they were small, flat, easily packed in valise or portmanteau and kept going in any position, it is reasonable to suppose they were also widely used as travelling clocks.

Every clock and watchmaker, or retailer, accumulates numbers of old watch movements, from those sold by impoverished owners for the value of the gold or silver cases, or bought in part-exchange for something in a newer fashion; and this accumulation must have accelerated early in the nineteenth century when the old verge watches, though still being made for the lower-priced market, were being at last ousted by those with the new-fangled duplex, detent and lever escapements. On the evidence of dials, hands, numerals and so forth, it seems that the first sedan-chair clocks appeared about 1800, or possibly a little earlier, and that most were made between 1820 and 1845 or a little later. It is fair to assume they were 'invented' by some unnamed genius who wanted to find a use for old but still serviceable movements, and found in them an ideal basis for a cheap but attractive and saleable article. A very similar process of making use of old watches also led to the production at, the same period, of attractive miniature bracket clocks of traditional shapes, in mahogany cases but with circular enamel dials. By about 1825, it seems that the circular sedan-chair clocks had become so popular that they were overtaking the supply of old watch movements, and 'purpose built' movements were made for them. These are known in the trade as 'square verge' movements, and they are similar to the obsolescent verge watch mechanisms except for being a little larger, and rectangular instead of circular.

Some very interesting early watch movements have survived because of these sedan-chair clocks, and they may therefore be forgiven their wholly misleading name, which appears to have been invented about 1890 when the antique trade may have been short on horological knowledge but did not lack for inventiveness over nomenclature. There are several reasons why a sedan-chair is the one place in which a sedan-chair clock is least likely to have been used. By the time they came into use, the sedan-chair was almost extinct. Sedan-chair journeys were generally too short for the occupant to be concerned about the time. Those who let out the public chairs on hire were too poor to equip them with unnecessary clocks; whilst those rich enough to have their own chairs and chairmen were rich enough to wear watches. The most serious objection to the theory that sedan-chair clocks were used in sedan-chairs lies in the fact that there are only two places in such a conveyance where a clock may be safely hung: one of them is on the door panel below the level of the occupant's knees, and the other is on the back panel behind his head.

Chapter Thirteen

Clock Care and Maintenance

THE craft of clock repairing and the specialised business of restoring neglected, broken or converted antique movements can not be dealt with adequately in a single chapter; but some guidance on handling antique clocks and on their care and maintenance may not be out of place.

A convenient starting point is to consider the removal and subsequent 'setting up' of a long-case clock. A start is made by removing the hood. The driving weights are then let down to their full extent, if possible, if the clock is not already run down. The object of 'unwinding' in this way is to avoid the lines jumping off the barrels when the weights are removed, as they can be awkward to coax back into position when the clock is reassembled and wound up. It may not be possible to see or get at the 'clicks' on the great wheels if they have stopped in certain positions, but if they are in favourable positions the procedure is simple. Place the winding key on one of the squares, and turn it slightly in the normal direction of winding; this will take the load off the click which may then be lifted clear of the ratchet by a slender pointed piece of wood, a thin screwdriver blade or other suitable tool; the winding key may then be allowed to turn backwards under the pull of the weight and, if it is of the proper crank-handle variety, it is only necessary to steady it until the weight is right down. If the key is of the bow or flat pattern, it will be necessary to stop after a half-turn, let the click back into engagement with the ratchet and take a fresh grip on the key in order to repeat the process of lifting the click again and allowing another half-turn to unwind.

If it is not possible to let the weights right down, it does not greatly matter, but before removing the weights from the hooked pulleys on which they hang, look to see whether the 'seat-board', to which the movement is attached, is screwed to the two upright members of the case which it straddles. It will usually be found that the screws are missing; therefore before removing the weights (which safely hold the clock in place) and pendulum, it is as well to ask someone to put a hand on the seat-board in case the clock movement and dial shows a tendency to tip forward and fall out of the case as the weights are removed. It is then a simple matter to unhook the weights. The method of removing the pendulum is also self-evident, but needs to be done carefully so as not to buckle or break the suspension spring as it is lowered through the loop of the crutch and manoeuvred out of the case.

With the weights and pendulum out of the way, it is easy to lift the movement, preferably by the seat-board rather than the dial, together with the dangling weight lines and pulleys, out of the case. It is unwise to put the movement down on its back as part of its weight may rest on the projecting loop of the crutch, and this can lead to bent or broken pallet arbor pivots. The easiest way to transport it is to fold pieces of soft paper to slip behind the hands, to keep them from touching the dial, and then to put the movement dial downwards on a soft duster or something similar either in a suitable box or on the floor or boot of a car. A wedge of newspaper should be put between the crutch and the backplate to prevent the former thrashing to and fro, and a similar wedge should be put between the bell and the hammer.

Care must be taken not to damage the pendulum suspension spring during a journey. It should be possible to unscrew the brass block, into which the spring is riveted, from the end of the pendulum, but the screwed joint is often reluctant to move and it is unwise to use force on it. Unless the journey is to be so short that the pendulum can be held out of harm's way, or laid flat, it is as well to remove the rating nut, slip off the bob weight, replace the nut and attach the rod, or at least its upper end and the spring, to a suitable piece of wood. A ruler and a couple of elastic bands, or something similar, does very well.

When setting the empty case, sans movement, dial, weights, pendulum and hood, in place, it is necessary to make sure it stands upright in both planes. There is no need to be mathematically precise about it, and in some old houses it will be found that if the clock is set carefully perpendicular by plumb line or spirit level it will appear to be leaning, because the walls, door frames or ceiling are not true. It will then be necessary to compromise a little. It is essential though that the clock should not lean so far back that the pendulum rubs against the case or so far forward that it brushes the weights, or that they catch on the still at the bottom of the trunk door; small sideways inclinations can be counteracted when 'setting the clock in beat', but they must not be so large that the pendulum bob strikes either side of the case.

It is always desirable, if possible, to screw the case to the wall or at least to ensure that the backboard of the case is in fairly firm contact with the wall for a good part of its length at the upper end. A few long cases, particularly some made in Wales, have the bases so shaped that they fit over the conventional skirting board and allow the upper part of the back to touch the wall, but these are unusual and if the normal base is pushed back to the skirting board there is a gap between most of the clock and the wall. Even with a perfectly flat base standing on a level, hard floor, the inertia of the heavy pendulum will be enough to make the clock rock. It can then happen that this constant if imperceptible movement will set the weights swinging on their lines as they descend and this will accentuate the movement of the case, until the tail wags the dog with sufficient vigour to stop the clock. At best, the timekeeping will be impaired, and there is always the risk of a clock being knocked over if it is not fixed to the wall in some way.

Having set the trunk in place, unravel the lines and pulleys of the movement, drop them over the open top of the case, put the movement into its place approximately and if it shows a tendency to tilt forward ask someone to hold it. Then put the driving weight on the left-hand, or striking side (or the solitary weight of a thirty-hour clock) and lower it gently to the extent of the line. If the line is, as it should be, of a length which just keeps the weight clear of the floor when fully extended, the pull of the weight will be enough to hold the movement safely in place. At this stage slide on the hood, and it will probably be found that the dial does not fit squarely into the frame behind the glass, or that it is so far back that an ugly gap is visible all round the dial, or that it is so far forward that the hood cannot be pushed right home without the glass touching the hands. With only one weight in place it will be possible to place a hand underneath the seat-board and juggle the movement and dial backwards, forwards or sideways until all is snug.

The hood is then removed again and the pendulum carefully manoeuvred into place so that its suspension spring can be guided through the loop of the crutch and then, with one hand holding the rod, the other can be used to coax the spring into its slot in the pendulum cock. Next check that the pendulum swings freely, and does not touch the back or front of the loop of the crutch; this simple fault is responsible for many troubles and can easily be cured by bending the crutch back or forward as necessary. If the case has been set tolerably upright in the fore and aft plane there will be no risk of the pendulum rubbing the back of the case, but if there is any doubt slide a piece of paper behind the bob whilst it is swinging. Finally put the weight on the going train side of the clock, wind it up half a turn and if the pendulum is still swinging the movement should start ticking.

It will almost certainly be 'out of beat', possibly so much so that the clock will not go. A clock out of beat, that is with unequal intervals of time between the ticks, is more apt to stop and less likely to keep good time than one which is properly set. It is also a constant irritant to those with a sensitive ear. Many people try to correct the fault by tilting the clock bodily to one side, perhaps propping up a mantel clock with pennies or putting wedges beneath one side of the seat-board of a long-case clock thereby making the dial sit askew in the opening of the hood. These expedients are not necessary as the iron rod forming the vertical member of the crutch was deliberately left soft so that it may be bent in the middle slightly, in dog-leg fashion, to one side or the other to set the escapement in beat and to counteract any slight inclination of the case. It will probably be necessary to make several attempts, bending the crutch only a small amount each time, until the clock ticks evenly and it must be tested at the smallest possible angle of swing at which it will go, as any tendency to be out of beat is more apparent at small angles than at wider ones.

The same principles apply to putting other types of pendulum clock in beat, and care must always be taken to ensure the pendulum rod does not touch the closed end, or ends, of the loop or fork through which it passes. Verge escapement bracket clocks with knife-edge suspension have no crutches to adjust and they generally have such widely swinging pendulums that they will be in beat without attention. If they sound uneven, however, they may be set in beat by slightly bending the pendulum rod itself. For bracket or mantel clocks with spring-suspended pendulums, the procedure is exactly the same as for a long-case clock, but it will often be necessary to turn a bracket clock hind side before on its shelf or table in order to get at the pendulum. It will then often be found that if it is set in beat in that position, it will be badly out of beat when it is again turned to face the room. This indicates that the shelf or table is not level and a few moments patient trial and error will be needed to achieve the desired result. Some chimneypieces slope downwards from front to back, and this may be enough to cause a large, heavy spring-suspended pendulum to stop by rubbing against the back of the case. It will then be necessary to resort to putting wood or cardboard slips of suitable thickness under the back of the case.

The part of the crutch through which the pendulum rod passes is closed to form a loop on ordinary long-case movements, as this makes a more rigid structure and the pendulum spring can be threaded through from underneath. An open-ended fork had to be used on bracket clocks where no such manoeuvre is possible, and rough handling may result in the two inner faces of the fork being no longer parallel. This should be corrected as it may lead to occasional stoppages which can be difficult to diagnose, as the slightest movement may remove the cause of the trouble, which is that in some positions the crutch binds against the rod. There must always be a small amount of sideways shake or play between pendulum and crutch; but too much leads to loss of impulse.

Many bracket clocks, and the finest regulator type long-case clocks, have crutches with a single stout pin passing through a slot in the pendulum, instead of the more usual fork or loop. It is essential that the pin, fork or loop is in axial alignment with the pallet arbor. Careless bending of the crutch rod to set a clock in beat may bend the operative part to one side, and even though the twist may be so slight as to be imperceptible it will cause the pendulum to wobble. The longer the pendulum, the more pronounced its departure from its proper path, and a bad wobble on a long-case clock can set the bob travelling in a figure-of-eight path which will upset the timekeeping and may stop the clock. If a pendulum still wobbles after the crutch has been carefully checked for axial alignment, it is probable that the suspension spring has been kinked and must be renewed.

To return to the business of setting up a long-case clock, once the beat adjustment is satisfactory, wind up each train fully but very slowly, making sure that the weight lines settle properly in the grooves in barrels. This precaution is not necessary with a thirty-hour clock, and if the lines settle properly during the initial winding, it is reasonably safe to assume they will do so on subsequent occasions. Some fine regulators have ungrooved barrels and these should be watched during the initial winding to see that each turn of line lies snugly against its neighbour, without overlapping.

Finally set the clock to time, making sure in doing so that the calendar ring will move during the night hours, and then set the calendar to the appropriate date. If the clock has a locking-plate striking mechanism, the strike may be out of phase with the hour shown on the dial. Early eight-day clocks with locking-plate mechanism usually have a small lever projecting from the nine o'clock side of the movement; pressing this allows the strike to run without moving the hands, so that the two may be set in phase. Thirty-hour clocks, nearly all of which have locking-plate mechanism, are generally without the little lever, but the count wheel is mounted on the back of the clock movement and the detent which rests upon it may easily be lifted to release the striking train as often as necessary.

Pendulum-controlled wall clocks, lantern clocks, tavern clocks etc may usually be set in beat by tilting them bodily to one side or the other until the ticking is perfectly even. If the clock then looks perceptibly askew it will be necessary to bend the crutch slightly; whether this is necessary or not, once the clock has been set in beat it is as well to anchor it to the wall (apart from its main suspension hook or staple), by any means which ingenuity suggests, in such a way that it cannot be shifted sideways and put out of beat again, when it is wound up or dusted.

The very heavy and often fragile pendulums of regulators may need a second pair of hands to steady them, whilst the suspension spring is manoeuvred into its slot. After about 1780, the best regulators were often made with the pendulum hung from a stout bracket bolted to the back of the case, as this gave a more rigid mounting than the back plate of the movement. Many regulators also have a screw device on the crutch which allows the escapement to be set in beat with greater nicety than by bending the crutch rod. Because regulators were often designed to work with a pendulum arc of only about two degrees on either side of the vertical line, they are particularly sensitive and need to be precisely in beat; and because the pendulum bob may weigh as much as 40lb, it is essential that the case be firmly attached to the wall.

The dead-beat escapement found in most regulators, and in some conventional long-case clocks of the early nineteenth century, is easily damaged and suffers bent escapement wheel teeth if the pendulum is allowed to swing after the clock has run down, or if the driving weight has been removed. No such damage occurs with anchor or crown-wheel escapements and the pendulum of an ordinary long-case clock, for example, may be set swinging before the driving weight is put on; but this must *not* be done with a regulator or other dead-beat clock.

When long-case clocks began to grow taller, early in the eighteenth century, advantage was taken of the extra 'drop' available for the weights to make the great-wheel barrels larger, thereby increasing the distance the weight descends for each revolution but correspondingly increasing the leverage. This meant that rather smaller driving weights could be used to give the same amount of power as before, with less friction and wear on the pivots and bearings of the great-wheel arbors. This theoretical advantage was not followed up in practice as often as it might have been. Throughout the eighteenth century and after, the 'average' eight-day long-case clock had driving weights of about 11lb for the going and striking trains; the quarter-chiming train, if there was one, would have a weight of 15lb or more to drive it. Eleven pounds is generous for the average striking train and positively lavish for the going train, which will comfortably work with a 6 or 7lb pull if it is properly adjusted, cleaned and oiled.

Two things resulted from giving long-case clocks such a generous margin of power. They won their reputation for reliability and for ticking away year after year without attention; but this very characteristic was a disadvantage, as they would continue going after the oil had dried and the whole mechanism was so choked with abrasive dust that pinions, pallets and other vital parts were subjected to unnecessary wear.

The eventual effects of long-continued neglect are familiar to every clock repairer accustomed to antique movements; pivot holes shaped like eggs, pivots worn almost to breaking point and pallet faces scored into the likeness of ploughed fields. A long-case clock which has been fairly regularly cleaned and oiled shows little signs of wear after more than two hundred years use; but once the deterioration starts it progresses quickly, and restoration when it is finally unavoidable becomes difficult and expensive. At all times though, it has been difficult to persuade the public that their clocks need occasional attention, and the sort of man who conscientiously takes his car to the garage for oil changes and routine adjustments every 3,000 miles is apt to become most indignant if his heirloom grandfather clock at last grinds to a halt after a generation without attention. Indignation then turns to fury when he is told that he will have to pay £30 or so for all the damage to be made good, and overlooks the fact that this represents less than a ha'penny a week over the thirty years of neglect.

Ideally a clock should be dismantled, cleaned, overhauled and reassembled every five years or so; and the process of 'cleaning', as a conscientious repairer understands it, includes re-bushing worn pivot holes, restoring by various means the correct working clearances in the escapement and making good other manifestations of 'fair wear and tear'. It often happens that non-specialist antique dealers who occasionally offer antique clocks for sale have them overhauled by semi-professional repairers, possibly members of their own staff with a taste for mechanics, who may leave the movements clean but in poor state. This type of half repair is often done in good faith, and the dealer may genuinely believe that the clock in question is, as he describes it, 'just cleaned and in perfect working order', in spite of which the buyer may find himself faced with a large bill for restoration work in two or three years time.

The buyer who is confronted by an obviously filthy movement

with rusted steel and corroded brass parts knows that he will have to pay for some repair work if he buys the clock, even if he is not able to judge the extent of the work needed to make all good. It is unwise, however, to assume that a brightly burnished movement is necessarily in good order. There are simple tests to gauge the general condition of a clock. Firstly, turn the hands forward through sufficient hours to see whether or not the calendar mechanism works, and in doing so check that each hour is counted properly and that the mechanism does not make much noise. Wear in the rack mechanism often shows itself by miscounting some numbers whilst getting the others right, and amateur or careless repairers often leave the fault uncorrected and hope the buyer will not notice. Early lantern clocks usually make a fair amount of mechanical noise when striking, but long-case, bracket and other eighteenth- or nineteenth-century clocks should be quiet; if they make a great to-do of grinding, whirring and clattering, they are obviously not as they should be.

A more important test concerns the escapement. If an ordinary long-case clock with anchor escapement is going with perceptibly vigorous recoil of the seconds hand at each beat, it is fairly safe to assume the escapement and going train generally are in good heart. If the recoil seems slight or non-existent, stop the clock and move the pendulum very slowly to one side or the other until a solitary tick is heard; release the pendulum and it should swing just far enough in the opposite direction for the movement to start going with the smallest possible 'action'. Keep an eye on it for three or four minutes, and if the escapement is in good order, the pendulum arc will increase so that it swings on each side perceptibly beyond the point at which the tick is heard. Most probably if there is little recoil evident the pendulum arc will not increase, and this will confirm that all is not well.

Where side glasses are fitted it is very often possible to watch the escapement of a bracket clock which has no seconds hand by which the recoil may be observed. Both verge and anchor escapement wheels should be seen to move with perceptible recoil, and the 'dance' of the 'crown wheel' of a verge escapement should be particularly vigorous. As we have seen, the recoiling action of these escapements is theoretically disadvantageous, but it is essential that they should recoil if they are to perform as well as they are able. When worn, both will continue to go with reduced recoil but they will be apt to stop, the wear which has caused the reduced action will accelerate and the timekeeping, particularly of the verge type, will deteriorate. If it is not possible to watch the escapement without removing the clock from its case, the test of the pendulum's ability to increase its angle of swing is again useful. The bob pendulum of a verge-escapement clock, for example, will probably allow the movement to start ticking with a swing of about 15°–20°, and if the arc does not quickly increase to some 30° or more the escapement will be worn or 'out of depth' (or both) and will not give good results. It was the ability of the verge escapement to keep going when worn or out of adjustment that earned the type its reputation for poor timekeeping, and led to so many antique clocks being converted.

After some experience, it will be found possible to judge the action of an escapement by ear, as the principle cause of poor action in an escapement is an increase in 'drop' with a corresponding reduction in impulse. With both the verge and the anchor mechanism, this fault produces a characteristic change in sound which may be compared to the difference between the note of a properly tightened drum and one which is slack. This does not apply so much to the dead-beat escapement, which is any event much less likely to keep going in poor condition than the other types.

A look at the three sketches of an anchor escapement in Figure 14 illustrates the point, and wear in a verge escapement has similar effects. In the first sketch, a tooth of the escapement wheel is just about to be arrested by the 'entry pallet', and when it is so arrested a line projected from the acting face of the 'exit pallet' will be midway between two teeth and this represents the proper amount of 'drop'. When the wheel is unlocked by the retreating movement of the entry pallet, the next-advancing tooth on the other side of the wheel has only to move one half tooth-space before the wheel is again arrested, and when the pendulum reverses its swing the whole of the movement of the tooth face upon the pallet face gives impulse. If the pallet faces become worn into ruts the 'drop' obviously increases, which increases the rate of wear not only on the pallet faces but on the tips of the wheel teeth which may even be bent backwards by the violence of the drop if there is much power available. The ruts or furrows cut in the pallet faces are deepest at the point of impact and grow shallower as they reach the end of each pallet; therefore in following the new path they cut for themselves the wheel teeth do not follow the original curvature, and some of the power which should be devoted to giving impulse is lost with a consequent reduction in pendulum arc. Contributory causes of excessive drop and weak action are that the pivot holes of the pallet and escape wheel arbors become worn so that wheel and anchor move further apart than they should be.

When examining or setting up an antique clock, it is as well to take a look at the catgut lines—the weight lines of a long-case clock or the fusee lines of a spring mechanism. If they feel hard to the touch, or show any sign of fraying or unravelling, it is unwise to wind the clock up. The lines of a long-case clock can be replaced without dismantling the movement, and 'bodgers' often take this short cut. As a general rule, though, worn or frayed lines provide clear evidence that the clock is overdue for a complete overhaul. It is not possible to reeve new lines into a spring-driven clock without dismantling it, and it is most unwise not to fit new lines to such a clock if it has to be taken to pieces for any reason. A broken line may do a great deal of harm as it flies round under the impetus of the spring; it is quite possible for the loose end of the line to wrap itself round one of the arbors and bend it or break the pivots. No such risk exists with a weight-driven clock, but the very heavy weights of a month, three-month or year clock could break through a floor board if a line should break when the clock is fully wound or nearly so.

Repairers often used to fit stranded steel wire cable in place of catgut, particularly in clocks of long duration with very heavy weights or in musical and quarter-chiming bracket clocks with powerful springs. These wire cables were much more reliable than gut, but they were apt to scratch and damage the grooves of fusees and they look rather incongruous. Fortunately there is no longer a need for them as modern technology provides nylon line in various thicknesses which looks very like catgut (which was often dyed green or red), but is very much stronger, unaffected by damp and easier to handle as it does not kink so readily.

The soft rope used in lantern clocks and thirty-hour long-case clocks, which employ the Huyghens endless rope or chain system, can very easily be renewed without dismantling the movement; but again it is fair to say that if the clock has gone long enough to chew through its rope, it is time to have it dismantled and overhauled. Many owners who have to replace a broken clock rope use sash line, or something of the sort, which lacks the softness of proper clock rope and is consequently more apt to slip and jump. The clock-material dealers to be found in the 'Yellow Pages' and other trade directories still supply rope in various thicknesses, and nearly every repairer has his pet method of making the necessary joint. Clock rope consists of so many strands, rather loosely braided round a three-strand core, that it is not easy to make a neatly spliced joint; it is essential that the joint should not be perceptibly thicker than the rest of the rope. If it is, it will tend to ride up the shrouds of the pulley, free of the pointed teeth, then slip for a few inches and pull up with a jerk from the heavy weight which may damage some wheel teeth. A rope should be well rubbed with beeswax before being put to work, as this will lessen its tendency to shed small particles of fluff, which settle in the movement and clog it.

The usual way of regulating a clock, by raising or lowering the bob of the pendulum, needs a little care with a spring suspension, as it is important to hold the bob whilst turning the 'rating nut' so that there is no tendency to twist the rod, as this might damage the spring. With knife-edge suspension, the whole vase-shaped bob is screwed up or down and this needs to be very cautiously done if it is stiff to turn. Clocks with a 'rise and fall' regulator on the dial generally show graduations from one to sixty, each being supposed to represent one minute's change of rate; but they are often more or less arbitrary and it becomes a matter of trial and error.

The reader who has patiently come so far will have realised that lubrication posed serious problems for the clockmakers and repairers of the past, and in our own time many clocks are needlessly damaged by working without oil, and many more suffer from having too much of the wrong sort of oil, in the wrong places.

Mineral oils being unknown in the seventeenth and eighteenth centuries, our forbears had the choice between vegetable and animal oils. Nearly all the common vegetable oils, such as rape, colza, linseed, castor or olive, become thick with a relatively small drop in temperature and fairly quickly evaporate into a sticky gum; animal fat derivatives, such as tallow, were difficult to liquefy enough for use in small mechanisms, so the choice was narrowed to fish oils. An oil refined from porpoise blubber gave good results, but most clock and watch lubricants were derived from whale oil (or train oil as our ancestors so misleadingly called it by faulty transcription of the Old Dutch *traen*, meaning a tear drop, because one of the valuable properties of whale oil is that its surface tension is such that it forms globules round a projecting pivot, or in a small depression, and consequently it stays where it is put). It was not until the nineteenth century that improvements in refining, liquefying and 'washing' oils produced a really fluid clock and watch lubricant which neither evaporated in a few months nor fluctuated greatly in its viscosity with the sorts of temperature changes to which a domestic clock is likely to be subjected.

'Straight' mineral oils are unsuitable for clockwork, as their surface tension is less than that of fish oils and they soon creep away from pivot holes and other places where they are needed. Also, in the ordinary light mineral oils, such as those sold for bicycles or sewing machines, a certain amount of fatty acid is present and this sets up electrolytic corrosion between brass and steel. Special mineral oils have been evolved for watch-factory use which do not cause corrosion and it is possible to prevent 'creep' by coating the surfaces to be oiled with a special inhibitor, but these are not really applicable to the ordinary antique clock. Unfortunately, as most houseowners have light mineral oils available, amateur efforts at clock oiling usually do more harm than good; particularly as the potentially corrosive oil is lavishly applied to surfaces which the professional leaves dry.

The wheel teeth and pinion leaves of clockwork should ideally follow cycloidal curves and therefore engage one another with no sliding friction; because the total forces are small the load on the teeth is light and the rolling friction between mating faces needs no lubricant. In practice, particularly in early clocks, the curvature of the teeth is not cycloidal, but the sliding friction which arises is so slight and the rubbing speeds so low that oil is still not needed on the wheel teeth. Indeed, it is positively harmful. In the lighter parts of the mechanism, at the escapement-wheel pinion or the final wheels of the striking train, surface tension of the oil may set up more drag than the friction it is supposed to relieve, and as few movements but those of observatory regulators are in hermetically sealed and evacuated cases dust settles on the surfaces made sticky by oil and is transformed into a grinding paste. The handyman who puts mineral oil all over the wheels and pinions of a clock quite often fails to reach parts which do need oil. Nevertheless this 'home treatment' not infrequently results in allowing a clock, which has stopped for want of oil in some vital part, to start going again and this convinces the operator that he has all the skill of Tompion or Vulliamy at his finger ends and that the professional who proposed to charge £5 to clean the clock is a villain. When the clock stops again a few months later it is all too often left untouched for some years, at the end of which time it will be badly corroded. Many antique clocks have been damaged if not ruined by such treatment.

Oil is needed in a clock principally at the pivots, and with a few exceptions each pivot is surrounded by a saucer-shaped depression known as an oil sink. One small drop in each sink is enough, and the smaller the sink the smaller the drop must be, otherwise the sink will overflow and the oil will quickly drain away. A drop of oil is also needed on the pillars on which the rollers of the calendar ring revolve; at the faces of the crutch where the pendulum rod touches it; on the pulleys of a weight-driven clock; and at the various parts of the striking work where there is sliding friction: for example, the tail of the hammer needs a touch of oil at the point where it comes into contact with the lifting pins in the periphery of the appropriate wheel of the striking train. The only parts of a clock which need oiling lavishly are the mainsprings, and it is not improper to put as much as an egg-spoonful of oil on the coils of a spring after it has been cleaned; but this is one of the points where a 'modern' lubricant is applicable and good results are obtained by smearing the coils of each spring with a light grease containing molybdenum disulphide. Obviously, this can only be done when the spring has been removed from its barrel and this is not a job to be undertaken lightly by an amateur.

The most vital points of sliding friction in a clock are between the escape wheel teeth and the pallets. As the loads are small and it is

Page 251 PLATE 37 A painted iron dial, the numerals and divisions repainted, showing the late-type calendar disc and a rocking ship automaton in the arch. Sold and signed Shortman of Newnham but made by Walker, Birmingham, *c*1830

Page 252 Plate 38 Early mural clock of the type mis-called 'Act of Parliament'. Made by Robert Berry of Hitchin, *c*1740

Plate 39 Unusual form of long-case clock based on a drawing in Chippendale's *Director*. The movement by Andrew Veitch of Haddington. The finely carved free-standing columns of the trunk are hollow and the driving weights pass inside them, *c*1775

impossible to exclude dust, many professionals advocate leaving the pallets dry in order to reduce wear. With jewelled pallets, as in good-quality regulators, or very highly polished ones of steel too hard to mark with a file, this advice is sound, but the unjewelled pallets of most antique domestic clocks are seldom 'glass hard' and work better for being lightly oiled. Provided the clock is not allowed to go on working when the 'drop' has become excessive because of wear at the pivots, the rate of wear is not excessive on the evidence of many clocks still working with original pallets after a couple of centuries. Regular cleaning and regular replenishment of the essential minute quantities of oil are needed to keep wear to a minimum.

The professional repairer having cleaned and burnished all the parts of a clock, re-bushed pivot holes if necessary and made good wear and tear by suitable means, then re-assembles the main trains and tests the action of the strike before oiling the pivot holes and other parts on the front plate. Then comes the time to put on the motion work and other parts attached to the front plate (many of which obscure the oil sinks), the dial and hands. All the oil sinks on the back plate are then filled, and finally the escapement parts are put in, oiled and tested. The oiling is done by putting a large drop of oil in a suitable 'oiling cup', which is generally a little agate saucer set in a suitable boxwood base with a cover. From the cup small drops of oil are carried to vital parts by means of an 'oiler', and a clockmaker's oiler is nothing more elaborate than two or three inches of burnished steel wire, flattened at one end and with the other set into a wood, ivory or plastic handle. With such an oiler the lubricant may be picked up in very small drops and put exactly where it is wanted, and all the advice in books of home hints about using a feather to oil a clock is nonsense.

'A touch of sweet oil and a feather', as the vulgar old music hall song had it, may be fine for oiling a lock but is all wrong for a clock. The mistake appears to have originated in the first edition of *Enquire Within upon Everything*, published about 1830 and has been solemnly repeated ever since. After nearly 150 years, it seems as though the feather may be going out of fashion as a clock oiler, and a recent article in a national Sunday newspaper advocated using a hypodermic syringe. The lubricants advocated by the self-styled authorities are often as bizarre as the implements they favour. Olive oil diluted with paraffin is often praised, and all that can be said of this lethal compound is that the low surface tension of the paraffin will spread the olive oil far and wide to do its worst. I have recently seen a fine seventeenth-century clock so lavishly oiled with this compound that the oil had crept along the centre arbors and spread a track of verdigrised corrosion down the gilded dial plate. It is one of the minor mysteries of life that the writers of home hints have apparently never asked a clock repairer for advice. Had they done so they would presumably have been astonished to learn that the best oil for a clock is clock oil, and the best implement with which to apply it is a clock oiler.

The antique collector or non-specialist dealer, particularly the former, who begins to take an interest in clocks will soon feel the need to tackle simple repairs. *Britten's Clock and Watch Maker's Handbook* is still amongst the best and most helpful of books, although it was written some eighty years ago. Even if the collector does not feel confident enough in his skill to go beyond dismantling, cleaning and re-assembling, he will be able to keep clocks in good order once major defects have been remedied; but most of those who feel able to go so far soon want to go further and to acquire the tools and the skill needed to undertake such work as re-facing and re-setting escapements, bushing worn pivot holes and making replacements for minor components like worn winding clicks or broken rack springs. Although they are being squeezed out of business by rising rents, the clock-material suppliers and specialist craftsmen of Clerkenwell and Birmingham still stock many replacement parts 'in the rough' for English long-case and bracket clocks.

In doing the simpler sorts of care and maintenance work the amateur will soon learn to recognise the presence of anachronisms and will become familiar with the evidences of past 'bodging'. Very few antique clocks have escaped the heavy hand of the bodger, amateur or professional, evident in punch and hammer marks round pivot holes as a poor substitute for re-bushing, or clumsy attempts to adjust the depth of an escapement by bending the pallet arbor or by enlarging the holes in the pendulum cock and removing the steady pins in order to set the cock lower on the plate than the maker intended. Steady pins are small pegs let into the cocks or brackets of escapements and parts of the striking and motion work, with corresponding holes drilled in the plates, so that the proper location of the part is independent of the screw which anchors it. Bodging escapements and other parts by such means is only a temporary expedient; sooner or later the work will have to be done properly and then the extra cost of removing the traces of the bodging (as far as possible) will also be incurred. It is almost impossible to remove all traces of punching round pivot holes and the injudicious use of soft solder also leaves its mark by causing a spongy corrosion in brass which makes it almost impossible subsequently to braze or hard solder the part. Soft-soldered joints are used for some parts of clock movements; but as a means of mending broken parts, they are generally undesirable.

The moral of all this is that the collector, even on the most modest scale, who does not feel inclined to become his own repairer, must employ a specialist. Great Britain is still relatively rich in craftsmen who could look Tompion or Knibb between the eyes without blinking and who thoroughly understand the proper repair and restoration of antique clocks. Their work is not cheap, and some of them actually command as much as the garage mechanic who screws spare parts into mass-produced motor cars, but in the long run the man who really knows his job and charges a fair price for his skill is cheaper than the incompetent. Without wishing to denigrate the ordinary High Street retailers' repair men, they do not usually have much experience with antique clocks. They may be admirably skilled in many ways but they often lack the historical knowledge to make replacements of worn, broken or missing parts.

Above all, the small collector or non-specialist dealer should beware of the sort of 'expert' who undertakes to tinker-up a clock on the owner's premises. A clock may stop because of some simple fault which skilled men may diagnose and rectify on the spot, but as a general rule if a clock stops after going well for some years it cannot be adequately dealt with unless it is completely dismantled, and this necessitates removal to the workshop. The do-it-on-the-spot tinkerers are still active, and long-case clocks in the past were frequent victims of itinerant repairers who went from village to village. A favourite trick was to restore life to a clock which had stopped because of general wear and tear by oiling it (on top of the dirt and dried oil in the pivot holes) and adding to the driving weight. This certainly set the clock going again but equally certainly accelerated the rate of wear. The process is comparable with putting a more powerful engine in a car as a cure for worn hub bearings which allow the brakes to rub; but it is still practised.

This is no place for detailed instructions on clock repairing, but one warning must be given to the owner who decides to take a clock to pieces. As soon as a weight-driven movement has had the weights removed it may be safely dismantled, but many a spring-driven clock, and no small number of fingers, have been badly damaged by incautious operators taking the main plates apart without first releasing the power.

It is quite easy to 'let down' the mainsprings of a French clock, or other type, with the usual 'going barrels' once the dial has been removed as the clicks, which are pivoted on the front plate, are furnished with elongated tails by which they may be held clear of the ratchet wheels, once the pressure has been taken off by slightly turning the winding key in the usual direction; with the click lifted clear of the ratchet teeth, the key may then be allowed to turn back for a half revolution, the click dropped back into place, a fresh hold taken on the key and the process repeated until the power is all released.

English spring clocks with fusees are less easily dealt with. The visible ratchets and clicks on the front plate are in line with the mainspring barrels and look similar to those of going-barrel clocks, but the power is usually greater and the squares much shorter as they do not have to protrude through the dial. These ratchets and squares are provided for the initial 'setting up' of the springs after assembling the clock, and it is unwise to try to let down a fully-wound spring by using them, as the squares are not long enough to hold safely with a key or hand vice when the springs are fully wound or nearly so. Nor is it often possible to let down the power by means of the ratchet and click of each fusee, as these are only accessible on the early type shown in Figure 3 (also found on some country-made clocks of a later date). Most eighteenth- and nineteenth-century fusees were made with the ratchet and click mechanism totally invisible, until the fusee was dismantled. On the best quality clocks, a small hole will be found between one pair of teeth on each great wheel, and a fine hard steel wire passed through this hole will come to rest on the tail of the click. By turning the key slightly clockwise to relieve the pressure, the wire may be pushed farther to lift the click clear of the ratchet, and the unwinding process can be gone through as described above. It is by no means certain, however, that the wheels will have stopped in positions that make these holes accessible and relatively few clocks have them. The safest course is to let the trains run. The strike and quarter-chime trains (if there is one) can be set running by wedging up the rack hooks and it is also as well to hold or wedge the hammers as far back as they will go. The fly will prevent a striking or chiming train running too quickly. To let the going train run, it is necessary to remove the escapement, and as soon as the pallets are out the train will start to run at ever-increasing speed. A finger or piece of soft 'peg wood' should be held gently on the arbor of the escapement wheel to keep the speed within reasonable bounds. When the trains have stopped running, the residual power can be taken off by holding the setting-up squares, generally too wide for a key, with a small hand vice or mole wrench, and releasing the screw-down clicks. When all the power is off, the fusee lines will slacken and it will be safe to remove the pins and take the main plates apart.

One other warning about spring-driven striking clocks must be given, which is that if they have to be packed for travelling steps must be taken to ensure they are kept upright, or nearly so, unless they have been allowed to run down completely beforehand. The reason is that the rack hook and warning piece of the striking train are gravity-operated, except in clocks specifically designed as travelling pieces, so that if the clock is placed in a horizontal position and moved about, the striking train will be intermittently released as the rack hook thrashes to and fro. Bracket or mantel clocks with heavy, spring-suspended pendulums should have these packed separately and not merely wrapped up and put inside the clock case.

To return to everyday matters, when turning the minute hand of a clock to set it to time, always do so by putting a finger near the root of the hand rather than the tip. If there should be any obstruction, the hand is much less likely to be bent or broken when it is moved from the root and there will be no risk of scratching the dial plate with the finger nail which so often happens if the clock hand is moved by its tip. Some fine-quality clocks of the early nineteenth century had particularly delicate hands, of a pattern originated by B. L. Vulliamy, with voided spade or heart-shaped tips; these are very fragile and need particularly careful handling. The McCabe clock in Plate 27 has hands of this type.

The hands of single-hand clocks are usually very stiff to turn; they always have, or should have, a counterbalancing tail and the safest way to turn such a hand is with one finger on the shaft, well clear of the tip, and the thumb on the tail. Never try to move such a hand by the tip.

The hands of a timepiece without striking work may be turned back with impunity, but it is unwise to turn the hand of a striking clock back past the numeral twelve; nor should the hand be turned back when it is within fifteen minutes before the hour, but it may safely be reversed slightly at other points in its journey. The minute hand of a quarter-chiming clock may be turned back for a space of about five minutes when it is more or less midway between quarters, but it is unwise to turn farther. If such a clock is more than a few minutes fast, the tedium of having to turn it forward through nearly twelve hours is best avoided by stopping it for a while. Similarly, when the clocks have to be set back an hour to change from summer to winter time, it is most easily done by stopping them; this is particularly applicable to those clocks with a day-of-the-month indicator.

It is true that English rack-striking clocks (unlike most of those developed in other countries) were provided with a safety device designed to allow the hands to be turned back without damaging the mechanism. This safety action was most ingenious. The pin on the intermediate wheel of the motion work which releases the strike does so by pressing aside a vertical 'tail' attached to the horizontal 'warning piece' which, as it rises, pushed up the rack hook. This tail on which the lifting pin acts was of brass, deliberately made thin just below the point where it was joined to the steel warning piece, and chamfered at its lower end in such a way that if the hands were turned back and the lifting pin approached it from the wrong direction, the flexible tail would merely be harmlessly flipped forwards as the pin was guided under the chamfered edge. As they were so thin, and sometimes became brittle with age, these flexible pieces were often broken during some repair process, whereupon many ignorant repairers failed to understand why they were made so flexible and made up new ones of much more solid construction. Whilst congratulating themselves on doing a nice honest job, they did not realise they had spoilt an ingenious safety device, as too brusque a reversal of the hands would now either break off the lifting pin or, worse, break a tooth out of one of the motion wheels. It is always as well to assume the safety action is not to be relied upon.

As described in Chapter 5, the ordinary day-of-the-month indicator is moved forwards once in twenty-four hours and is free of the device which moves it for about twenty hours; in those months with fewer than thirty-one days it has to be set forward by hand. This should be done from behind the dial and is a simple matter with a long-case clock once the hood has been removed; except on the smallest bracket clock, there is usually room to pass a finger between the movement and the side of the case in order to turn the calendar ring. Clocks are often found with the calendar rings badly scratched by attempts to prod them round from the front with a penknife or some other pointed implement.

It is often desired to prevent a clock from striking. Where the strike is controlled by the rack type of mechanism and fitted with a strike/silent switch there is obviously no difficulty. Nor is there any difficulty with a locking-plate mechanism, as the striking train may be allowed to run down or the appropriate driving weight may be removed from a long-case or other weight-driven clock. Neither expedient is suitable for a lantern or thirty-hour long-case, with a single weight driving both trains; but it is easy to make the striking train inoperative by placing a suitable wedge of folded paper to prevent the 'fly' turning. No harm will be done to the going train with the strike put out of action, and when the clock is required to strike again the business of reconciling the locking plate with the dial is easy (see page 242). Difficulty can arise, however, with those rack-striking clocks which are not fitted with a strike/silent control.

As will be seen by looking again at Figure 18, the number of blows counted by the rack mechanism depends on the distance the tail of the rack falls on the 'snail', which is mounted upon or moved by the hour wheel. When the rack is released in preparation for striking twelve, as shown in the drawing, the tail sits in the deepest step of the snail, and if for any reason the clock should fail to strike that number (either because the train has been allowed to run down deliberately, or because of some fault) the advance of the snail will bring the edge of the high step, up to the one o'clock position, firmly against the stout peg projecting from the hind side of the rack tail. This contact takes place between twenty and forty minutes after twelve on those clocks with the snail mounted directly upon the hour wheel, and shortly before one when it is mounted on a 'star wheel and flirt' device. So that the clock shall not be stopped by the edge of the snail jamming against the rack tail, the latter was made resilient and the leading edge of the high step of the snail was chamfered to provide a safety action, similar to that of the letting-off lever, which allows the rack tail to be pushed harmlessly forwards out of the way.

Unfortunately, as with the other safety device, careless repairers have often replaced the resilient rack tails with stout ones which will not budge. Therefore the clock stops at some time between about 12.20 and 12.55, and if the owner incautiously pushes the minute hand forward the resistance may be enough to break the hand or, worse, to rip one or more teeth out of the hour wheel. If a rack-striking clock is found to have stopped at any point in this suspicious period therefore, do not put much effort into pushing the minute hand forward; if it is reluctant to move, turn it slightly back and investigate to see whether the striking train has run down or failed to operate.

Even if this safety device has not been tampered with and works as it should, it is unwise to put the strike out of action merely by letting it run down or by wedging the fly, as the effort of pushing the rack tail aside will put an extra load on the going train. In default of a strike/silent control, therefore, it is desirable to shut off the striking by tying or wedging the rack so that it cannot move from the 'neutral' position. A suitable thickness of indiarubber or cork wedged between the rack and the front plate answers the purpose very well.

Many Dutch and Austrian clocks with rack-striking mechanism

closely follow the English pattern, and were fitted with similar safety action to the rack tail; so, too, were many provincial French clocks, particularly those of the Neuchâtel district which have vertical gravity-operated racks and the maddening habit of striking each hour twice over with the object of letting an awakened sleeper be woken enough to count the second performance if he misses the first. The typical Paris, or provincial city, movements still used locking-plate striking mechanism until about 1850 and were thereafter fitted with a type of rack mechanism with no safety action. As the wheelwork of these French clocks was finely made and very delicate, many have suffered broken hour-wheel teeth merely because of the failure to strike twelve, with the consequent jamming already described.

As we have seen, a mantelpiece is not a good place for a mantel clock, particularly if a coal or gas fire burns beneath it. Modern electric storage heaters offer a tempting flat surface which should also be avoided if possible. Dust should be excluded, although it must be admitted that lantern clocks cannot be protected except by enclosing them in glazed cases which spoil their appearance, and many long-case clocks are so open to the atmosphere that a couple of years after cleaning the machinery resembles a gravel-crusher rather than a timepiece. Much can be done to improve them, as the usual fault is that age and warping have produced cracks in the thin panels and joints in the upper structure of the hood behind the façade, and these may easily be sealed by glueing a layer of thin canvas or other light fabric over them. Similarly the gap between hood and backboard will usually have become much wider than the cabinetmaker intended, and strips of self-adhesive spongy 'draught excluder' will be found useful to keep dirt and spiders at bay. The back-board of most long-case clocks will be pierced by numerous holes where screws have been inserted to anchor the case to the wall, and all of these but the one intended to be used should be stopped with plastic wood or putty.

A spring clock with verge escapement and knife-edge suspension may be gently moved from place to place, during spring-cleaning for example, with impunity; but an anchor-escapement clock with spring suspension and the usual heavy pendulum can easily be damaged by quite slight jerks. The safe way to carry such a clock is to tilt it slowly forwards until it stops ticking and then to carry it in the tilted position so that the heavy pendulum rests on the back-plate of the movement and cannot thrash to and fro. Set the clock down, still tilted forward and very slowly restore it to a perpendicular position. To start it going again, tilt the case slowly sideways for a few degrees and let it drop smartly back to the horizontal position, which should be enough to set the pendulum swinging without having to open the case.

As we do not live in an ideal world, the ideal of having clocks dismantled, cleaned and overhauled at intervals of not more than five years is largely unattainable. As an acceptable compromise, it will be found that most ordinary clocks, apart from fine regulators and very delicate small pieces, survive remarkably well if they are properly re-oiled every two or three years and most collectors are able to do this. Oiling in this sense entails taking the movement out of the case, removing the hands and dial and dismantling most of the 'under-dial work' in order to get at the pivot holes in the front plate. It is particularly important to remove all the motion work to expose the oil sink surrounding the long centre arbor. The professional repairer will object to the idea of putting new oil on top of the drying remains of old, but provided the movement is reasonably free from dust, and modern oils are used, the results are tolerable and certainly better than leaving the clock to run dry.

The owner who is confident enough to go so far will also feel confident enough to remove the escapement, polish the pallets and clean out the pivot holes from which he has removed the pallet arbor with 'peg wood'; which is a stick of soft dogwood (sold by material dealers) cut to a suitable point and twirled around each pivot hole until the freshly cut surface of the wood comes out as clean as it goes in. With an anchor escapement it is not possible to do more than take out the pallet arbor without going the whole hog and dismantling the main plates, but the normal construction of a verge-escapement bracket clock allows the escapement wheel itself, together with its two supporting pivot-brackets or 'potences', to be removed without disturbing the rest of the movement. Before removing the pallets of any spring clock make sure the train is prevented from running; an easy way to do so is by hooking a piece of soft wire round the rim of the third wheel (the contrate wheel of a verge clock) and attaching the other end to one of the pillars of the movement.

Most verge-escapement clocks have a means of adjusting the 'depth' of the escapement, which usually takes the form of a square-headed screw in the underside of the lower potence on the hardened, flat end of which the bottom pivot of the escapement wheel turns. Turning this screw slightly clockwise moves the escapement wheel closer to the pallet arbor and small amounts of wear on wheel teeth or pallet faces may be counteracted. With all the parts of a verge escapement removed, it is possible to 'peg out' and re-oil the pivot holes in both potences and to clean and polish the knife-edges thoroughly; but if the pivot holes have worn enough to allow noticeable side shake to the escapement wheel arbor, or if there is more 'drop' on one pallet than the other, it is time to have the whole clock dismantled and thoroughly overhauled.

Perhaps this chapter should end with a cautionary reminiscence. I was once called to attend a much-prized sick 'grandfather' which had 'suddenly stopped', the indignant owner could not think why, after 'keeping *perfect* time' for more than twenty years. The immediate cause of the stoppage was that the weight line of the going train had finally given up the unequal struggle and snapped; retrieving the weight disclosed that the bottom of the case contained a nest of mice, whilst a large colony of spiders had spun their webs over and round the movement and a pet parrot apparently liked to perch on top of the hood which was, alas, far from parrot-proof. The indignation of the owner turned to fury when he was told the clock must be removed for a complete overhaul, and he was not amused to be asked to read the old inscription, almost indecipherable for dirt and corrosion, in the arch of the dial: 'Keep mee clean and use mee well, And I will strive the truth to tell.'

Chapter Fourteen

Restoration and Faking

THE dividing line between restoration and faking is often so thin as to be invisible, and what is known and accepted as a piece of legitimate repair work at the time it is done, may pass for original work a few years later. Whether it then steps over the line and qualifies as a piece of faking is open to question. The point may be illustrated by describing the work done on a very nice seventeenth-century long-case clock by Charles Gretton which passed through my hands some years ago, and which had lost the original base to its slender 'oyster veneered' walnut case. It often happens that long-case clocks suffered damage or rot in their lower quarters, as they are apt to be knocked by brooms or scrubbing brushes or left damp from too enthusiastic swilling of stone floors. It is not unusual, therefore, particularly with early examples, to find the plinth, or sub-base, missing, or obviously replaced with one of different colour or style, or the base itself looking out of proportion because its lower edge has been cut off and the plinth, or a replacement, put back. The entire base and plinth of this Gretton clock from the lower edge of the trunk downwards was a replacement.

With that total disregard for congruity which nineteenth-century repairers, and those who paid them, so often displayed, this elegant walnut clock of about 1685 sported a beautifully made *mahogany*-veneered base which was probably made about 1820 in a late Sheraton or Regency style, complete with an inlaid oval cartouche set with the typical shell motif and a shaped 'apron' base with out-turned feet. The effect was rather that of an admiral in full-dress uniform wearing army boots and leggings; something had to be done and the case was sent to a sympathetic cabinetmaker-restorer who had a carefully hoarded stock of old veneers. He made for it a new base and plinth in the correct style, using the proper methods and materials of the period and laboriously coloured and polished the new parts to match the old (and those who say that only time can produce the characteristic patina on old furniture do not comprehend the skill of the expert restorer). The man to whom the clock was sold knew that the base was a replica, indeed he had seen it before it went to the cabinetmaker, but it is doubtful now whether the most expert eye could detect the new work and any dealer through whose hands it may pass in the future will be able to describe it as genuine in good faith. Presumably this restoration borders upon faking, but there are few who would say the case had suffered an illegal operation.

It is probably true to say that few seventeenth-century long-case clocks, if any, exist in wholly original condition, and the majority of early eighteenth-century examples have also been damaged, repaired or altered in some way. There is no substitute for experience in the business of distinguishing between original work and a clever restoration. The collector or dealer must often rely on intuition and general background knowledge of different period styles. In other words, he will often have to decide whether such-and-such a moulding or other detail could have been used at a given time, or ask himself whether such-and-such a part, which appears original, could really have withstood so many years of use in such condition.

A simple example is afforded by the bun feet of the clock in Plate 18 which are modern replacements of the originals, fitted about ten years ago. As such feet were nearly always turned from beech wood, which is soft and appetising to the furniture beetle, it is reasonable for a collector to assume that bun feet on a seventeenth-century clock are almost certain to be replacements and he will scarcely need to examine them. This same clock has suffered an alteration of its original lift-up hood which has been made to slide forwards, and has been reconstructed so that the front frame opens on hinges. This alteration was probably done very early in the clock's life and it is not possible to say whether the pillars of the hood are original or not. It belongs to the period when spiral-twist pillars were just going out of fashion in favour of plain ones, but there is something about the present ones which suggests they are not original. Details of this sort need close examination, and experts often disagree about them.

The lift-up hood arrangement was altered on many clocks to make them usable in low-ceilinged rooms, and other ways of reducing height were commonly practised. If removal of the cresting or other superstructure did not suffice, the base would be 'cut and shut'. Removal of the plinth or sub-base, which was likely to be rotten anyway, was sometimes enough, but very often the bottom few inches would need to be removed from the base itself whereupon the plinth, or a new, smaller one, would be replaced. Quite apart from the proportions of the clock being spoilt, this reduction would obviously upset the symmetry of a panelled or veneered base and was particularly regrettable if it had to be done to a marquetry case. It seems to be a perfectly legitimate restoration to rebuild truncated bases as far as possible. With plain oak there is no great difficulty but cross-banded veneers and inlaid work may be almost impossible to match properly.

A less common method of reducing the height of a clock was by removing the base, taking a few inches off the bottom of the trunk and trunk door and replacing the base. This could sometimes be done without making the clock look unduly squat but left the disposition of the door lock and hinges asymmetrical; conscientious craftsmen would then cut a new lock rebate and keyhole, fill up the old, and shift the hinges. The marks left by this work give the game away, but evidence of changed hinges, or a shift of their position, are fairly common and taken on their own do not necessarily mean that the trunk has been cut. It is obviously much more difficult to restore lost inches to a trunk and door than to renew a plinth or superstructure and only on an extremely valuable clock would the expense be justified. Generally the clock must be accepted as it is, but the buyer should always look for alterations of this sort as he may be able to use them as a means of reducing the price.

Structural alterations to bracket clocks are less common than to long-case clocks, but the earlier they are the more the dealer or collector must be on his guard, as all manner of strange things do happen. It is not unknown, for example, for plain domed or caddy-topped cases to be adorned with basket tops, and the quotation in Chapter 7 from Mr Lee's monograph on the early history of the pendulum clock, in which he mentions the transmogrification of a Hilkiah Bedford clock into an Edward East, indicates that early portico-topped cases were sometimes modernised into the domed fashion of a later period. Therefore it may be assumed, or at least suspected, that some of the early portico tops now seen are restorations.

Whether such a restoration is considered legitimate or not depends on various considerations, and one can only give a personal opinion, which is that it is proper to restore the original appearance of an antique if it is possible to do so, provided a substantial part of the finished article is genuine. How substantial the substantial part must be is a matter for the individual conscience; making a new drawer to replace one missing from an antique chest of drawers is clearly permissible, but the construction of a new chest round one surviving antique drawer is clearly a fake, and it is at the intermediate stage that the dividing line becomes so thin. There is a great temptation to make a clock look thirty or forty years earlier than it is in some instances, as this may greatly enhance its value.

Half fakes of this sort are more difficult to detect than outright fakes, and detection is more difficult in a clock than in most other domestic furniture as it has to be considered both from the horological and the cabinet-making aspects. This is one of the reasons why so many dubious specimens are sold, often in good faith, by non-specialist dealers. Conversely the horological expert, when examining a clock in an antique shop or sale room, may concentrate too much on all the details of the movement, dial, hands and so forth and miss a quite obvious anachronism in the case.

Old bracket-clock cases not infrequently lost top or bottom mouldings, frets, finials and other parts and have had replacements of the wrong period or proportions fitted. A surprisingly large number of those which originally stood on gilt-metal bracket feet, similar to those of the clocks by Allam and Clements and Leroux, (Plate 27) or the example by Moore (Plate 43) turn up without them. The feet were presumably removed in order to make the clock fit into some particular place, and were then put aside and forgotten. If suitable cast-brass feet cannot be found or made, it seems a legitimate restoration to have a cabinetmaker fit carved wooden bracket feet, which many clocks had, or some form of stepped block foot which is easier to make. A clock which was intended to have feet always looks wrong without them. As the McCabe clock in Plate 27 shows, gilt metal bun or ball feet came into use for small clocks in the nineteenth century and these too are often missing, but they are fortunately much easier to copy than bracket feet.

Legitimate fields for restoration which affect external appearances rather than mechanism are dials and gilt-metal case mounts, and some understanding of the appropriate gilding and silvering processes is essential. Antique dealers are sometimes confused by the different methods of gilding on wood, leather, plaster, glass and metal and refer to the fine original finish of metal furniture mounts, or clock spandrels, as 'water gilding'; but this refers to a method of laying goldleaf on wood or gesso surfaces which is used when it is desired to burnish the highlights. The term is wrongly given to gilt metal work which can also be burnished, or partly burnished, to provide contrast with the areas left matt or frosted. Except as a means of making good small areas, goldleaf gilding is not applicable to metal; those brass parts of clock dials and cases which were gilded were done by a mercurial process, which was ousted by electro-gilding by the middle of the last century.

Mercury gilding, sometimes known as fire-gilding, involved many operations of cleaning, polishing and 'pickling' the surface to be treated according to the nature of the finish required, and similar processes are needed if the gold is to be electrically deposited. When the surface was ready, gold dust mixed to a spongy consistency with mercury was rolled, brushed and dabbed evenly over the surface, and well worked into all the crevices of chased work. The proportions were such that there was sufficient 'free' mercury in the amalgam to start amalgamating with the brass or bronze. The piece would be left for a while to let the mercury bite well into the base metal, carrying the gold with it and the longer it was left, within reason, the thicker and more durable the gilding. The surplus would then be carefully washed off, and the washings recovered from the water for further use; whereupon the piece (or, in practice, a batch of pieces) would be raised to considerable heat in a small charcoal forge fire in order to vaporise the mercury and drive it off. Then would follow several more processes of washing, first in

Page 269 PLATE 40 (*left*) Miniature mahogany bracket clock of 1790 style, but made about 1840 by Payne of New Bond St. It is a travelling or portable clock with lever escapement and carrying case, only 5½in high; (*centre*) fine, three-train quarter chiming clock by Andrew Dunlop, Master of the Clockmakers' Company, *c*1735; (*right*) miniature repeating and striking bracket clock, with moon phases indicator in the arch, and day-of-the-week shown below the usual calendar aperture. By William Bell, *c*1790

Page 270 PLATE 41 (*left*) Mahogany clock in the 'Egyptian taste' popularised by Thomas Hope; maker, Thomas Bagshaw, London, *c*1820; (*centre*) London-made bracket clock of *c*1770, conventional except for having a late example of Knibb's 'tic-tac' escapement; maker Martin Dohoo, unrecorded, probably 'Hood'. Compare with Eardley Norton who occasionally signed his clocks 'Yeldrae Notron'; (*right*) inlaid mahogany timepiece with pull-wind alarum by John Ham, *c*1830 weak acid or cyanide of potassium dissolved in alcohol, followed by water, before the piece was dried in heated sawdust in readiness for finally burnishing of the appropriate parts with bone or agate burnishers. The last process was to put on a thin coat of clear lacquer to give the delicate gold some protection against handling.

This fire gilding process was long and costly; and in the days before powered fume extractors and closed furnaces, the gilders suffered from their exposure to poisonous mercury fumes. The results were very durable and varied in quality of texture from good to superb, according to the amount of preparatory and finishing work done. The colour of the finished article could vary from reddish gold to a sort of honey blonde. Apart from a few craftsmen doing restoration work of the highest quality, metal gilding is always done now by electro-deposition which gives almost as good results whilst being very much cheaper and safer—cheapness being only relative, of course.

Because of the expense of mercurial gilding, a cheaper alternative was sought and found, very early on, in gold lacquering. By using suitably tinted lacquer varnish over brass which had previously been pickled to a matt finish, or burnished as required, the metal can be preserved from oxidation and coloured to a variety of shades from pale gold to bronze. Gold lacquering was very extensively practised in the eighteenth and nineteenth centuries, not only on clocks but on furniture mounts and handles and on microscope tubes and other scientific instruments. Gold lacquering is not quite so effective for chased and matt surfaces as it is for giving a burnished gold effect on plane surfaces, on which it is virtually indistinguishable from true gilding. Given reasonable care, and particularly if it is behind glass as on clock dials, it is surprisingly durable.

Many antique dealers are unaware that the 'nice original gilding' they point out to their customers is sometimes gold lacquer, often of quite recent origin. Some years ago I bought a fine early nineteenth-century bracket clock, profusely adorned with gilt metal mounts of admirable quality but in shocking condition, with nearly all the gold rubbed off by injudicious use of metal polish. To have had the pieces fire-gilt again would have cost too much, and as the ordinary electro-gilding process was not able to achieve the desired colour, the mounts were carefully burnished and gold-lacquered, very cheaply, by a firm of metal finishers who specialise in such work. I then had the pleasure of selling the clock to a world-renowned London firm of goldsmiths and jewellers who also have a fine stock of antique clocks. After the price had been agreed, and whilst waiting for a minion to write a cheque, the clock buyer condescendingly told me he did not usually buy clocks made after 1800 but that he had been finally tempted to have this one by the 'beautiful original condition of the gilding'. He assured me that the expert could always tell old mercurial gilding by the colour and silky texture which no modern gilding could equal, and I solemnly agreed with him.

The collector or dealer will often come across bracket clocks with the gilt metal mounts so darkened by dirt or oxidation that they are scarcely visible. This is particularly the case on ebonised cases which, if the mounts are black, will probably be shabby and dull anyway. It used to be thought very bad practice to do anything about discoloured mounts, but there is no merit in dirt and the reason for the long popularity of black cases with gilded mounts cannot be appreciated unless they are seen as they were intended to be, with the gleaming black in contrast with glowing gold.

It is useless to attempt to do anything with blackened mounts whilst they are *in situ*. After they have been removed, often a rather difficult process as many are held on by panel pins whose heads break off, the owner or restorer may be agreeably surprised to find how well they respond to washing in one of the many cleaning compounds advocated for the job. Every repairer has his own pet 'soup', but the amateur will do well to start with warm water, pure soap flakes and a liberal lacing of liquid ammonia. It is sometimes advantageous to follow this, if repeated *gentle* brushing in the suds still leaves the metal dull, with a paste of cream of tartar. Gilders' cleansing solutions, based on various mixtures of cyanide and spirit, are effective but unpleasant and rather dangerous. The clock by Penton in Plate 30 is an example of one on which all the blackened mounts were restored to their present splendour simply by washing in one of these compounds, which removed the dirt and old darkened lacquer and revealed that, except on a few high spots, the gold was still intact.

More often the preliminary washing reveals a less happy state of affairs, and greater or lesser areas of the mounts are down to the bare metal. The most usual cause of this is that at some time in the past an attempt has been made to clean the darkened metal work (whether the original finish was gold lacquer or real gilding protected by clear lacquer), in too harsh a way, so that most of the gold has been scrubbed off with the dirt and old lacquer. Metal polish is the most frequent destroyer of gilding and the new shiny surface that is revealed, as well as looking too brash, soon tarnishes. When sending mounts to be re-gilded, it is essential to seek out a firm which understands and specialises in antique restoration work. Straightforward electro-gilding seldom produces the properly mellow colour, and ordinary commercial electro-plating and gilding firms usually subject all the work to machine-polishing processes which give too bright and even a finish. As stated earlier, gold-lacquering will often give excellent results, and it is a process within the scope of the 'do-it-yourself' handyman. It is by no means easy to achieve a good result, without streaks, on large areas such as dial plates, but as the lacquer is easily washed off with solvent no harm can be done. The amateur will find the old-fashioned spirit lacquers easier to work than modern cellulose or synthetic lacquers as they are not quite so quick-drying. For the best results a dry atmosphere is essential, and the metal to be lacquered with old-fashioned spirit lacquer should be warmed to blood heat.

The chapter rings of some early lantern and other clocks were occasionally of solid silver or, as described in Chapter 4, of 'close plated' brass. 'Close plating' involves soft soldering or tinning and fusing a thin sheet of silver to a thick sheet of brass, and may be described as a one-sided Sheffield plating. With few exceptions, however, from the mid-seventeenth century onwards, English clockmakers always finished their engraved brass chapter rings, seconds rings, calendar rings and so forth by a chemical silvering process which is cheap, simple and non-toxic. As with gilding or gold-lacquering, much of the final effect depends on the preliminary processes of cleaning the plate or ring, and 'stoning' it with various grades of abrasive stones to make an evenly grained matt surface which, after silvering, will show neither high lights and hollows nor the slightest pitting or unevenness of texture. These processes of 'laying a grain' are done after the ring or dial plate has been heated, so that black sealing wax applied to it melts and runs into all the engraved numerals, decoration and signature.

The prepared parts are then wetted and sprinkled with common salt, and a small quantity of the silvering compound, generally in the form of a paste, is rubbed quickly all over the surfaces, whereupon the combination of silvering compound and salt immediately turns the grained brass a dirty blackish brown. The parts are then washed and gently wiped with a paste of cream of tartar and water, which turns the dirty-looking surfaces white. According to the type of silvering compound and the amount of final wiping with cream of tartar, the operator can vary the finish from a misty silvery grey to almost dead white. The latter is appropriate to a plain regulator dial, but the slightly grey silver is preferable for separate chapter rings mounted on gilt- or gold-lacquered brass dial plates.

Proprietary 'silvering salts' can be bought; but as they tend to give rather too bright a finish for antique clocks, the enthusiast can easily make his own compound by dissolving a small stick of nitrate of silver (lunar caustic) in about a pint of water (preferably distilled), then precipitating the chloride by adding a tablespoonful or so of common salt. The chloride of silver is then repeatedly washed by allowing it to settle, pouring off most of the water, adding more, stirring and repeating the process some twenty times. After washing, pour away as much of the water as possible and to the remainder, with the chloride in suspension, add enough cream of tartar, and a little more salt, to make a fairly sloppy paste which must be kept in a darkened glass jar as the material blackens immediately on exposure to light.

Because this chemical silvering is very sensitive to atmosphere and light, the silvered parts must be given one or two *very* thin coats of clear lacquer as soon as possible after they have been thoroughly washed in running water to remove all trace of silver salts which have not combined with the brass. To coat a fairly large area absolutely evenly with lacquer is far from easy, as any surplus, or overlapping of strokes, will show in certain lights as ripples or ridges. Too thick a single coat over the whole area will make the surface shiny and spoil the effect; any areas not covered, which are difficult to see whilst brushing on the lacquer—which must be done quickly

—will turn black very soon, and too thin a coat over the whole area will show a rainbow effect in certain lights. As the best results are had by applying the lacquer to warmed surfaces it is fatally easy to make the chapter ring or plate slightly too hot, so that the wax in the engraved lines runs out in black streaks as the lacquer brush passes over them.

Because of these difficulties many repairers who undertake antique restorations send dials or rings to one of the few remaining professional 'dial writers' in the trade. These professionals unfortunately do too good a job; 'antique work' is only a sideline to them and they prepare the work for silvering on rotating discs or tables, and generally get too highly burnished a surface, in place of the even grain required, so that the result looks more like silver plating than silvering as it should be. However, the growing interest in antique clocks is leading more and more specialist dealers and repairers to undertake their own silvering, so it should not be too difficult to find someone to do the job in the eighteenth-century manner.

According to the care taken not to scratch it, and the degree of atmospheric pollution, chemical silvering lasts for anything between ten and fifty years, perhaps even more if the conditions are particularly good. It was always recognised in the past that the silvering had to be renewed from time to time. Careless handling hastens the decay; and allowing the fingers to brush against the dial whilst turning the minute hand wrongly by the tip will sooner or later cause black streaks or lines to appear where finger-nails have cut through the lacquer. The microscopically thin coat of silver will then disappear and, if the atmosphere is only slightly corrosive, the blackened areas of brass will become more or less pitted. Even if the protective lacquer is not scratched, it gradually perishes and allows part or all of the area to be first darkened and then corroded. Whilst the silvered parts are suffering in this way over many years, the gilt-brass or gold-lacquered dial plate and spandrels will also be growing dark (and possibly corroding if much lacquer perishes) until the whole dial looks shabby and is very difficult to read.

Before World War II, most antique dealers, all museum curators and many collectors of the old school refused to have clock dials restored and re-silvered and there are still those who believe that such restoration 'destroys the original surface'. Far from destroying a surface which is most unlikely to be original, occasional renovation is essential to preserve the true originality of the engraved chapter rings and chased spandrels. This is particularly true of the chapter rings or one-piece silvered dials; as once the silver has disappeared, the numerous small pits caused by corrosion are extremely difficult to remove, and in 'stoning down' to eliminate them and to lay a fresh grain the more delicate lines of engraving, particularly of the signature, may be rubbed away. Also, if the dial, denuded of its protective surface, is exposed to atmosphere so corrosive that green lines or streaks of verdigris appear (and this is not uncommon), it may be almost impossible to undo the mischief. On the other hand if a dial is taken in hand when the first signs of discolouration appear, it may not be necessary to do more than wash away the remaining lacquer with methylated spirit (or amyl acetate, if a cellulose lacquer has been used), wipe the silvered surfaces with cream of tartar, wash and re-lacquer. This is obviously the best way of preserving the original grain of the surface; and if gently rubbing with cream of tartar does not suffice, it is often possible to make a good job of re-silvering with very little preliminary stoning, provided the job is done promptly when dark streaks appear.

Unfortunately, the belief that it is almost immoral to re-silver dials or chapter rings still lingers, and the process is so generally misunderstood that many auctioneers catalogue clocks with 'steel' or 'steel-mounted' dials. Thirty-hour long-case clocks often had the centres of the dials engraved, not matt gilt (see Plates 23 and 34), and these areas were originally silvered, as were the chapter rings, leaving only the areas outside the chapters and the spandrels to be gilded or gold-lacquered. Many restorers leave these engraved centres as polished and lacquered brass, which is not only incorrect according to the usage of the eighteenth century but reflected light from the bright area makes it less easy to read the time and spoils the decorative effect of the engraving.

Painted dials are often found in very bad condition, sometimes because the background has started to flake away but generally with the background tolerable and numerals, divisions, circles and signature more or less obliterated by incautious washing. Painted long-case clock dials, as noted earlier, usually had the decorative corner pieces or arch paintings done in oil colour, which would stand cleaning; but one sometimes comes across long-case dials, square or arched, wholly devoid of any ornamentation, and this indicates that at some time the whole dial was in such bad condition that the flaking background had to be renewed, and, for economic reasons no doubt, the dial-writer merely put in the essential divisions and numerals on a bare expanse of white paint. Similarly, one often finds dials on which the numerals etc have been renewed by an amateur with relatively little success, or by a professional who has paid no heed to the original style and proportions.

The business of scribing all the circles and divisions and writing the numerals, particularly the Roman type with their hair-thin diagonals, is generally beyond the amateur. The help of a professional dial-writer must be sought, and even the best professionals seem unable to produce such elegant script or 'black letter' for the signatures and place names as their predecessors. Unless the background paintwork is perished and flaking, it should aways be kept and the dial-writer be instructed only to renew the divisions, numerals and signature; the old backgrounds seem never to have been dead white but to have had a faintly greenish-creamy tinge which age has often darkened, whilst also adding hair-line crazing which cannot be reproduced. If the background is too far gone to save, as it very often is with bracket or wall clocks which have been used in kitchens or near gas lamps in the last century, the dial-writer must be strictly instructed to make the new surface as near as possible to the old colour, otherwise he will send it back dead-white which always looks incongruous. Similarly, unless he is very carefully instructed about the size and shape of the numerals, he will tend to make them of the heavy and very elongated style of the later Victorian period, which will throw the proportions of the whole dial out of balance. These elongated numerals look very well on mid-Victorian watch dials, where the diagonals are a miracle of painting, so thin as to be almost invisible, and where the hands are suitably proportioned, but they are totally at variance with the hands, bezels and other details of eighteenth- and early nineteenth-century clocks. The disparity is particularly noticeable between, say, a good circular-dial hanging clock of about 1810 on which the numeral IIII will be only a little longer than it is wide and an ordinary 'office dial' of any time after about 1870, on which the figure IIII will be at least twice as long as its width with the other numerals similarly drawn out. The scale and thickness of the minute circles and numerals, where applicable, and the seconds and date circles are also very important. The fairly general rule is that the tip of the minute hand should reach just short of the outside diameter of the minute band; that the width of the minute band between the two circles (or if there is only one, outer, circle, between that circle and the lower edge of the minute divisions), should not exceed one-half of the distance between minute marks; and the tip of the hour hand should not overlap the inner edge of the hour numerals by more than about a sixteenth of an inch on bracket-clock dials of average size. A slightly bigger overlap, up to a quarter, is permissible on a 12 or 14in wall dial. Given that the hands are original, a most important point, it is possible to calculate the correct proportions from them.

As the professional trade dial-writers still adhere to the maddening custom of their predecessors of using water-soluble black pigment for their work, it is as well to ask that the finished dial be given a coat of clear lacquer or synthetic varnish so that subsequent attempts to clean it will not again damage the markings.

It is with the signatures on painted dials that the honest dealer is faced with his greatest dilemma and the dishonest one with his greatest opportunity. Although we call them signatures they were, of course, the work of the original dial-writer and not in the actual calligraphy of the clockmaker; it is consequently a great temptation to the unscrupulous to have the superscription of J. Snooks, Hogsnorton, transformed into, say, Dwerrihouse and Carter, Berkeley Square. The honest dealer or restorer who is faced with a painted dial plate from which the name and place of the maker have disappeared, or been so damaged as to be illegible (a frequent occurrence), is faced with the choice of having the dial re-written without signature and 'address', in which case he will know that it will look unbalanced and incorrect, or of having some maker's name and town written in at random, which smacks of faking.

If the back plate of the movement is signed, which is rare, there is obviously no difficulty. As the nineteenth century advanced the names on clock dials increasingly represented retailers who bought clocks ready finished from wholesale suppliers; even makers of the calibre of Vulliamy sold a number of clocks which were wholly made for them by others, and it is always worthwhile, if the signature on the dial is missing or illegible, to examine the front plate of the movement which may yield the stamped name or mark of the actual maker. Thwaites and Reed were one of the principal suppliers and if their mark be found, it seems quite proper to have 'Thwaites and Reed, London,' written on the dial.

Where there is no signature on the back plate and no stamped mark on the front one, patient study of the dial at various angles under a strong light may reveal enough for the owner or restorer to work out the name. If the clock is a country-made one, it is sometimes possible to make out the name of the town or village even if the maker's name is illegible. Consultation then with the published lists of clockmakers (those of Britten and Baillie being the most comprehensive) or with old directories, taken in conjunction with the known period of the clock, often leads to the tolerably certain conclusion that the clock must have been made by so-and-so. This was the case with the painted-dial long-case clock in Plate 37. Before the numerals etc were re-written, the only parts of the signature to be legible were an initial letter 'J' or 'F' and a final 'on' or 'an'; but there was just enough left of the place name to make Newnham a strong possibility. As the original owner of the clock was known to have been a native of Kent this lead was followed, and reference to the lists showed that a J. Samuel Shortman worked in Newnham, Kent, at the time when this clock would have been made. It therefore seems a legitimate restoration to have had the signature and place re-written as they now appear.

If it is quite impossible to find the name by this sort of detective work, it may be proper to have the name and place of an unimportant maker of the appropriate period written in to balance the dial; but this is open to misuse and a better alternative, probably, is to invent a fictitious name and address. A word of warning about spelling is needed. By the time the painted iron dials were in use, the spelling of proper names was pretty well fixed, but modern dial-writers often make mistakes over them unless they are clearly given the correct form. For example, the famous London partnership of Grimalde and Johnson made their best clocks with engraved and silvered dials on which the name Grimalde is so spelled as may be seen in Plate 29; but they also supplied pieces of slightly lesser quality with painted iron dials and these quite often appear re-written as Grimaldi.

One of the most profitable fields for the smart operator is in the production of so-called 'grandmother' clocks. Some of the earliest long-case clocks were so small as almost to qualify for this title; but the term is generally taken to mean a scaled-down long-case clock, preferably less than 5ft tall with all other dimensions to suit, with a suitably reduced long-case movement complete with driving weights and long pendulum; or with verge escapement and bob pendulum if of the very earliest period, but these are probably to be counted on one hand.

Genuine examples of all periods do exist but they are exceedingly rare and, leaving out of account the twentieth-century specimens, which are no more than spring-driven mantel clocks perched on non-functional trunks, nearly all are fakes or mixed marriages of one sort or other. Some were made by amateur or professional cabinetmakers as an exercise in skill, and these are often beautiful pieces of work marred by bodged-up movements and dials from various sources. Towards the end of the last century a number were produced commercially in a very well-executed reproduction Chippendale style. These now have considerable value in their own Victorian right; but despite the fact that their characteristically Victorian movements give the game away to those in the know, they are often passed off as antiques.

As the 'grandmother' size of case allowed less than the usual 'drop' for the weights, an eight-day duration could only be given by adding an extra wheel to each train or, most often, by making the barrels about half the usual diameter. Either of these courses entailed increasing the mass of the weights; but as the small dimensions of the trunk already posed problems in finding room for two weights and a pendulum, the design of an eight-day grandmother presented difficulties which partly account for the rarity of genuine specimens.

Consequently, most of the faked or married examples have thirty-hour movements. Old lantern clocks were one source, very often with the striking work removed, and wall clocks similar to that by Elizabeth Hunte in Plate 22 were favourite candidates. Indeed, as stated earlier, this type of clock is not difficult to turn into a 'grandmother' by the addition of a trunk and base, and if these are made by 'cutting and shutting' an old oak 'grandfather' case of full size so that all the mouldings, hinges, panelling etc are indisputably old the result can readily be passed off as a genuine antique. The shortness of the case, necessary to keep it in proportion with the upperworks, will probably prevent the clock going for much more than sixteen hours, and the need to wind it night and morning will expose the imposture.

Movements from 'Act of Parliament' wall clocks have also been used for bogus grandmothers, as they were designed to go for eight days with only a short drop for the weight. They are therefore very suitable, but the shape of the movement plates, usually a truncated triangle but occasionally L-shaped, gives a clue to their origin.

In the sense of taking supplies of raw material and making an antique from the ground up, the outright faking of antique clocks is rare. Unlike the better sorts of reproduction furniture, reproduction antique clocks are so little like the real thing that they are unlikely to deceive anybody. Even 270 years ago or more, a certain amount of jiggery-pokery went on, however, and the names of the more famous English makers appeared on pieces in which they had had no hand; but these forgeries were mostly done abroad, or at least for foreign consumption. This is less true of clocks than of watches, which were extensively faked on the continent. Early examples are very close copies of the real thing, so much so that experts disagree, for example, as to whether some of the watches signed 'Qüare' or 'Quaré' are German or French forgeries or whether Daniel Quare obligingly put in some foreign-looking minor details and added accents to his signature to further his export trade. By the middle of the eighteenth century, 'faking' of a much cruder sort was practised and large numbers of watches, and a few clocks, were made in Holland of indisputably Dutch style but for the 'signature' which represented one of a number of fictitious London makers. These watches were of poor quality, obviously intended for the type of customer who would have had little opportunity of handling a real English watch and who would consequently be deceived by the inscription of Jos. May, London, or Tarts, London; these being two of the names most often used.

Dealers and collectors must be much more on their guard against 'marriages' and 'improvements' than against any outright fakes; although the latter undoubtedly exist and the fact that specialists openly advertise the engraving of back plates or dials and exact copying of various 'antique' components indicates the extent of the 'improving' business. At one end of this trade is the substitution of 'antique' engraved and silvered dials for the painted iron ones which are less sought after, whilst at the other end are clever practitioners who will engrave for their customers a 'typical' Knibb or Tompion dial or back-plate, complete with signature, so perfectly as to pass the closest examination. It is fair to say that the craftsmen who do this sort of work are mostly concerned with making up and suitably engraving replacements for missing parts, which is perfectly proper, but their skill can be harnessed by unscrupulous dealers to transform sows' ears into silk purses, or to make complete clocks by famous makers materialise out of a few genuine pieces. One of the most skilled engravers makes it his business always to include certain 'secret' markings in the ornamental curlicues of his work which, in effect, constitute his own signature.

Fortunately the expense of faking the works of famous makers, either directly or by 'improving' well enough to deceive the expert, is expensive enough to be something of a deterrent. Also, the smaller collectors and non-specialist antique dealers for whom this book is intended are not able to buy in the Tompion class; but the rising value of all antique clocks is increasing the number of mixed marriages which constitute the most common pitfalls for the unwary.

Starting with the ordinary long-case clock it is necessary to consider the following questions:

1. On the lines already indicated, how many alterations or restorations, signs of cutting down etc can be found in the casework?
2. Does the dial belong to the movement, and if so, are the spandrels and hands correct for the dial?
3. If the maker's name is engraved on a separate plate or boss, is the putative maker one who is likely to have made such a clock at such a period?
4. If the dial is of the 'break arch' form, is the arch formed in

one piece with the rest or is it separate and attached by metal straps and screws or rivets?

5. On the evidence of the shape and style of the pallets, wheel collets etc (see Chapter 10) how much 'new' material can be seen in the movement?
6. If calendar and/or lunar or astronomical indicators are present on the dial, are the necessary wheels etc to activate them still in evidence? They will nearly always be found, if present, between the dial and the front plate and with some levers, detents etc mounted on the back of the dial itself. If in doubt, turning the hands forward through 24 hours will indicate whether or not the usual simple calendar and lunar indicators are working.
7. If the clock is a country-made one, with a fairly short case (under 6ft 6in for example), particularly if of simple flat-topped form to accommodate a square dial, and if the movement is of eight-day duration was it not originally a thirty-hour clock which has been converted?
8. If movement, dial, spandrels, hands etc all seem to belong together, do they also belong to the case? This is the most difficult question to answer.

The apparently obvious answers to some of these questions can be misleading. Concerning No 2, for example, it is easy enough to detect wrong spandrels if they are grossly out of character or obviously of the wrong size (and many 'marriage makers' are careless about details), but even if they are apparently correct it is as well to examine the back of the dial plate to see if there are any surplus holes for screws in the neighbourhood of the spandrels, or larger holes for 'feet' of chapter ring, seconds ring, maker's nameplate etc. If there are none it is tolerably safe to assume all is well, but the presence of spare holes does not *necessarily* indicate jiggery-pokery. Craftsmen sometimes made mistakes and drilled holes in the wrong places. It is also not unknown for chapter or seconds rings to have been wrongly engraved, turned over, re-surfaced and re-engraved. This necessarily entails altering the feet, from one side of the ring to the other; and for one reason or another the engraver may have put the new markings out of axial alignment with the old ones and this will entail drilling a fresh set of holes for the feet in the dial plate. These innocent reasons for surplus holes are exceptional, and they should always be looked upon with suspicion.

The question of deciding whether the hands are right is one which can only be answered after intensive study or long experience. Examining illustrations of hands and dials, particularly the dated examples of the former shown in the earlier editions of *Britten's Old Clocks and Watches and their Makers*, and other sources, is helpful; but the study of actual clocks eventually brings about the instinctive ability to spot a wrong 'un at a glance. The hands which are only slightly 'wrong' are the most difficult to discover and it may be helpful to say that of the clocks pictured in this book, two with hands which are incorrect, but not glaringly so, are in Plates 33 and 37. In the former, the fine dial by Benjamin Merriman, *c*1700, has the original very slender seconds hand, usually the first to be broken, but the minute hand, although of appropriate style, was intended for a slightly bigger dial and has been shortened and thrown out of proportion; the hour hand is some fifty years later than the clock, fractionally too long and not of good enough quality for the dial. In Plate 37, the painted dial clock by Shortman, neither the minute nor the hour hand belongs to the clock, being about twenty years earlier, and the observant eye will detect that they are not a pair anyway.

On the question, No 3, of the clock having the wrong signature, it is obviously much easier for the faker to do his worst if the signature is on a separate plate or cartouche, and these should always be removed if possible and examined for signs of alteration. It is not unknown, however, for clocks to 'grow' new chapter rings with important signatures upon them; if this has been done by grafting on a genuine ring from another source, vacant holes in the plate (or holes filled in with metal of a different colour) may give the game away; but a new ring purposely made up and engraved by a skilled craftsman may be almost impossible to detect. Here the buyer can only rely on his instinct, and ask himself whether such-and-such a maker could have made the clock in question taking all the other details of style, quality and finish into account. There are many examples of clocks on which the faker has made such glaring mistakes that they cannot deceive the collector with even a little experience. I have for example seen a lantern clock with a Victorian spring movement and the name of Thomas Mudge, who certainly never made a lantern clock, on the dial. Nevertheless, the clock fetched several times more than it was worth at auction and the catalogue carried a eulogistic note about the famous Thomas Mudge and his invention of the lever escapement.

When faced with question No 7 it is not usually difficult to decide whether a small country-made, eight-day clock was originally made with a thirty-hour movement. Marrying a new, or different, movement to a dial nearly always involved drilling new holes in the front plate or shifting the feet, or short pillars, on the dial plate; as these conversions were mostly done when the clocks had very little value, the practitioners concerned seldom made any attempt to hide their traces. Careless or ignorant dealers often married an eight-day movement, almost without exception made for concentric hour and minute hands, to a dial made for a single-hand clock. The presence of quarter and half-hour divisions on the inner edge of the chapter ring, with *no* minute divisions on the outer edge, gives the game away immediately. Nearly all eight-day movements were made to carry a seconds hand, but very few thirty-hour dials were engraved or inscribed for seconds, and therefore the presence of an elongated arbor to the escapement wheel to carry the 'pipe' of the seconds indicator behind a dial with no provision for a seconds hand, is another sign of conversion. Finally, a large majority of eighteenth-century thirty-hour clocks had engraved dial centres; so, too, did many eight-day ones, but if the dial was intended for an eight-day clock the position of the winding holes would be marked, and they would be drilled before the decorative engraving was done. Therefore the engraver would be able to fit the holes into the pattern, and an engraved dial with winding holes and squares incongruously pierced through the bellies of cocky-olly birds, or cutting across the stems of flowers, is an almost certain sign that the movement and dial do not belong together.

The answer to the eighth question is sometimes provided by answering the fourth: 'Has the arch been added to the dial or is it integral with the rectangular part?' As indicated in Chapter 10, the arch and rectangular part of a dial were very occasionally made separately, and joined together by the original maker as a means of adapting old-stock, unfinished, square dial plates to the new fashion.

A few square-dial clocks were converted to the new style fairly early in their lives by making a new hood, or re-building the old, and adding an arch to the dial; but in the majority of cases the arch has been added in order to adapt a clock to a case which may be as much as a hundred years younger. The incongruities of style should be fairly obvious, but many non-specialist dealers pass on such marriages as 'all original' in good faith. At a time when painted-dial long-case clocks of run-of-the-mill quality were not much esteemed, many were fitted up with 'new' gilt and silvered arched dials made up from those removed from unwanted square-dial thirty-hour clocks when they, too, were almost valueless. Thus the buyer can end up with a pleasant late eighteenth-century mahogany case housing its eight-day movement, hitched to a square thirty-hour dial, pierced with winding holes and augmented with a screwed-on break-arch. The results of such multiple inter-marrying may properly be called bastards.

Where regulators or long-case clocks of unusual type are concerned, there is much greater chance of clock and case belonging together. Long-case clocks with oval or hour-glass-shaped dials, for example, are occasionally seen and will only fit into the cases designed for them. Also, some of the most important seventeenth- and early eighteenth-century clocks are numbered both on the movement and the case, and although obviously a clever faker will not be put off by the need to stamp a number into a case structure, it is a favourable indication to consider with the other details.

As the clock mechanism and dial were made by one team of craftsmen and the case by another, it is not improper to marry together a clock and a case from different sources, always provided they are of appropriate age, style and quality. Similarly, most collectors are not deterred from buying a particular clock if they discover, or are told, that it has only recently moved into its present case; but if it can be assumed beyond reasonable doubt (and it is not often possible to be certain beyond all doubt) that clock and case really belong together, it adds to the value of the clock and the pleasure of owning it.

Nearly all dealers who specialise to any extent in antique clocks accumulate one or more long-case movements and dials of good quality, and anxiously hunt for suitable cases of the right period.

Page 287 Two provincial bracket clocks: PLATE 42 by Thomas Marshall, Lincoln; countryfied but pleasing; PLATE 43 a more sophisticated style with the curious combination of bell-top and square dial. Probably London made and only signed and sold by Moore of Ipswich. Both clocks *c*1785–90.

Page 288 PLATE 44 Miniature, 5in high, lancet or Gothic clock having portable movement, with watch-type verge escapement, with striking train and hour-repeat; enamelled dial. By the same Richard Comber of Lewes who made the clock in Plate 34, *c*1800

PLATE 45 Small bronze and ormolu timepiece 'in the French taste' with enamel dial, by Desbois & Wheeler, Gray's Inn Passage, *c*1810

The search may take twenty years or more, or may never succeed, and less conscientious dealers in pursuit of a fast buck will put any old clock into any old case and are not ashamed to offer the resultant hodge-podge for sale.

If the customer knows what he is buying and is happy to have, say, a good London square-dial eight-day or month clock, originally housed in walnut or marquetry, in the deal case made a hundred or more years later for a country thirty-hour clock, no great harm is done. Indeed, if a dealer or collector has a particularly fine and important dial and movement, there may be no choice between having a reproduction case made for it at great expense or putting it into one of a later period. Where these badly-mixed marriages are to be deplored is when they impose upon buyers who are simple-minded in the sense that they have not had the inclination or opportunity of studying enough to notice the incongruity. Indiscriminating buyers of this sort include those who buy or hire clocks for television productions of 'costume plays', in which though most of the furnishings are commendably accurate, the clocks are generally laughable. It is also odd that the effects department, usually so accurate, frequently make long-case clocks apparently beat three-quarter or half-seconds, instead of seconds, and cause sonorous 'Big Ben' chimes to boom from clocks which purport to have been made a hundred years or more before the great Westminster clock made the familiar chime popular.

The more experienced antique collector, even if he has not previously paid particular attention to horology, will not generally be taken in by the obviously incongruous marriages, and the real problem for him concerns minor discrepancies. Such as deciding whether the dial does not fit snugly to the 'mask' behind the hood door because of some innocent repair, or because clock and case, though apparently compatible, are living in sin rather than holy wedlock.

Similarly a new seat-board for the movement, or new upright members in the case to support it, may be innocent but should always be viewed with a certain amount of suspicion. Examine also the means which which the movement is attached to the seat-board, and look to see whether new holes have been drilled in the latter to accommodate new fastenings.

There were two principal methods of clamping movement and seat-board together. One was to drill vertically through the lowest pillars holding the movement plates together, to tap the holes with screw threads and to drill corresponding holes in the seat-board so that suitable bolts, sometimes square-headed and slotted for a screw-driver and sometimes formed into a 'wing' or 'thumb-screw' shape, passed up from underneath, could firmly clamp movement and board together. The commoner method avoided drilling and tapping the pillars (and until the eighteenth century was well advanced, screw cutting was a chore which clockmakers avoided as much as possible) and comprised a suitable length of rod, turned into a hook at one end and given a few turns of thread upon the other. With the short hooked end over the pillar and the elongated threaded portion passed through a hole in the board, a square nut screwed on the latter clamped the hook tightly over the pillar. For this cheaper, simpler, method of fixing, the holes in the board obviously had to be drilled off-centre in relation to the pillars. It has been said in a recently published book that 'in all movements up to *c*1700 the lowest pair of pillars are drilled and tapped'. This implies that all movements without drilled pillars must be later than '*c*1700'; but readers should be very wary of dogmatic assertions of this sort as there are so many exceptions.

One can only counsel the reader to look closely at the fastenings. Absence of any signs of alteration, such as vacant holes in the board, will be favourable but the presence of alterations must not be taken automatically as proof that clock and case do not belong together. There are many innocent reasons why the clamping screws, or hooks, or the seat-board itself may have been altered. As for the statement that 'all movements before *c*1700' had screwed pillars, many of the earliest long-case clocks do not, and are secured by quite different means; but screwed and tapped pillars never quite went out of use and are to be found on some clocks as late as 1820. The only fixed rule about almost every detail of clock construction is that there is no fixed rule.

The eight points about different aspects of long-case authenticity apply also to bracket clocks; but some others must be added. It is not possible to judge a bracket clock in detail without taking it out of its case. The earlier, more important and valuable the clock, the more necessary this is; and provided the potential customer seems reasonably knowledgeable, few respectable dealers will object.

The very removal of the movement brings the first question to light. Most early bracket clocks had a wooden platform or stool below the movement, supporting the weight, and this obliged the latter to sit with its dial plate exactly square with the opening in the case. On either side of the back of the dial plate were two rotatable eccentric discs, forming latches, furnished with protruding slotted bosses by which they could be turned to enter slots cut in the side members of the case structure. This arrangement was rather frail, as the parts of the case engaged by the latches had to be fairly thin and often broke away. Therefore many clocks of the period 1680 to 1720 approximately have been altered to one or other of the methods of fixing most usually found on eighteenth-century clocks. One method was to drill and tap the lowest pair of movement pillars, so that stout bolts could be screwed into them from the bottom of the case, passing through the seat-board; or L-shaped brass straps, engraved to match the back plate, could be attached by screws to the back of the movement and the sides of the clock case. This became the commonest form of fixing, and straps of this sort found on clocks of the early period are usually later additions. Fixing straps may be seen in the view of the movement in Plate 28.

If an early clock is removed from its case and evidence is found that the case is, or once was, slotted for latches but no traces of the latter are visible on the back of the dial plate, there is reason to question whether clock and case truly belong. Finding the latches, or traces of them, with no corresponding slots in the case is not necessarily evidence of malpractice as the original slotted members may have had to be replaced, and the repairers usually decided not to renew the slots but to adopt a new method of fixing.

Probably the most important points, apart from the original eight, to consider when examining a bracket clock concern the conversion and possible re-conversion of the escapement, and the removal of repeating mechanism from clocks once fitted with it. The signs to look for have already been outlined in Chapter 11. It is easy enough to recognise a Victorian anchor escapement and pendulum in a Georgian or earlier clock, but very much less easy to determine whether the verge escapement one finds is original or a re-conversion.

Absence of wear on the pallets is no criterion, as the replacement or re-facing of such parts is a legitimate and often necessary repair. The new contrate wheel of a re-conversion fits back into the original pivot holes and the new top and bottom potences for the 'scape wheel are also anchored to the original screw- and steady-pin holes. If the work has been done by a good craftsman who is not only skilled with his tools but has a sense of period, it may be almost impossible to tell except by metallurgical analysis.

As it is recognised that so many bracket clocks, possibly half of all those made, were converted, and as the re-conversion can be done in the manner appropriate to the period, it is generally regarded as a proper part of restoration. Most of the reputable antiquarian clock dealers have no hesitation in telling their customers that they have had a particular clock re-converted, but of course they cannot always vouch for those they have bought with verge escapements which may or may not be original. If a clock is discovered in generally poor and dirty state, with a crown-wheel escapement showing plentiful signs of wear and bodging, it is fair to assume it is 'right'.

The collector or dealer who buys a clock with a Victorian anchor escapement has to decide whether to have it re-converted. The job is far from cheap; with prices so swiftly rising it is difficult to put a figure on it but, allowing for the general overhauling and cleaning to be done at the same time, one must not expect much change from a hundred pounds. Therefore, the question is partly answered by considering the potential value of the clock after restoration in relation to the price paid, or asked, for it in its present condition. Obviously, the earlier and more valuable the clock, the more suitable it will be as a candidate for the operation; particularly if it has, or had, a mock pendulum. A clock dial designed for a mock pendulum never looks right with a vacant space where it should be, or with the little disc listlessly wagging over the small arc dictated by the anchor escapement. To the real clock fanatic the restoration of the characteristic *sound* of a crown-wheel escapement is another reason for abolishing the Victorian interloper.

Replacing missing repeating work (or other ancillaries such as complex calendar mechanism) is very much more difficult and expensive than re-converting an escapement, and is probably less justifiable ethically. On a seventeenth-century clock, by one of the more sought-after makers, worth between £5,000 and £20,000, it may make sense commercially to spend £500 or more on making new repetition work, but it is obviously less sensible with clocks of less exalted values. Part of the expense arises because removal of the original repeat mechanism will have left many vacant pivot and screw holes in the movement, and the restorer will have to ensure that his new work fits all the spaces occupied by the old. This will mean many hours of design and experimental work, as no two early repeating mechanisms were exactly alike, trying to work out what were the shape, size and function of the missing pieces. This is a much more expensive business than simply designing and making a quarter-repeat mechanism from scratch, and this aspect of repeater restoration leads some unscrupulous practitioners to add repetition work to clocks which started life without it. This is not infrequently done to timepieces without striking work as they are generally less valued than striking clocks, have plenty of room for the extra mechanism, and their extra value as repeaters justifies the expense.

This particular form of 'faking by addition' is often done without proper regard for period accuracy of detail, and it is therefore detectable. It is also sometimes done without much regard for engineering considerations and I have seen an example in which the repetition work was bogus to the extent that it did not work and never could be made to do so. However, it looked impressive through the glass side of the case, and the clock appeared at auction in dirty condition so that on cursory examination it would be thought the repeater was merely out of order.

It sometimes happens that a clock survives with its repeating mechanism more or less intact, but put out of action by removal of the under-dial work, or most of it. This is a much more encouraging prospect for restoration as the existence of the repeating train between the plates, complete with the pin-barrel hammers and bells, means there need be no qualms, ethical or monetary, about making replacements for the missing pieces.

The re-conversion of lantern clocks to verge escapement and

wheel-balance control is also one which poses moral problems. The practical aspects of this have already been touched upon, and the re-conversion of an indisputably genuine balance-wheel clock seems justifiable. Unfortunately the recent spectacular rise in the value of lantern clocks of all kinds has led to the 're-conversion' of many that never were balance-wheel clocks in the first place. As very few early lantern clocks have survived without loss of some original part or other, frets and side doors being particularly apt to go astray, and as most of them show signs of damage, careless handling, bodging or modernisation, they provide many opportunities for the faker to do his work. It is a large subject and one which cannot be dealt with very fully here; the collector who wants to add one or more lantern clocks to his hoard would do well to study as many examples as he can in other collections or museums. One of the leading experts, Mr K. Williams, is currently writing a book on the subject.

Other forms of restoration which often border upon the fraudulent, such as the transformation of plain cases into lacquered ones, the over-restoration of japanned 'Act of Parliament' clock cases and the stripping and staining of ebonised cases so that they appear to be mahogany or walnut, belong in the general field of antique furniture 'improvement'. This rather depressing chapter can be ended with the suggestion that it might be helpful to the collector if the words 'Tempis Fugit' which appear on so many clocks of rather dubious ancestry were replaced by 'Caveat Emptor'.

Chapter Fifteen

English Influence and Decline

If there were space enough, it would be interesting to follow the ramifications of different national influences in matters of clock design throughout the world. It would be possible, for example, to dismantle an early eighteenth-century Austrian clock and demonstrate that *this* detail derived directly from English practice, whilst *that* came from Holland and the *other* was of French origin but modified by German influences.

By the end of the seventeenth century the Dutch, having 'invented' the pendulum clock, were producing long-case clocks which would be difficult to distinguish from English ones, were they not signed. As time went on, these Dutch tall clocks became more obviously Dutch as such characteristics as fiddle-shaped trunks, *bombé* bases and very florid marquetry became typical of a Dutch school of cabinet-making. The English did not follow these fashions, which also manifested themselves in the best quality long-case clocks of France, Austria and South Germany. By the middle of the eighteenth century, the long-case clocks made by 'town' makers in those countries, in Paris, Vienna, Munich etc, were generally much too florid and bulbous for English taste, whilst the 'country' productions of all continental countries tended to be very much cruder than their English counterparts. This is not to deny the presence of ingenuity and a certain rustic charm in many of the Dutch, French, German and Italian 'peasant' clocks; but it is notable that the gap between city and village practice was narrower in England than elsewhere.

In outward appearance Dutch spring clocks did not have much in common with thosc of English make from about 1685 onwards, though there was strong similarity between Dutch and French spring clocks up to about 1740. Despite the historico-political link of the Austrian Netherlands, Dutch influence on Austrian spring-clock design was much less than on their weight-driven examples. Late seventeenth- to mid eighteenth-century Austrian and Bavarian bracket clocks closely resemble English ones both mechanically and in appearance. The proportions were subtly different and as time went on the differences became more marked; the Austrian productions also tended to be rather more gaudy with, very often, a large paste brilliant flashing to and fro on the mock pendulum and a profusion of rather badly executed gilt-metal work. Sometimes, the gilt-metal mounts were simulated in carved wood or plaster.

By the end of the eighteenth century, what came to be known as the 'Vienna' mantel clock, also made elsewhere in Austria and South Germany, was very much more French than English in appearance, and the Viennese masters rivalled the best that Paris could do in elegance of case design and fine-quality bronze and ormolu work. Mechanically, these late Vienna clocks are a mixture. The movements are generally rectangular like the English, but with no fusees like the French; the pendulums hang on silk loops like the French, but the rack-striking and repeating work is in the English manner. Wholly Viennese and wholly perverse was the need of even the finest quality Vienna spring clocks of this period to be wound every day or every two days. This curious abberation is as inexplicable as it is annoying.

By contrast with their long-case clocks, which are so often clumsily proportioned or vulgarly ornate (or both), and these delicate and very 'Frenchified' decorative mantel clocks, the Vienna school also produced a splendid, new form of wall timekeeper—known in the English trade as 'Vienna regulators'. Although designed for accurate timekeeping, they had conventional dials, not those of English 'regulator type', but in outward appearance the early examples (*c*1800–20) of these delightful clocks have a very English flavour. A furniture expert would see Sheraton influence in the casework. Mechanically, these clocks were superbly made with very delicate wheelwork, Graham escapements modified with adjustable pallets, often jewelled, and wood-rod pendulums. Many of them had striking work, with rack mechanism laid out on the English plan. Their popularity led to their being copied throughout

Germany, and they survived into this century, in sadly debased form, made down to a price for the mass market.

Apart from Bavaria and the other southern provinces, in which Viennese influence was dominant, German clockmaking in the eighteenth century generally followed native and French influences rather than British. Except, that is, for the use of anchor or dead-beat escapements. As in Holland and France, the gap between 'city' and 'country' clocks was far wider than in England. The latter, particularly those from the Black Forest cottage-industry craftsmen, perpetuated all-wood construction until very late and often combined a kind of folksy *gemüthlichkeit* of carving and painting with ingenious, but very primitive, mechanism. The Black Forest craft spread and laid the foundations of the Swiss mass-production clock industry, exemplified by the cuckoo clock which the Swiss are curiously happy to claim as a native invention, although the Black Forest craftsmen had been making bird-call clocks of various kinds for a hundred years before their well-organised cottage industry spread over the border. As noted earlier, very large numbers of Black Forest wall clocks were exported to England in the nineteenth century, where semantic confusion led to their being called 'Dutch'.

As we have seen in Chapter 3, some writers have suggested the English long-case clock was not a new 'invention' but in direct line of descent from the sixteenth- and seventeenth-century German 'pillar' clocks. In his recent book, *The Grandfather Clock*, Ernest L. Edwardes states positively that this is so, and cites a specific example, the Kremsmünster pillar clock, as the common ancestor. Other authorities point to the very strong probability that the pillar or case structure of this splendid astronomical chamber clock is of later date than the clock itself; other 'pillar' clocks of the late sixteenth century give no impression of having been designed 'all of a piece', as English long-case clocks were. Nevertheless, there was a tradition in Germany for having enclosed, standing, weight-driven clocks, and many examples of late seventeenth and early eighteenth-century make resemble contemporary English long-case clocks. As Germany was the birthplace of the spring clock, it is not surprising that there is no German equivalent of the English bracket clock; and, on the whole, English horological influence in Germany was represented by watches rather than clocks. On the evidence of surviving examples in collections, relatively large numbers of English watches were exported to Germany. Equally large quantities of indisputably German watches survive bearing the name of the much-plagiarised Daniel Quare.

The same applies in France. Contrary to popular notions of France always leading the way in refinement, delicacy and elegance, until the eighteenth century was more than half spent, the average French watch, the *oignon*, was extraordinarily clumsy and bulbous and usually with only an hour hand. This was strangely in contrast with the conventional Paris, or Paris-type, clock movements which were already rather smaller and more delicately constructed than their English counterparts. In broad terms anybody who was anybody in France wore an English watch until nearly the end of the century, when Breguet, Le Roy, Lepine, Robin and others, but principally Breguet, introduced a new concept into French watchmaking to such good effect that by the end of the Napoleonic War, anybody who thought himself anybody, anywhere, had to have a Breguet watch, or the nearest thing to it that his resources would command.

In clockmaking, though, the French preferred their own way and apart from the use of the anchor escapement, French clocks, spring- or weight-driven, were distinctively different from English ones in almost every mechanical detail from the end of Louis XIV's reign onwards. Apart from those of the *Comtoise*, *Capucine* or *Pendule d'Officier* types, the French makers did not adopt the rack striking mechanism until half way through the nineteenth century and then, as we have seen, used a form which could give rise to damage if the clock failed to strike twelve for any reason. For precision timekeepers, either weight- or spring-driven, the leading French makers preferred the pin-wheel to the Graham type of dead-beat escapement, and for ordinary domestic clocks they clung to silk thread or cord pendulum suspension until very late in the day. This inhibited the use of heavy pendulums, but for precision timekeepers in which a weighty pendulum was essential they often used a form of inverted knife-edge suspension which was superior to the English variety as dust was less easily able to get between the fixed and the moving elements. Very large numbers of French clocks of all sorts made between about 1760 and 1860 have, or appear to have, gridiron pendulums; but this gesture towards John Harrison is more apparent than real, as the French attribute the invention to Le Roy and a very large proportion of the gridiron pendulums are bogus with the alternating brass and steel rods assembled for decorative effect and not for temperature compensation.

Although the English makers had the lion's share of the export trade to the Middle East, to Portugal and to Spain at one time, this does not seem to have influenced any native school of English-type horology in those countries. Exports to the Scandinavian countries and to Russia did inspire a certain amount of copying and the trade with China led to the production of some remarkably English Chinese bracket clocks at the end of the eighteenth century. These made no concessions to English fashions externally, and the form was that of a plain, shallow, rectangular box of shitan wood, standing on a carved support similar to those used for table screens. The glass front of the box did not open but revealed a convex circular enamel dial, with centre seconds hand (always a *sine qua non* for the China trade), surrounded by fretted brass ornamentation. Because of the Chinese liking for centre seconds hands, most of the English clocks made for the trade had been arranged to wind from the back, and this was copied for the home-made variety. Raising the sliding panel at the back of the case revealed a typically English-looking bracket clock movement of rather old-fashioned type, with rack strike, bob pendulum, crown-wheel escapement, fusees (of a most peculiar shape which suggested they were copied without true appreciation of their function), engraved back plate and maker's 'signature', in meaningless mock-European characters.

The very large subject of American horology is dealt with in a number of books on the subject, and it can only be summarised here by saying that it was not until the eighteenth century was nearing its end that a native school of clockmaking was established. Nearly all the American clockmakers up to that time were of English origin, first, second or third generation as the period dictated, and they closely followed English practice. Because of the need to import springs (almost wholly from England), nearly all the clocks were weight-driven, either thirty-hour hanging clocks or eight-day long-cases. There were some fine early eighteenth-century American bracket clocks, very similar to their English counterparts, but they are very rare.

The mechanism of American long-case clocks did not differ materially from contemporary English examples; and until the century was well advanced, many of the components appear to have been imported from England 'in the rough'. Naturally enough, the American cabinetmakers developed their own styles of casework, though they seem never to have departed very far from English forms and, at first glace, it would always be possible to mistake an American grandfather clock for an English one. Some of the characteristic American details, such as 'whale's tail' cresting over the hoods of arched-dial clocks, are very pleasing.

Chauvinism and the growing demand of an expanding population for low-priced clocks after the War of Independence led to the production of the first true American clocks by Eli Terry. These were weight-driven clocks with wooden wheels and other mechanical parts which owed nothing to English example and more than a little to the Black Forest craft. The interesting thing about the American clock industry is that from its inception, it was devoted primarily to low-cost quantity-production.

Popular history gives Henry Ford the credit for 'inventing' mass-production, but he merely carried to a logical conclusion the process which was started early in the nineteenth century in the Connecticut brass-clock industry and was developed by the small-arms industry later in the century. The all-wood construction of the Eli Terry type of clock did not lend itself readily to production on a scale large enough to meet the demand, and by the third decade of the nineteenth century a number of factories were producing 'patent brass' clocks in great numbers. Whether they were produced under names of individuals, such as Chauncey Jerome or Seth Thomas, or by amalgamations such as the Ansonia Clock Co, the basis of these clocks was the machine production of interchangeable components designed to need a minimum of handfitting. At the same time that these concerns were beginning to cater for the mass market, Abraham Willard and some others concentrated on better quality clocks, often of very elegant design, which were good enough and cheap enough to edge imported English or French clocks out of the more expensive end of the business.

It was the Chauncey Jerome type of operation which produced the weight-driven 'shelf clock' which was as typically American as the Mississippi steamboats which Mark Twain piloted before the Civil War. By that time the Yankee shelf clock was as firmly entrenched in popular use and mythology as the Model 'T' Ford became sixty years later; and it was a timepiece of this type which Mark Twain caused one of his characters to describe, in the deathless phrase: 'Why, sometimes I've known that clock to strike as many as one hundred and sixty-eight right off before she gets tuckered out.'

The merit of these attractive shelf clocks, and their smaller spring-driven successors, was their cheapness. Though the conception was entirely American, many details of construction were similar to those beginning to be practised in Germany, with stamped, rolled-brass frames and wheels, lantern pinions and bent wire or strip construction for most of the parts which traditional English or European makers still fashioned from steel laboriously forged, cut and filed to shape.

By the middle of the nineteenth century when 'Dutch' wall clocks and 'Yankee' shelf clocks began to arrive in England in great numbers, the English makers had rested on their laurels too long. After 150 years of making the best clocks and watches in the world, they dismissed the products of Connecticut, Neuchâtel, La Chaux de Fonds, Geneva and the Black Forest as cheap and nasty, without seeing that, in many ways they were cheap and astonishingly good. Like the Model 'T' Ford, the Yankee shelf clock may have flouted engineering or horological propriety in many ways but it would stand unlimited abuse, it could be tinkered-up after a fashion by any handyman and it was provided with such a generous margin of power it had no option but to go or bust.

The choice of 1850 as the closing year for this account of English domestic clockmaking is arbitrary. The trade did not come to a sudden stop in mid-century and English horologists still had important contributions to make in the fields of precision timekeepers, turret clocks, marine chronometers and in the infant science of electrical horology, well represented by the pioneer work of Alexander Bain, whose first electric-clock patent was granted in 1841.

Ten years later the horological displays at the Great Exhibition, despite the partial failure of Shepherd's too-ambitious electric master-and-slave clock system, would have seemed to confirm the continued supremacy of the English industry. At least, this would have been the superficial impression given by the elaborate, beautifully-made clocks and the array of watches for the traditional markets of America, Spain, Turkey, Persia, and Egypt.

The export trade was shrinking though; a native American watch industry was coming into being, producing both low-priced and fine pieces and it could not be foreseen that it would succumb to Swiss competition after a relatively short life. A shrewd observer at the Great Exhibition might have seen that the English no longer made watches specifically for the Chinese market. This business had passed to the Swiss who were already beginning to dominate the watch business throughout the world, not by any particular superiority of horological expertise but by their ingenuity and superior organisation of production methods. Success in clock and watch manufacture came not from having the best-designed product to offer but in applying the best methods of production engineering.

A significant straw in the wind was that although long-case clocks of ever more elephantine and ill-proportioned sorts continued to be made into the twentieth century, the traditional thirty-hour 'cottage grandfather' did not long survive the accession of Queen Victoria. It was supplanted entirely by American and German imports, and it was not only the quickly expanding working class, the new urban poor, who bought foreign clocks but the great majority of the middle class as well.

By the 1880s, the furniture of a typical, prosperous middle-class household would have included an inherited grandfather clock of greater or lesser merit in the hall, a monumentally ugly black marble French clock to take away the appetite in the dining-room, and, a more frivolous ormolu and 'Sevres' porcelain mock-Louis XVI French clock under a glass shade in the drawing-room. In the master's study, if he aspired to one, there might have been an English mantel clock in a state of decay, but more probably an even bigger and uglier French marble clock than that in the dining-room; the kitchen clock would have been American or German; a French 'carriage' clock would be found in the best bedroom, with a lesser

French timepiece probably broken and kept for decoration, in the spare room. A Swiss cuckoo clock might have graced the nursery, whilst the servants' bedroom needs would have been met by a German 'tin-ticker' alarm clock made, tested, transported, taxed and sold retail for less than three shillings.

It is not too much of an exaggeration to say that Victorian design is seen at its best in such crafts as decorative engraving and 'engine turning' and at its worst in the general run of domestic furniture made after about 1850: there are the usual exceptions and decorative small metal work could sometimes be too fussy and some of the later Victorian furniture, chairs particularly, if the scale is small enough can be quite pleasing. Taking the general rule though, we find extremely attractive small, engraved travelling clock cases, and engine-turned dials for small mantel clocks and similar objects as fine in their way as anything done in the seventeenth and eighteenth centuries, hand in hand with 'furnishing' clocks, mantel or grandfather, so ill-proportioned and overlaid with meaningless, uninspired carved mouldings that one can scarcely repress a shudder at the sight of them. The late type grandfather clock reached the nadir in its nastiness under Edward VII, when many of the leading furniture houses supplied monstrous clocks, often 9ft tall or more, in debased 'Sheraton style' cases supporting traditional gilt and silvered dials so over-decorated as to be almost unreadable, and exposing through multi-paned bevelled plate-glass trunk doors an array of nickel-plated tubular gongs for quarter-chimes whose saccharine sonority of tone matched the fairground vulgarity of their appearance. Clocks of this sort were, apparently, sold for use in private houses but they are particularly associated with the lush vestibules of the Grand Hotels of the era. By some extraordinary quirk these monumental monstrosities have recently captured the favour of the public, or a section of it. Having been regarded as unsaleable for some years, they are now becoming valuable, and one was sold at auction in December 1971 for £600. The figure makes the £16,000 paid for a Knibb long-case in March 1972 look like a bargain.

Some of the leading early Victorian makers revived a form of quarter-chiming mechanism which had been used by Charles Gretton, and others, in the late seventeenth century. This system was known in the clock trade as 'quarter striking' and although it was quite widely used on the continent, it is rare in eighteenth-century English clocks. It provides an elaboration to the normal hour-striking mechanism so that the quarters can be signalled, usually on two bells but sometimes on a full chime, without adding an extra train of wheels with another driving weight or mainspring and fusee.

The system generally sounded only the first three quarters, omitted the fourth and went straight into the hour striking. The mechanism usually involved some arrangement, known as 'pump action', to slide the quarter hammers (on very early examples the bells themselves) out of engagement when the hour only was to be struck. The system certainly saved a certain amount of space but it is doubtful if it saved much money, because it involved complication and it only worked reliably if it was made to the highest standards of finish. Consequently, although it apparently provides a 'cheap' way of making a quarter-chiming clock, it is only found on very high-grade examples. Viner, Frodsham, Barwise and Dent favoured quarter-striking for some of their best portable or travelling clocks; and Viner made a few superb month-duration quarterstrike clocks, with lever or marine chronometer escapements.

Where Victorian design excelled was in purely functional things which could also be made decorative, but with the decoration subordinate or complementary to the function. These manifestations of high-Victorian art are often seen in works of engineering and the splendour of the Egyptian-columned inverted-compound beam engine, at the Whiteacre pumping station in Staffordshire, is matched by many Victorian clockmakers' 'shop regulators' (which were not infrequently sold for use in private houses), and in the best skeleton clocks.

The history of English skeleton clocks has been handsomely recorded in a book by Royer-Collard. They originated in France towards the end of the eighteenth century and the idea was taken up with enthusiasm in England, where many very fine examples were made in the first half of the century. As the name suggests, a skeleton clock is an uncased timekeeper, protected by a glass shade or case, with its plates cut away in various decorative shapes to expose all the wheels and mechanism to view. In early examples, the wheels were often of very large diameter with six or eight slender 'crossings' and very delicate rims cut with large numbers of fine teeth. This delicate array of wheelwork was set in a correspondingly delicate skeleton frame, perhaps lyre-shaped or of some other elegant form, with a highly polished pendulum seen flashing to and fro behind the rest of the burnished mechanism. Many makers combined the skeleton form with some experimental or unusual type of escapement, to heighten the interest; and one of the popular variants was a type of detached detent chronometer escapement, adapted to work with a pendulum. Most skeleton clocks were time-pieces, but striking and quarter-chiming examples are seen and these obviously provide an even more impressive display of intricate-seeming and highly finished machinery-in-motion.

The skeleton clock remained popular throughout Queen Victoria's reign, but with numerous honourable exceptions (many of skilled amateur construction) the late specimens are very dull, stereotyped and badly finished by comparison with those of the first half of the century. Many were turned out, some for home assembly it is believed, by Clerkenwell jobbers with meagre-looking wheels and other parts from standard 'kitchen dial' type clocks.

Apart from the best skeleton clocks, Victorian horological innovation was chiefly expressed in improvements to methods of temperature compensation, to marine chronometers, regulators, to turret clocks and watches. These developments only marginally affected domestic clocks as, for example, in some of the superior travelling clocks with marine chronometer-type escapements made by such firms as Frodsham or Dent. There were some pretty early Victorian Gothic case designs for small mantel clocks, and some very fine quality Louis XVI-style ormolu clocks, with engine-turned gilded dials, sold by some of the leading West End retailers such as Payne of Bond Street and Viner of Regent Street; but on the whole the case-making side of bracket or mantel clock design increasingly lacked inventiveness and elegance.

It seems that a number of the better makers realised this, because during the second half of the century a large number of the finest quality spring-driven clocks were made in a Victorian adaptation of a mid-Georgian style. These clocks are not so much reproductions as exercises in nostalgia for a glorious past and amount to a confession, perhaps subconscious, that the clockmaking trade had nothing new to say. The usual form was that of a conventional mid to late eighteenth-century bell-topped bracket clock, usually ebonised and profusely adorned with gilt-metal mounts which contrived to have an indisputable if indefinable air of their Victorian origin, in spite of being cast in the exact patterns of their eighteenth-century prototypes. With that extraordinary lack of an eye for good proportions which marred so much Victorian design, these cases are invariably considerably deeper from front to back than is appropriate to the other dimensions. The dials harked back unashamedly to the traditional style, with gilt brass backgrounds and spandrels and separately mounted silvered chapter circles and subsidiary dials. The subsidiaries, grouped in the break-arch, usually included strike/silent and chime/silent controls, a rise-and-fall pendulum regulator and a selector to change from eight- or ten-bell chime, to Whittington or Westminster chimes. For nearly all of these clocks had three-train chiming movements, made regardless of expense, and some of them were arranged to chime at the owner's pleasure either on the traditional bells or on the newly fashionable coiled steel rod gongs.

In addition to the curious exaggeration of the front-to-back dimensions, these 'Victorian-Georgian' bracket clocks were usually very large, often more than 2ft high, and extremely heavy. Only the most massive of marble chimneypieces or console tables could support them, and the beautifully finished triple-fusee movements would not have seemed out of place in the engine-room of the *Great Eastern*. So generous, so needlessly generous, are the dimensions of all the mechanical parts that it is not unreasonable to suppose they will withstand five hundred years or more of use. They make no concessions to the need to supply a mass-market, and although their outward appearance signifies lack of artistic sensibility in their reliance on old forms, curiously distorted or blurred, they are sublime manifestations of Victorian stability and confidence in the future.

Tempus Rerum Imperatur, 'Time rules all things', was the motto chosen by the Worshipful Company of Clockmakers in 1631, and by the enduring nature of their best work their Victorian descendants seemed to express the belief that they could defeat time.

Acknowledgements

THE author and publishers wish to thank all those who have lent or given photographs for use in this book, and for their permission to reproduce them, namely:

Dr and Mrs David Bennett, Plate 37

The Trustees of the British Museum, and Beresford Hutchinson, Esq, Plates, 1, 2, 3, 4, 6, 7, 8, 9 and 10

Herr Dieter Pesch and Aubrey Brocklehurst, Esq, Plate 11

Peter Henley, Esq, Plate 43

The Owner, Plate 21

Brigadier Meyrick Neilson and Peter Harding, Esq, Photographer, Plates 12, 13, 14, 15, 16, 17, 24, 26, 29, 32, and 40

Messrs 'Strike One', Plate 38

Index

Italic figures refer to illustrations